THE LANDS WITHIN ME

the lands within me

Titles by the Canadian Museum of Civilization can be purchased in bookstores or by calling (819) 776-8387 or, in North America only, 1 800 555-5621, by e-mail to publications@civilization.ca or through our Web site at www.cyberboutique.civilization.ca or by writing to Mail Order Services, Canadian Museum of Civilization, 100 Laurier Street, P.O. Box 3100, Station B, Gatineau, Quebec J8X 4H2

National Library of Canada cataloguing in publication data
Main entry under title:
The lands within me: expressions by Canadian artists of Arab origin

Issued also in French under title: *Ces pays qui m'habitent*.
Includes bibliographical references.
ISBN 0-660-19088-5

1. Art, arab — Canada — Exhibitions.
2. Arab Canadians — Exhibitions.
3. Art, Canadian — 20th century — Exhibitions.
I. Kaouk, Aïda.
II. Bourque, Dominique, 1962-.
III. Canadian Museum of Civilization.
IV. Title: Expressions by Canadian artists of Arab origin.

N6549.5A65L36 2003 704.03'927071'074714 C2003-980297-3

PRINTED IN CANADA

Published by
Canadian Museum of Civilization
100 Laurier Street
P.O. Box 3100, Station B
Gatineau, Quebec J8X 4H2

Manager, Publishing: Deborah Brownrigg
Co-Publishing Coordinator: Louis Robillard
English Editing: Sheila Singhal
French Editing: Christian Bérubé
Graphic Design: Bleu Outremer communication/design
Cover Design: Bleu Outremer communication/design

Canada

TABLE OF CONTENTS

table of contents

P P

Alexis Nouss

EFACE

PREFACE

The world is now uninhabited. Populated, overpopulated, yes; explored, conquered, certainly; cleared, devastated, assuredly. But inhabited, no.

More precisely, it is the concept of habitat that is uninhabited. It is empty; we have abandoned it, though we are the only ones to give it meaning. For it is only the world, the human world, that can truly be inhabited. The celestial spheres are home to no one, except by way of metaphor.

We inhabit the earth the way we inhabit our mother: a body that is foreign and yet ours, a body that nourishes us, a related body. The umbilical cord is now cut.

Humans vacating it, the concept becomes void. And so ends the haunting litany of philosophy, the venerable old woman who — whether she speaks the language of Plato or the language of Heidegger — made of the earth a world. "How to live in the world?" she kept repeating.

We inhabit the earth the way we inhabit our mother: a body that is foreign and yet ours, a body that nourishes us, a related body. The umbilical cord is now cut. The affluent live in the virtual and the global, deterritorialized possessions; the disinherited live in territories that they no longer possess, with resources exhausted or confiscated. "Wrong life cannot be lived rightly," [1] Adorno had already concluded at the end of a reflection on the impossibility of inhabiting anything anywhere today. Individuals can no longer find places of their own that would allow them to elude the grasp of the control-and-consumption society. No more self, no more home.

For refugees, exiles, illegals, for those who "inhabit" exclusion, the world is a place where they cannot stay. Residence on earth is prohibited. The gravity of these words resounds all the more as they take on meaning for the whole world — the planet and its inhabitants — if we think of the ecological and environmental threat, the acuteness of which is now recognized. To no longer be able to inhabit the earth threatens to become the fate of all.

And the desert, which partakes of eternity, teaches its inhabitants the ephemeral nature of every dwelling place

There are others among us, children of Shem or of Abraham, who share a knowledge that religious discourse has known how to symbolize. For Judaism, the "four cubits" of the *halakhah* practice of ritual observance are sufficient to encapsulate the world so that it can be inhabited responsibly; and for Islam, the prayer rug reminds the one who prays of this same consciousness. These are peoples who have known the desert. And one does not inhabit the desert the way one inhabits a city. One resides *in* a city, but one sojourns *on* the desert. The desert does not restrain those who live there, since it knows no boundary. And the desert, which partakes of eternity, teaches its inhabitants the ephemeral nature of every dwelling place.

The artists of **The Lands within Me** have retained this memory. Their Arabness is not a symbol of exclusionary ethnicity, but rather an emblem of exile experience. Most have lived in many countries in the course of their migratory wanderings as if, with the departure from their place of origin, they were abandoning all origin in place and all identity attached to a territory. *Métissage*, or cultural mixing, thus comes naturally to them, and they remind us that it is a process which begins at origin, not a sort of crossbreeding between originally pure or intact entities. *Métis* are nomads who circulate between places of belonging. To live in the world as a poet, Hölderlin's injunction, must be understood as living in the world as a nomad, which he anticipated by turning from the words of reason to the words of silence, the words of the desert.

However, the artworks in the exhibition are not devoid of representation. They do not give way to abstraction, which can astonish us if we remember the ban on figurative imagery in Semitic traditions. They are always representing, as much in broken mirrors as in suspension bridges; as much in the failure as in the success of the encounter. In these works, reality is both expressed and perceived — that is, reality dwells in them. "With the dwelling the latent birth of the world is produced," Lévinas tells us.[2] This place — the house, the habitation — marks the interruption of the continuum. It is the stopping place that allows distancing, that allows the subject to objectify the world, to gather it in and to welcome the other. Since the dwelling place assures this function of gathering in and of welcoming, it is not subordinate to a material habitat, and art can become a dwelling place, can assume this office of opening to oneself and to the other. The artwork as a dwelling place will not only be visible, but, in the words of Klee, will make visible.

The world is no longer a habitat. Then let it be a binnacle.[3] Do not judge this word ungracefully technical or disparaging. Poets use it — it rhymes with *tabernacle* — and if there is something of the technical in it, it is the technique of voyagers, in the air or the cosmos, and on the seas. Sailors protect their lantern within a binnacle. It shelters the flame. The fragility and ephemeral nature of beauty must not frighten us, but inspire us. As the "dove poet" writes: "Furtive rose inhabiting appearance / Thus perhaps we live / And only fire for us is substance / Between the sands and the retreat of the sands."[4]

[1] *Minimamoralia. Reflections from Damaged Life,* trans. E.F.N. Jephcott (London: Verso Editions, 1989), p. 39.

[2] *Totality and Infinity*, trans. Alphonso Lingis (Pittsburgh, Pa.: Duquesne University Press, 1969), p. 157.

[3] *Binnacle*: a built-in housing for a ship's compass (*The Canadian Oxford Dictionary*, 1998).

[4] Salah Stétié, *Fièvre et Guérison de l'Icône* (Éditions Unesco/Imprimerie nationale, 1998), p. 71.
The author's family name means "dove" in the dialect of Aleppo, Syria.

ACKNOWLEDGEMENTS

This book is the result of the collaboration of many people to whom I would like to express my deepest gratitude.

I would like to thank, first of all, the authors of the texts in this book: Abla Farhoud, Rawi Hage, Alexis Nouss, Serge Ouaknine, Lamberto Tassinari, Camille Zakharia and Laura Marks.

Thanks also to all the people who collaborated in the translation and editing of this book: Claudine Vivier, Harriet Ellenberger, Daniel Mroz, Judith Terry, Sheila Singhal, Christian Bérubé, Daniel Zamorano, Ghassan Aris and Catherine Germain. I would like in particular to acknowledge the contributions of Claudine Vivier and Harriet Ellenberger, who have worked with me on this project since the beginning, and who have brought to the manuscript an undeniable level of quality.

I would also like to acknowledge the skills, the devotion and the determination of the team that worked tirelessly on the exhibition itself. They include exhibition designer Chantal Baril, interpretive planner Monique Carnell, project managers Danielle Goyer, Christiane Saumur and Michele Courtemanche, and assistant curator Constance Nebel. I could never thank Constance enough for giving me the benefit of her experience, and for her constant support throughout the long process of conceiving and organizing the exhibition **The Lands within Me** — from which this book has also benefited.

I would also like to express my gratitude to the Museum's photographer, Harry Foster, for the quality of his work and the beauty of the photographs which illustrate this book so wonderfully.

I must also mention the contributions of Deborah Brownrigg, publications manager at the Canadian Museum of Civilization, and of Louis Robillard, coordinator of co-publications at the Museum, both of whom have shepherded this publication project so carefully throughout the process of production.

My colleagues in the Museum's Research Division — particularly Carmelle Bégin, former head curator, and Andrea Laforet, director, Ethnology and Cultural Studies Division — also provided me with their generous support throughout this journey, and I would like to express my sincere thanks.

I would also like to recognize the many colleagues and friends who have encouraged, advised and inspired me, including Denise Côté, Danielle Boutet, Pascale Galipeau, Johanne Despatie, Marcel Martel, Anne Latendresse and Michelle Séguin.

This work has benefited as well from the assistance of Dominique Bourque, who has worked closely with the authors, including myself, and has helped them to polish their texts. Her literary talents and good judgement have proven invaluable, and I would like to express my deep gratitude to her.

Of course, this project would never have seen the light of day without the generosity of the artists took part in the exhibition **The Lands within Me**, and the generosity of the artists and collectors who agreed to loan their works to the Museum.

And finally, my thanks to all the staff of the Canadian Museum of Civilization who have made contributions large and small to the realization of this book.

Aïda Kaouk
Gatineau, Quebec
October 2003

INTRODUCTION

INTRO DUC TION

aïda kaouk

"People often ask me if I am Amerindian or South American; if I come from the Middle East or from Portugal . . . And I find that rather nice; I can be from anywhere." These words from the artist Bernice Lutfie Sorge might have been mine. But they might just as easily have been those of other people who speak Arabic or Spanish or English or French — those who have left their native country to live elsewhere: in this instance, in Canada.

We are All Culturally Mixed Beings

If migrant art testifies today to the massive displacements of individuals and populations across the planet, it also takes into account the phenomenon of *métissage*: a phenomenon as ancient as human societies, and one that touches not only migrants, but each of us to different degrees. For there exists no culture, and thus no cultural identity, that is not "the outcome of intermixing and interbreeding", the result "of an opening to the other." [1]

Métissage refers, not to a simple juxtaposition of various elements, . . . but to a meeting in the strongest sense of the word . . .

The present work has been conceived as a space for personal testimony, creation and reflection about *métissage*: a notion too often disparaged in this age of multiplying demands based on identity, the standardization of the world, and globalization. *Métissage* refers, not to a simple juxtaposition of various elements (as in the concept of multiculturalism, for example), nor to their recasting as a homogeneous whole (the melting-pot model), but to a *meeting* in the strongest sense of the word, to "a permanent confrontation that not only links but transforms both sides." [2] To favour this type of meeting, in which no one has to deny himself or herself and in which each can evolve, it seems to me necessary — today more than ever — to broaden the view we have of others: different in their ethnic origins, but similar in their human condition and in the richness of their cultural backgrounds.

Along with the exhibition **The Lands within Me**, this work does not seek to underline the "exoticism" of works by Canadian artists of Arab origin — rather, and emphatically, the contrary. The variety of works presented in this exhibition, and reproduced in part here, attest above all to the unique character of each artist. To put it another way, the works are approached, not as testimony to the "ethnic", but rather as expressions of a social experience in which the specific and the universal are revealed one with the other, and not one without the other. It is not a question of treating immigrant experience, which is at the heart of the project, anecdotally, but of seeing in it a human experience that can be shared by all citizens of a plural society.

The Lands within Me

It was in 1993, during my meeting with the artists Shwan and Alnaser, that the desire was born to write two works that would showcase their respective creations. This double project never saw the light of day, but it opened the way, in 1996, to a more ambitious project: an exhibition on migrant experience and *métissage*, as expressed by 26 Canadian artists of Arab origin. The Canadian Museum of Civilization accepted this new project, and the exhibition opened in October 2001.

At first entitled **Letters Home**, evoking both distance and the intimate connection that exists between the artists and the countries that have marked them (all have "traversed" several countries before and after making their homes in Canada), the final project was called **The Lands within Me**. This title disrupts the meaning habitually given to the words. In fact, *land* or *country* is no longer assumed to be the place inhabited, but becomes an entity that "inhabits" beings — an entity that is carried within them. In this sense, the title does not refer to an original or unique land, but to the "cultures" that contribute to moulding our lives and the worlds of our imagination. Rather than insisting on belonging to one land in particular, it evokes the importance of the diverse places, roots, attachments and memberships that shape us, transform us and enliven us.

When ethnic and religious belonging is being used — often with devastating effect — for political ends, and when questions of identity become the order of the day in social discourse, it appears to me important to be aware of the fact that cultural identities in the contemporary world are at once multiple and complex, and that cultural hybridity is a reality of our time.

Conceived as a *chant d'amour*, a love song to the culturally interwoven worlds of the imagination, **The Lands within Me** celebrates opening up to others, whoever they may be. It also extends a hand to each and every person, to invite their participation in efforts to bring together diverse peoples, societies and cultural groups.

Established in the different regions of Canada, from the Maritimes to British Columbia, the artists of **The Lands within Me** are originally from Arab countries or territories as diverse as Algeria, Egypt, Iraq, Lebanon, Morocco, Palestine, Syria, Tunisia and Yemen. They have chosen different means of expression — photography, painting, ceramics, jewellery, video, installation, sculpture, calligraphy — and work in diverse artistic currents. Born between 1930 and 1970, they belong to different age groups; and although some are just beginning their careers, the majority have already created a body of work, and several are pursuing international careers.

All the same, neither age nor the success of these artists played a role in their selection for the exhibition. In fact, many others could have been added to these creators. It was not a question for me of organizing a talent contest, but of leaving the door wide open to the ensemble of artists and to diversity — including a diversity of styles, schools and artistic media.

Moreover, the 80 works that make up the exhibition have been grouped, not by their belonging to a particular category of art (modernism or postmodernism, institutional art or handicrafts, classical or naive art), but by different themes. This arrangement allowed, to my mind, a truer appreciation of *métissage* as "individual experience of the . . . recognition of otherness in ourselves." [3]

***Métissage* at Work**

One can do no more, in a few lines, than give a brief survey of *métissage* in the works of **The Lands within Me**, while also indicating the variety of its manifestations. The culturally-intermixed dimension of works by Yasser Badreddine and Aldin Rashid is already expressed at the level of intention, for both are anxious to carry on classical Arab calligraphy in the context of North America. In works by Taouffik Semmad and Shwan, cultural intermixing appears more in the playful and audacious approach they adopt in the face of this traditional art. Semmad's invention of a hybrid calligraphy style and Shwan's representation of inscriptions belonging to everyday life, and spilling over onto the frame of the painting, bring into question the rules and borders that define all art.

Between these two poles, the formal and thematic hybridization proves to be infinite. It can be found even in the very process of fabricating the work, as when Liliane Karnouk uses a computer to design and cut out a folding screen with traditional geometric motifs, which she then spends hours painting. Hybridization can also be connected with the sources of inspiration. Such is the case for Marc Eliany, who makes a spontaneity characteristic of certain Moroccan painters interact with the lines and forms of Amerindian painting. Or for Ali Kichou, who brings together elements of primitive, Berber and other arts promoted by the Italian group Movimento Trattisto. But *métissage* can also reveal itself in the choice of media or of subjects. Thus, Sanaa M. Wassef gives "Canadian" colours to her Egyptian-inspired ceramics, and Nicolas Zeitouni, in his gouaches inspired by the Eastern decorative motif, breaks with the symmetry that characterizes that motif. In the same way, the painter Abd Hanafi gives to his Montreal streets the allure of the *souks*, and Joseph Moukhtar makes the rectangular architecture of North American urban landscapes dance and undulate. Finally, it also happens that materials and subjects clash with each other, the better to meet. This is the case with the jewellery by Nihal Mazloum — created by North American methods in a North American style, but bearing Arabic script or Pharaonic symbols — or the installations by Jamelie Hassan, who gathers together videos, *objets d'art* and artifacts from here and abroad, to make visible the "small histories" which History incessantly erases. Bernice Sorge, for her part, superimposes, in a quest for identity, imprints of red-veined leaves, yellowed family photos and stories evoking the memory of her Syrian-born mother.

In addition, a number of works present themselves as veritable bridges between the two or three — or more — worlds that coexist within the artists. Sami Zubi's re-creation in transparent plastic resin of the motif of a massive old wooden door in Jerusalem, for example, calls up the possibility that clarity (open-mindedness) can prevail over obscurity (closed-mindedness) in that region of the world. The acetate on which Hanna Alpha chooses to paint the "fires of Kuwait" during the Gulf War contrasts with the opaque screen that a television set can sometimes become in the face of reality. The representation, by Hadjira Preure, of a young Algerian woman on the cross evokes the charge of hope associated with the symbol of the sacrificed Christ. The clear line that Adel Alnaser favours confers a great transparency on drawings that combine diverse architectural and symbolic universes. This idea of passage between coexisting worlds is also found in Laila Binbrek's mirrors without glass or silvering; in the telescoping of squares, one square within another, on the canvases of Ishrak Sahar; and in the recurring of an oblong form evoking openness in work by Farouk Kaspaules, and the recurrence of the red house in Mirella Aprahamian's paintings. Similarly, the installation video of Jayce Salloum formally sets into dialogue, through the projection of landscapes and moving skies, different spoken accounts dealing with experience or the representation of it. Finally, by photographing himself as he photographs Inuit hunters or the ragpickers of Morocco — that is, full-length, clothed in the traditional costume of his native country, and in black-and-white — Karim Rholem chooses to represent himself and to represent the other in himself, becoming in his turn a bridge between cultures.

But the culturally-mixed perspective of the artists can also appear in the versatility of their creative actions. Thus, beyond their own works, the photographers Rawi Hage and Camille Zakharia not only made portraits of the exhibition's artists (with the exception of Karim Rholem), but also wrote a text describing that experience. Without consulting with each other, both dealt with the question of heritage: the inheritance one receives, and the inheritance one passes on. In choosing to tell the story of his meeting with the painter Wadie El Mahdy, who died in 1999, Rawi Hage pays homage to a master whose work would appear in the exhibition. For his part, Camille Zakharia asks what immigrants can or should pass on to their children.

An Open Book

It seemed to me important that this book, like the exhibition, offer a variety of approaches and forms, and not be restricted to presenting photos of the works and artists, accompanied by "a word from the curator". Just as in the exhibition project, I had wished to decompartmentalize artistic categories and movements so that a real interaction could take place. I also wanted to associate different types of texts in the publication in order to bring together a wide variety of people, rather than a small group of specialists. To put it differently, I insisted on making this book a space conducive, not only to reflection, but also to the meeting of diverse points of view and — why not? — delight. That is why I can only echo the wish that Lamberto Tassinari expresses in these pages: to see art move "from the museum to the street." In this connection, I would like to touch on the memory of an experience that well illustrates the power art possesses to bring together human beings, even the most different.

During a brief stay in my native city of Aleppo, Syria, I was invited to an evening of music organized in the inner courtyard of a house in the old city. This weekly concert has been held for two generations in the same place. When I arrived with friends, the door was wide open. Amateur musicians were gathered around the central pool to sing and play an instrument. In that usually private and intimate space, the music united instrumentalists, singers and listeners, and drew together people who scarcely knew each other. I felt then that lively pleasure which is called *tar(a)b* in Arabic, and which is indissociable from a relationship of sharing and exchange.

Opening wide the door to that other "private" place which is the book, I wished to bring together, in this work, authors who, like the musicians of Aleppo, were able to call out to, join with, perhaps even touch the readers passing by. These authors come from different backgrounds — in the arts, criticism and research — and are "inhabited", like the exhibition artists, by other countries. The playwright and novelist Abla Farhoud brings to life her grandmother, born in Lebanon, who came to Canada in 1930 to make her home. Claiming the heritage of this skillful seamstress, Abla devotes herself to stitching and restitching for us the fragments of memories that remain to her of this captivating and endearing individual. In an entirely different style, Lamberto Tassinari, professor at the Université de Montréal, novelist and former director of the avant-garde magazine *ViceVersa*, offers us a reflection on the *traces* left by works of art, and the place that these works must occupy now that artists are becoming, not only "voyagers", but also "voyages". Serge Ouaknine, writer, dramatist and professor at the Université du Québec à Montréal, audaciously challenges himself to define Eastern and Western cultures from that "encounter with memory" which art represents. Finally, Laura Marks, critic, curator and Dena Wosk professor of Art and Cultural Studies at Simon Fraser University, has set herself the task of understanding — while paying particular attention to the materiality of the works in **The Lands within Me** — what it is that gives migrant art its luminous grace.

Let us make a place, then, for their words and their visions of the world!

1 François Laplantine and Alexis Nouss, *Le Métissage* (France, Flammarion, 1997), p. 46. To put it another way: "*Métissage* is a composition whose composing parts keep their integrity" (*op. cit.*, p. 9), or "Métissage lays out a third way between the homogeneous and the heterogeneous, fusion and fragmentation, models aiming at total integration and those advocating separatism on the part of minorities," François Laplantine and Alexis Nouss, *Métissages de Arcimboldo à Zombi* (Pauvert, 2001), back cover.

2 *Traces of Images*, *Dialogue*, *Where Am I From*, *All these countries . . .*, *The Third Place*.

3 François Laplantine and Alexis Nouss, *Métissages de Arcimboldo à Zombi*, *loc. cit.*

PART ONE

PART ONE

1

Abla Farhoud

JANA

JANA

I have never called her by her name. I have never heard anyone call her by her name. My father would say *immé*, Mama; my mother called her *mart aamé*, wife of my uncle. Among those who spoke Arabic, she was known as *Oum* Chafic, mother of Chafic, the name of her eldest son, as tradition would have it; and among francophones, Madame Farhoud, as custom would have it. I have never heard anyone call her Jana. Jana is my grandmother's name. I called her *sitté*. I could have said *sitto* or *téta*, but in Aïn-Hirshy, the village in southeastern Lebanon where I was born, we used *sitté* or *ya sitté* when addressing our grandmother, and *sitté* Jana when speaking of her to someone else.

Sitté Jana was born in 1900. On precisely the first day of the year 1900. If I dwell on this, it is because hardly anyone in my village knows the date of their birth. I myself have a fictitious date: "When you were born," my mother told me, "the goats were outside." (I concluded from this that I was born in spring or in summer. But which year?) The inhabitants of my native village have a phenomenal memory for the slightest details of each person's life; but strangely, no memory at all for birthdates. "I was born before the big famine or after the Great War, or just before the French arrived in the village, or two days after my cousin Nabil" — this is more or less what you would receive as an answer if you asked someone's age. But the woman who repeatedly said that the century was born with her had good reason not to be forgotten!

My grandmother arrived in Canada about 1930. She wasn't the first; on my father's side, the family had been emigrating since 1885. But these peculiar emigrants who were my ancestors had the curious habit of always leaving behind one of their children in the village. The child would grow up, emigrate in turn, and leave behind one of his or her children . . . who would grow up, emigrate, and . . .

Strong of character, independent, determined, free, Jana is the sort of rare bird who makes tongues wag in the village.

In about 1903, my grandmother's parents depart, in accordance with family tradition, leaving their daughter Jana behind in the village. Jana grows up with grace, as the saying goes, but *not* with wisdom — although, in the end, that depends on one's point-of-view. Strong of character, independent, determined, free, Jana is the sort of rare bird who makes tongues wag in the village. She succeeds in learning to read and write, which is quite rare at the time, especially for a girl. Well before feminism, she knows that emancipation comes primarily through knowledge and financial independence; she knows that freedom is not given, but taken. Conventions and customs, often stifling, are of little consequence to her; and, at the risk of provoking scandal, Jana always follows what her head and her heart dictate.

In this year of 1915, her heart is intimately linked to a young man, the handsomest in the village, by the name of Daher. She will marry the love of her life, and they will have three children.

But what is it with these Lebanese who are always wishing to leave!

Daher is no different from the others. He too leaves country, wife and children, and a few years later, he returns to die in Jana's arms — the honeymoon was too short, and Jana remains inconsolable for life. She never remarries. And it is not for lack of suitors. Have I told you that she was beautiful?

At thirty years of age, she too departs with two of her children, leaving Chafic behind in the village — Chafic: the boy who would become my father.

But what is it anyway with these Lebanese who are always leaving a child in the old country! To stay or to go: at some point, one must choose.

She arrives, probably in Montreal, and then (we know neither why nor how) finds herself in Havre Saint-Pierre, a small village lost on Quebec's North Shore, where she opens a small shop. Why Havre Saint-Pierre? Why so far? The new Lebanese community had already begun to settle around Berri and Craig streets in Montreal's south end — why go so far away? My questions always remained unanswered.

Several years ago, I made a pilgrimage to the places where my grandmother had lived and worked for so many years. I went to Havre Saint-Pierre by boat, since there was at that time no practicable land route. What a surprise! I even met people who remembered her and her children. It was as if memory transformed into the words of these persons made her alive and genuine for me. My grandmother really had lived here. Not that I was thinking she had lied, but at the moment they spoke to me of her, what had been for me a story became reality. As if, to exist, it were necessary to be present in the memory of another.

I walked the streets of Havre Saint-Pierre; her shop had become a post office, I believe. In the distance, it is true, the river and the landscape are very beautiful. But what was she doing, *sitté*, without husband, without friends, with two children to feed? What was she doing in the evening, when night falls, when the children are asleep, when customers are in their own homes, where there is no book, no newspaper, written in her language, where even the radio speaks and sings in another language — a language she barely knows? What was she doing, *sitté*, alone?

The first time I saw *sitté*, it was in 1951 or 1952; I was six or seven years old, and she was nearly the age I am today. Good Lord, how old I thought she was! We had just arrived from Lebanon. Father, mother and children. Without exception. Thus, we had just broken with the family tradition which dictates that one child remain in the village as the guarantor of our roots in our native land. I do not know, at the time, if my parents have really made the choice to leave for good, but I know they have not left behind in the village a single one of their five children. All of our family was there, ready to face a new life, a new world. Grandmother had just sold her shop in Havre Saint-Pierre to open an entirely new one in Saint-Vincent-de-Paul, in the suburbs of Montreal. It was in her home above the store that she welcomed us upon our arrival.

She was not the sweet and loving woman I remember today, but a woman who was valiant and hardworking, courageous and meticulous. Have I told you that she also knew how to sew? I saw her one day stitching and unstitching a dress, stitching and unstitching thirty times the neckline of her dress so that it would fall exactly as she wished it to fall. Have I told you of her unremitting determination, her patience, her taste for beauty? This neckline stitched, unstitched and restitched thirty times — I often think of it when I rewrite again and again the same paragraph so that it will be exactly the way I hear it in my mind.

Jana, who taught me how to stitch, unstitch and restitch necklines, words, sleeves, paragraphs, blouses, short stories, dresses, plays, coats, novels . . . just for the pleasure of accomplishing our lives.

My grandmother, as I was telling you earlier, was not a woman who allowed anyone to tread on her. She had a nasty temper, as some people said behind her back, but never to her face. Nevertheless, when I was alone with her, I felt like a princess being welcomed by a queen.

One day, several years after our arrival, she came to visit us in the small city of Sainte-Rose, where we were living then. She took me aside and asked me in Arabic, "Abla, do you want to come spend a few days at my house?" I immediately said, "*É ya sitté* — yes, Grandmama." I remember the big bed just for me, with oh-so-white cotton sheets, the spotless bedroom that smelled good, just for me. (In all my childhood and adolescence, I had never had a room of my own.) The next day, she woke me with a voice so sweet that I thought I was dreaming. I still hear her unique way of calling my name: "Abla, Abla, *fiï ya tou'brini', fiï* — wake up, my darling, wake up." Breakfast was already on the table: fresh crusty bread, still hot, that I could dip in *crème fraîche* — which I love most in the world, still to this day.

Each time I look at the patchwork she gave me a few years before dying — a superb satin bedspread which reminds me of the textures and colors in *The Arabian Nights* — I think of those thousands of hours that *sitté* spent restitching her life, alone, in her shop, dreaming perhaps of her love who had died and her daughter who died a few years later. Each time I look at the satiny diamonds on top of my bed, I think of that *crème fraîche*, that hot bread, of her unique way of calling me Abla, which I long to hear again. I think that never could *sitté* Jana have imagined I would one day transpose memory into words to pay her homage — at nearly the same age she was when I saw her for the first time, when I called her "*sitté*" for the first time, not yet knowing that her name was Jana.

Jana.

Jana, who taught me to do *only* what my head and my heart dictate. Jana, who taught me how to stitch, unstitch and restitch necklines, words, sleeves, paragraphs, blouses, short stories, dresses, plays, coats, novels, just for the pleasure and the beauty that make us forget death — just for the pleasure and beauty of reaching the very farthest limits of self; just for the pleasure of accomplishing our lives.

TRAVEL NOTES

TRAVEL NOTES
(EXCERPT)

Rawi Hage

In 1999, the team preparing the exhibition **The Lands within Me** commissioned me to photograph 13 Canadian artists of Arab origin in different regions of the country. My journey began in Vancouver and continued to Kitchener-Waterloo, then to the Atlantic coast of Canada and back to Montreal, where I live. Before my departure, the curator, Aïda Kaouk, asked me to keep a record of my trip and my encounters with the artists.

Years before, in Beirut, I had written a poem in French that my instructor displayed on the wall. Then the war came, I forgot the words of the poem, and I stopped writing. I no longer found my voice through the written word; it was the light reflected by objects and persons that became my mode of expression.

In the course of my journey to meet the artists, I felt like one of the angels in Wim Wenders's film *Wings of Desire*. Aloof, invisible, silent, these immortal spirits witness the life of travellers, exiles and lost mortals. Unable to speak here of all the exiled mortals I encountered, I will content myself with evoking only one among them: the painter of Egyptian origin, Wadie El Mahdy, now deceased.

On the road to Kitchener-Waterloo, where Wadie lived, I passed many trees and a million cars. I ended up finding the painter's home — after having driven by wide cornfields and over the bridge that they'd told me about at a gas station — and I parked my car filled with electrical wires, film, cameras and the remains of junk food. I rang the bell. The door opened. I picked up my bags and entered the building. Wadie was waiting for me in the long hallway. I smiled; he waved and offered to help carry my bags. I declined the offer, thanking the Almighty. He insisted, swearing by the All-Merciful, and I had to surrender.

Aloof, invisible, silent, these immortal spirits witness the life of travellers, exiles and lost mortals.

He took my black bag and showed me into his apartment. In the living room, a woman he introduced as a friend was sitting on an old green couch. In her late fifties, with dyed hair, she was wearing an oversized sweater and had an ordinary name. She asked me questions, and I answered: "Montreal," "Water, please," "Here." I drank the water while walking around, examining the space. She began to talk about art, galleries, small cities versus big cities, a catalogue; then she mentioned her daughter, excused herself and left the apartment. All this time, Wadie had remained quiet and distant, as if by design — as if he had planned in advance to leave the lady in charge. I was now alone with him. In his mid-sixties, calm, with graceful manners, he moved slowly and spoke in a low but steady and clear voice. His face was smooth, with long ears that extended below the jawline. His lips were moulded in the thick shape characteristic of a godlike figure.

"I lived in Montreal once," he said.

"Really, where?"

"I stayed for ten years. Maybe I should never have left," he added, ignoring my question.

"Nice city," I said compulsively, and then regretted my words, not knowing if they would intensify his remorse.

We chatted in short phrases. Our topics included Egypt, Lebanon, Canada, painting, maybe the weather — I cannot recall. Outside, it was a sunny day. A blunt shaft of harsh light invited itself in to settle partly on the wooden floor, partly on the furniture. On the other side of the living room, away from the windows, a sombre hallway led to other rooms. Besides the large living room, the apartment contained two bedrooms and a kitchen that opened onto a dining room. The dining room held a retro-style table surrounded by a few metal chairs coated in bright vinyl, the whole encircled by a series of statues painted in vivid African colours. The walls were covered with paintings, all by Wadie. For some reason, the painter seemed eager to show me around the apartment. He gave directions with small gestures, pointing a finger or lifting his head. There were canvases everywhere, on each wall, each armchair, each piece of furniture.

"Here is where I work," he said.

"Here is where you work," I echoed.

The room seemed too well-ordered. I assumed that everything had been arranged the day before by the lady, for the photography session, because Wadie was too weak to lift things. As he later explained to me, he was recovering from two medical operations, simultaneously, and had to restrain himself. Slow were his movements, motionless were his rooms, and serene was his presence.

"I use a knife," he whispered to me.

"A knife, eh!" I said.

He nodded, and we walked into a second room. There he led me to a painting of a train station filled with Egyptians of all classes and backgrounds. On the canvas one could see the swift traces of Wadie's knife that gave life to people and to trucks. Women, men and objects coexisted in a chaos of movement: there were ladies veiled and unveiled, gentlemen turbaned or with heads bared, merchants and buyers, fruits and vegetables, cars and donkeys, noise and calm *chicha* smokers, their long hookahs descending towards the ground.

"That one will be in the show," he said, pointing at the canvas.

Nearby, but faraway from the world of his paintings, lay Wadie's bedroom, facing east. In it, a desk, a double bed, an old TV, a mirror, a closet and two large windows all seemed to bow before a painting, a portrait of his wife.

"My wife died here, in this city. She had left Montreal to come here. After awhile I decided to follow her, and when I got here, she died. I have not left town since."

I kept quiet, not blinking or making a sound. The many funerals back home had taught me how to behave, how to stay still through the long chants of women hidden in black, surrounded by men with long, mourning faces.

"I wanted to go back to Egypt, but now I am too weak," the painter said. "Maybe this will be my last show. Maybe I will die here. I had a heart attack, down in the street. I was watching a marathon and felt weak and dizzy. I asked an officer for help. I was taken to the hospital."

Later on, after we were done with the photo session, Wadie invited me to a local restaurant.

We took my small red car, and I drove through the streets of Waterloo, following his directions. At the restaurant where he was a regular customer, he led me to a table next to a large window. We sat down and waited. A very tall waitress appeared, with the broadest smile on earth and the longest legs in the universe. She offered us the menu and recited the specials of the day. To Wadie's questions she would respond with splendid enthusiasm, listing and explaining the ingredients carefully. We ordered soup, salad, spaghetti, bread and beer; then, armed with our shiny utensils, we attacked the meal with an ancient appetite. I was thirsty, and the beer was cold and dark. I carried it to my mouth with both hands and drank to the fullest. That made Wadie smile.

"Are you married?" he asked.

"No," I said, "but I almost got married once."

"I have never felt so alone in my life as these past two days," he said in a low and humble voice. "My wife was Italian. She died. I am alone in this land. Here no one cares. I should never have left Egypt."

''You work in photography?"

"When I need the money."

"How old are you?"

"Thirty-four."

"It is the right time to get married," he said in Arabic. "Don't stay alone." Then he repeated in an Egyptian dialect, "Get married. It is better."

"I get married every other day," I said jokingly.

"That does not count," he replied.

The waitress reappeared, asking if everything was OK.

We each ordered a slice of apple pie and a strong cup of coffee. I tried to take the bill, but Wadie insisted on paying, all along calling me: "*Ya Bacha! Ya Bacha!*"

We returned to Wadie's place. I picked up my equipment, saluted the painter, and began driving back east.

The sun was at my back, rushing in the opposite direction, towards the west. It was the time of day when one can feel a delicate and rosy light touching all that has been created — all that has existed, none hidden nor spared. It was the hour when all creatures face destiny and bravely wait for darkness to fall.

It was the hour when all creatures face destiny and bravely wait for the darkness to fall.

I thought of Wadie's life: the image of him surrounded by his artwork, alone, like a pharaoh buried among his servants and belongings.

Then I thought of myself and all those mortals who had passed through my life, their presence retained in fragmented and vague recollections, accompanying me in my long exile. And I thought of how I have always, persistently, chosen solitude.

WHERE TO START?

WHERE TO START?
A PARENT'S SOUL-SEARCHING

camille zakharia

Through this project I have met many generous people who have let me, not only into their homes, but also into their lives and hearts, sharing with me their most intimate possessions: their memories. Their personal stories have propelled me through an emotionally exhausting journey of self-exploration that has left me questioning, yet again, who we are as immigrants.

Why did we leave home? We all left for the same reason: a better life. Each of us has achieved it differently; yet none of us seems to believe that he or she has been perfectly successful. We have all clung, in one way or another, to a nostalgic notion of home: a romanticized past that no longer exists, and may never have existed as remembered.

As a result, through the generations, we persist in holding on to the ghosts of tradition, each generation imposing itself on the next for fear of losing its identity: an identity that has become so confused. Did this vicious circle begin in our fear of losing who we are to a foreign culture, or did it begin in response to a foreign culture's fear of who we are?

Church has become our refuge in so many ways other than spiritual. We congregate to hear our language spoken, to share our foods and our troubles and our joys, to cling to the remnants of who we were. Here we practice a religion of a different sort. We worship the motherland, choosing to forget what it was about it that drove us away in the first place.

Do I want this for my children? Do I have something better to offer them than the self-imposed enclosure of one community within another community: a self-sustaining quasi-reality of Arabic music muted in the winter snow, faded photos of cousins unknown, cups of Turkish coffee turned over with fortunes unrevealed, the disillusionment of finding out that their parents' home is not the utopia we described to them?

We have a fierce need for family. My wife talks about having six kids if we could only afford them. She is trying to re-create the family she left behind, and I have heard the same feeling echoed from countless others like her. We procreate in an attempt to combat the loneliness of our self-imposed exile (much of the time, I do feel exiled, my choices made for me by wars, economics and family pressures). We bring our children into this world determined that their childhoods should replicate ours, refusing to acknowledge that our own early lives weren't as idyllic as we like to think. And in this paradoxical state of selfishness, mixed with the selflessness of our desire to protect them, we deny our children who they are.

Where must our children exist so they can truly have the best of both worlds?

Where is the middle ground we often talk about? Where must our children exist so they can truly have the best of both worlds? How can we show them when we ourselves don't know?

Must my son be Lebanese, I constantly question myself, when he is only partly so? What choices should I let life present him with? What choices should I make for him?

I feel an overwhelming desire to protect him, and a crushing helplessness at the knowledge that I don't even know where to start.

PACKING LIGHT

PACKING LIGHT

Laura Marks

What packs well? If you could carry only one thing on the journey, what would you choose?

Most of the artists whose work is represented in **The Lands within Me** have moved multiple times in their lives; they have had to learn to travel light. An element of portability, of being able to pick up and move again, remains in some of their materials. In the following, I will discuss two important media of travelling art, both as real objects and as metaphors: metal and calligraphy. Both are small, and both can be "melted down" if necessary.

Metals have been described as the ideal nomadic art material, as metalwork is convertible from tool to weapon to *objet d'art*.[1] Metal remembers, but it is also capable of transformation: a useful analogy for the migrant himself or herself. Similarly, calligraphy is compressible, the word capable of springing into a shape and of collapsing back into itself.

The expandable and contractible quality of metals and writing is a fine paradigm for the capacity of art in general. For a believer, art is the rendering "effable" of the ineffable, giving material shape to a spiritual entity. For anybody, art has the capacity to compress history and knowledge into its very form, for a patient viewer to decompress or "unpack". The artwork telescopes the journey into the point of arrival. This pliability and compressibility of the artistic means informs all the work in **The Lands within Me**, whether the artwork doubles as useful object, is made from the materials associated with travel, or is meant to travel itself. Of course, as we shall see, no matter how light one travels, the voyage between the Middle East and Canada forces excess baggage on the traveller. This will inform my third point about travelling art. Newly perceived as exotic or threatening in the context of North America, these artists may choose to persist in their survival acts of importation, or they may make the process of cultural translation the object of their work.

Metal Travels

Although the only actual metalwork in **The Lands within Me** is the jewellery by Nihal Mazloum, many of the exhibition pieces are fundamentally "metallic" in that they are malleable according to the needs of travel. The utilitarian arts, in particular, make sense to pack on a journey. In a welcome gesture, the exhibition places "craft" works, such as ceramics and calligraphy, alongside works in contemporary, conceptual forms that would be at home in any exhibition of international art (for example, at the National Gallery of Canada). The separation of art from craft — the idea that art continues to change, while craft is stuck in the past — is a modern European notion. This distinction serves the well-known colonial strategy of relegating a colonized culture and its traditions to a time outside time, modernity and "progress".[2] But in Middle Eastern and North African tradition, calligraphy and other useful arts such as ceramics, weaving and bookbinding were pursued as the highest creative forms until the end of the Ottoman Empire, and are still valued alongside art for art's sake. In **The Lands within Me** we may see works in craft media as spirited revivals of a tradition in which art and life are not separate.

Functional objects also have the metallic property of being conductors between "there" and "here". As Liliane Karnouk says, furniture is a mediator; standing between the carpet from home and the computer from here, the furniture she builds "connects two worlds of experience." These useful things are examples of what I've termed the "transnational object": objects that are created in cultural translation and transcultural movement.[3] In Laila Binbrek's *Mirror, Mirror*, a pair of vanity tables covered with transnational objects offers a comparison of the elaborate beauty rituals women perform "over there" and "over here".[4] On one table, frankincense, cubes of musk, and incense balls are evidence of the time-honoured cultivation of scent as a form of beauty. A big bottle of Chanel's Amarige on the "Canadian" table, and a tiny sample of the same perfume on the "Yemeni" table, may indicate that European products are hard to come by, or it may suggest that bottled fragrances are not so coveted in a region that, at the inception of the perfume industry, provided methods and ingredients to the relatively scent-ignorant Europeans. Here are two different cultural ideas of beauty: one more olfactory, one more visual. Sugar hair-remover and rose-petal scrub on one side, Nair and The Body Shop on the other, remind us that in the globalization of the culture of beauty, everything comes with a brand name. Yet each side of the table hints of the life on the other, and we sense that the same woman sits on either side of the table — on one side donning the lace-trimmed black veil; on the other baring her exfoliated skin for all to see.

Among these artists we also find *bricoleurs*, scavenging materials pertaining to shipping and housing: linoleum floor tiles, burlap sacks. The transitory nature of these materials suggests that being in a place cannot be separated from the journey, even for artists born in Canada. Ali Kichou's *La vache des orphelins* is a voluminous tapestry made, not of precious silk or fine wool, but of rough burlap coffee sacks, stamped with export information. Immediately we know this is art about transit and translation. Kichou has painted the sacks with a scattering of forms borrowed from Berber women's fabric designs, in brown, white and shocking neon colours. These are travelling materials, nomadic designs; the eccentric pattern itself, growing over the surface of the burlap like a hardy weed, seems willing to travel indefinitely. *La vache des orphelins* is a highly optimistic work of art, testifying to the migrant's ability to adapt knowledge to new situations. The single dark note, squatting in a corner of the tapestry, is a very tall, stylized wooden stool with a brass spike on the seat: a menacing instrument of worship or torture, or both. The screaming yellows, greens and pinks of the new synthetic dyes recall how artists in colonized cultures traditionally take advantage of trade to incorporate European innovation, as when in the eighteenth century First Nations artists began incorporating glass beads alongside quills in their embroideries. Connoisseurs and art historians may wring their hands at the demise of authenticity, but the artists themselves, one imagines, are restless to innovate with whatever new tools become available. The bright chemical colours are a testament to the lively impurity of art. "Promise me that you will not sell the cow, that you will always keep it for the little orphans," Kichou quotes the tale; this cow appears to be an endless source of sustenance.

Postcards, the art form destined for transition, are a medium contingent upon a journey, and the possibility of never reaching a destination. Rawi Hage produces his black-and-white photographs as dozens of postcards, rejecting the notion of works of art as precious objects. What is seen in the photos in *Care of Raymonde* is different from the usual tourist snaps, however: many are taken at touristic sites, but the view is skewed and particular. Others capture transient moments: a destroyed movie theatre with some seats still intact; three children's sandalled feet; light streaming through a half-open door. Submitted to the post, the cards become little traveling bodies, arriving, if they do arrive, battered and weary from the journey, and stamped with the permissions, costs and surveillance of border-crossings. Hage sent these cards, intimately inscribed in Arabic, French and English, to a friend before submitting them to be viewed by us, so we remain aware that our viewing of them is bound up with the look and touch of another.

Writing Travels

All the above objects are fundamentally "metallic", in their ability to change form, conduct, and melt down for travel. The other medium of travelling art that I emphasize here is calligraphy. The painted word is the privileged art form of condensation; ever since the Islamic prohibition on illustrating the word of God, artists have learned to compress the divine into that most abstract of figures, the written word. In principle, the word has no substance beyond its cognitive function. In practice, the word always invites embodiment on the one hand, and transcendence on the other. The word is the membrane between the mortal and the immortal. When we read a word, we speak it mentally, giving it form on our lips, tongue and throat: speaking it, we connect the word to the physical world through our bodies. As Maurice Merleau-Ponty wrote, "Words most charged with philosophy are not necessarily those that contain what they say, but rather those that most energetically open upon being."[5] At the same time, however, the word — especially the words of a spiritual book such as the Koran — points beyond the material world. The calligraphic medallions that decorate mosques are a special kind of window which allows worshippers to see straight through to the divine. In the history of Islam, the word became a figure, in order both to connect with the material world and to hint at the transcendent realities it conceals. Even when the words are not names of God but useful maxims, they manipulate the relationship between word as thought and word as embodied action. As a meditation, calligraphy concentrates the artist's activity, in order that viewers may later partake of its meditative properties. In the hands of Yasser Badreddine and Aldin Rachid, words shimmy into figuration and then innocently slip back into word.

The word is the membrane between the mortal and the immortal.

Bookbinding is another of the traditional arts that came under siege during the speedy industrialization of North Africa and the Middle East in the early twentieth century. Taouffik Semmad's exquisite book *Histoire de Sindbad le marin : premier voyage* (*History of Sinbad the Sailor: First Voyage*) is unbound. Semmad's work, being copperplate etchings, is a bridge between writing and metal. Unlike the exquisitely-controlled calligraphy of Badreddine and Rachid, Semmad's ink seems to have flown from his brush in bursts of inspiration, divine or otherwise. Some of his spontaneous figures recall the "flung ink" (*sui boku*) paintings of Ch'an masters: artists who subsumed their egos and concentrated their bodies so that the will of the universe could take form in a single fluid gesture. For his series *L'Avant-Babel* (*The Time before Babel*) Semmad incorporates gestural writings from many cultures: Arabic, Cyrillic, Chinese. He seems to suggest that it is the body that ultimately bears the weight of mixed cultural knowledge, and that it is the body, again in an act of meditative concentration, that can achieve and express the synthesis of this knowledge.

Words need exercise. That the word revels in the freedom of travel is most evident in the joyous painted tiles of Shwan. From a tradition in which precious enamelled tiles celebrated the names of God, Shwan extracts two elements — tiles and celebration — and the rest is invention. These sayings are thoroughly secular: chestnuts of wisdom like "Nobody buys fish in the water" and epigrams borrowed from shop windows. Shwan has chosen the humblest of mass-produced materials — linoleum floor tiles — and has integrated their easy-clean pastel aesthetics into his work. Although the bright colours and crude forms look childish, there is a concentrated wisdom in these works: a sort of existential celebration of the life that insists on continuing to be reborn from tired phrases and utilitarian materials. "Love is blind" is knowingly inscribed on faux-brick tile, while forgiving hearts wink around the phrase said of intolerable people, "God must have had a good reason to create him/her." Shwan rejects the traditional stylized calligraphic forms, preferring to let the word dance from the brush. In his recent framed paintings, the lines and colours spill onto the frame, too exuberant to be contained.

Like Shwan's casual calligraphy, many of these works are deceptively modest: it is the task of the viewer to retrace the steps of their travels. Meanings change in transit. Something that was part of everyday life in one place becomes laden with other kinds of significance in another. Many of these works testify to what Igor Kopytoff calls the "cultural biography of things"[6] — the changing value objects gain in the course of transit. What was common in one culture becomes a treasure when it is carried to another. Objects and ideas shapeshift over the course of a voyage, collecting new and unforeseen meanings. Spending time with these works, you begin to learn their biography.

Baggage Travels

A third aspect of travelling light is its converse: "having a lot of baggage". Being in the West requires constant acts of translation and correction: a Middle Eastern artist in Canada can never simply be in the present because the Western present is coded against him or her; thus, there is a continual demand to retranslate, to explain oneself. Camille Zakharia's revolving collage, *Lebanon-Canada, via Bahrain*, suggests the triple worldview constantly negotiated by the émigré. Consider the will it takes to keep inhabiting a beloved and well-known culture in the midst of a disorienting and re-Orienting new one. I write re-Orienting, for suddenly in the new context these artists and their memories are considered exotic. The most optimistic of these works defy charges of exoticism and splash the hues, scents and exuberant lines of the homeland onto chilly, monochrome Canada. Hadjira Preure's *Houria* is ablaze with sublime colour. Mirella Aprahamian washes the monochromatic landscape with leaf green, while in Joseph Moukhtar's paintings, Quebec architecture takes on curving lines as though full of mosques.

What was common in one culture becomes a treasure when it is carried to another.

Part of this baggage of cultural translation is the negotiation between traditional and modern (Western) styles and media. The internationalization of the art world has led to a certain uniformity in the criteria for what is good art. Yet in recent years, artists have incorporated the practices of their non-Western traditions into erstwhile "Western-style" art, producing hybrid art practices. Works by Nicolas Zeitouni, such as the charming *Mona*, incorporate the traditional surface-organized composition (as opposed to illusionistic depth), traditional iconography, and the blue of the Egyptian sky, into the European medium of easel painting.

Works in the contemporary vocabularies of conceptual and installation art are, interestingly, also the most overtly concerned with addressing the process of cultural translation. These works ask whether it is possible to translate between cultures and over time: whether some understanding can arise, or whether memory is buried in the place it originated. Jamelie Hassan's elegant *L'espace de l'alphabet – II* (*The Space of the Alphabet — II*) works literally with translation: the transformations of Arabic script as it was adapted to transcribe languages such as Berber and Farsi. Her works hint at what is lost, and what is retained, as local languages are incorporated into the dominant Arabic. Jayce Salloum's five-screen video installation *everything and nothing* (from the ongoing project *untitled*) weaves together the voices of exiles: former Yugoslavians reflecting on their shattered nation; and the fragile yet magnetic Soha Bechara, a Lebanese National Resistance fighter who was jailed and tortured at the Khiam detention centre and now studies international law in Paris. This powerful work communicates effectively because harsh is framed by gentle. The long words of the Eastern European intellectuals are cushioned by a screen of clouds. As Bechara caresses the rose Salloum offers her, the intimate context of the interview gently frames her impassioned description of the ideal of cultural translation: "It goes beyond acceptance, beyond tolerance, it is the capacity to reach an empathy with the other in a way that encompasses everyone, democratically, with liberty, equality, and justice."

In the work *and at night we leave our dreams on the window sill: memory of a place*, Farouk Kaspaules uses the silkscreen technique to literalize the buildup of histories of cultures and colonization. Each panel in this array of printed panels pictures a fragment of sculpture, a painted miniature or an architectural edifice, juxtaposing rich and expressive forms from many eras. Some of these images are overlaid with a menacing matrix of stylized forms suggesting cruise missiles, testifying to the destruction of cultural treasures during the Gulf War, as well as to the longstanding pillage of the Middle Eastern cultural heritage by European museums. In the centre of each panel, an oblong form suggests a window, or perhaps a prayer mat. Kaspaules makes it clear that the treasures of his cultural heritage are lost from view, whether owing to his displacement or to their physical destruction. Nostalgia is out of the question, for nostalgia suggests it is possible to return. In contrast, Bernice Lutfie Sorge gives a tentative access to memories of the past — covering, or uncovering, faint family photographs under a pattern of blood-red philodendron leaves. In these works, as in works by Binbrek, Salloum, Hassan, and Sami Zubi, the act of expression is inextricable from the effort to clear out a space, in the Canadian context, from which to express.

The question for the travelling artist thus becomes: Should I work to clear out a space from which, eventually, migrants like me will be able to express, or should I go ahead and express, even if it might be misunderstood? These two different tasks — expressing and making room for others to express — are best carried out cumulatively and collectively, as in the shared space created by **The Lands within Me**. The choices each artist has made rely on a deeper question that accompanies preparing for a voyage: When you packed to leave, why did you bring *this*?

1 Gilles Deleuze and Félix Guattari, "Treatise on Nomadology — The War Machine," *A Thousand Plateaus: Capitalism and Schizophrenia*, trans. Brian Massumi (Minneapolis: University of Minnesota Press, 1987), pp. 401–402.

2 Johannes Fabian, *Time and the Other: How Anthropology Makes Its Object* (New York: Columbia University Press, 1983).

3 See Laura U. Marks, "The Memory of Things," Chapter 3 of *The Skin of the Film: Intercultural Cinema, Embodiment, and the Senses* (Durham N.C.: Duke University Press, 2000).

4 Binbrek is of Yemeni ancestry, was born in Kitchener, Ontario, and grew up in Saudi Arabia; the products on her table were collected by aunts in Yemen and in the United Arab Emirates; so "here" and "there" mean many places.

5 Maurice Merleau-Ponty, *The Prose of the World* (Evanston, Ill.: Northwestern University Press, 1973), p. 20. Originally published as *La Prose du monde* (Paris: Gallimard, 1969).

6 Igor Kopytoff, "The Cultural Biography of Things: Commoditization as Process." In Arjun Appadurai, ed., *The Social Life of Things: Commodities on cultural perspective* (New York: Cambridge University Press, 1986), pp. 64–94.

THE ART OF LEAVING TRACES

THE ART OF LEAVING TRACES

Lamberto Tassinari

Which Lands Live within Them?

The exhibition **The Lands within Me** and its 26 artists give us occasion to attempt a diagnosis — to advance hypotheses on what today's art heralds. The exhibition is itself an unusual event: something other than the customary visual arts exhibition that demands recourse to aesthetic theories, to the coded language of the art critic.

There are several good reasons, other than aesthetic, for commenting on this exhibition. The first is that, being *without a country* twice over, as artists and as migrants, these creators witness, with overwhelming clarity, the universality of the artistic quest and its symbolic substance. Secondly, through the infusion of their "cultural identities" into the universal space of artistic play, they demonstrate (alas! this is still necessary) that the time has come to destroy our mindset of *modern* classification which persists in qualifying artworks, attributing to them a place and a time — an "ethnic" identity. Finally, the status of these creators as non-protagonists, non-stars, in the international arts system — even if certain of them benefit from international recognition — constitutes one of the most convincing demonstrations that this is an era in which it becomes necessary to redefine the meaning and the role of art. For, although the world seems to be running quickly towards its own demise,[1] the artist remains generally perceived as the bearer of visions capable of changing this world. Because they know how to see, how to perceive and how to create works, artists are called upon to "witness".

To affirm the worth of personal testimony in art is all the more important, since, as I will try to show, it is necessary to democratize art, once and for all, by euthanizing its *aura*.[2] One of the artists in the exhibition, Adel Alnaser, shares this conviction with me. On the Plateau Mont-Royal in Montreal, in his small apartment — which seems hewn from stone, white as a whitewashed wall, tortuous as an alley in Bagdad (his city of origin) and, strangely, giving the impression of an Italian Renaissance painter's studio — Adel spoke to me of his life, which is his art. Therein lies the sublime virtue of art: its unifying strength, its truthful character. We are forced to remain utopian and to believe that there will arise a society in which "the artist will not constitute a particular sort of man, but where each man will constitute a particular sort of artist."[3] It is the microphysics of

One day, this son and grandson of artisans . . . picked up his suitcase and transformed himself into a voyager becoming poco a poco, as he puts it, the voyage itself.

the existent that proves the soundness of such a view: the secret life of an artist working outside the noisy and illusory world of the media — the calm and harmony of his gestures, his words, the subject matter of his works, his world.

Adel Alnaser, during the travels that led him from "the land between two rivers"[4] to Canada, stopped over in Italy, where he lived for several years and studied art in Rome. The Italian language, which he still speaks very well, was our lingua franca, and gave our meeting a surprising taste of universality. The personal testimony of an artist such as he can be summarized in a single word: *freedom*. One day, this son and grandson of artisans tied up his camel in the desert of ancient Assyria, picked up his suitcase and transformed himself into a voyager becoming *poco a poco*, as he puts it, the voyage itself.

At that time, painting was already his life, and even if life is greater than art, art constitutes the centre of it, its heart, its meaning. If he has followed his vocation, his passion, as other artists do, he has, nonetheless, known how to avoid the anguish that paralyzes the majority among them, which derives from a desire for recognition, a need for consecration by critics, the thirst for success. It is in this way that he has remained free. A nomad, he never stops travelling, crossing borders that he does not see because he does not believe in them, so convinced is he that his roots extend over the entire earth and intermingle with those of other men and women who live with us on the same planet — our "earth-nation" as Edgar Morin calls it.

The calligrapher Taouffik Semmad allows us to touch upon that other aspect of art, which is tradition. Tradition: that is to say, memory, method, attachment to names, attachment to a place. If all that is not opposed to travel, still it is not founded in travel. Expatriated without being a nomad, Semmad is an authentic weaver of cultures, languages, signs: the Orient, the Latin world, the Hellenic world — he draws them all, in spiralling scrolls of colour. In fact, this studio artist adopts an analytical approach to art, in which research and experimentation are associated with the lessons of the past. The man, as much as the artist, has settled his accounts with nostalgia, having succeeded in integrating the diverse cultures that make up his personality, and that never cease to work upon him as he ceaselessly works with them. He does not really miss the odours, the colours, the sounds of his native Algeria: his laboratory is his country.

Uprooting, Disorientation and Art

If we believe that there are as many nomadic artists as sedentary artists, we know, all the same, the point at which, in the history of civilizations, travel has become an experience that creates meaning, producing symbols and myths. On the individual level also, as we have seen, the voyage is a gesture charged with ethical and aesthetic consequences. To leave the paternal home, the mother-fatherland, to uproot oneself in order to inhabit the voyage — the "somewhere else" — plunges us into the territory of imagination: imagination of the Other and of the faraway, whether it be the unknown, still to come, or that lost place to which we must return — the features of which fade from memory, the remembering of which is itself a kind of suffering. In the Greek language, *nostalgia* means *pain provoked by the thought of return*. Ulysses is the symbol of the man-artist, and *The Odyssey*, the narrative of his return to Ithaca, is the founding model, the archetype, of the adventure story.

The Romantic movement reappropriated this theme of the voyage at the beginning of the nineteenth century and, towards the end of that same century, symbolism was only the exacerbation and theorization of this aesthetic and of a visionary art whose great practitioners are Baudelaire, Rimbaud and Mallarmé. In their writings, we find again such words and expressions as *pure art*, *spirituality*, *alchemy*, *artist-hero-genius*, *predestined being*, *aesthetic sainthood*, *prophecy*, *seer*. According to these poets, art — "pure art" — is the tool capable of uncovering the spiritual in nature, transforming "mud into gold". If the mystical formulation of some expressions can provoke a certain discomfort within us, we must, nonetheless, recognize that art became modern through its refusal of modernity; that is to say, through its disavowal of the bourgeois world and its ethical and political values. Discomfort aside, how can we not adhere to this artistic vision which, together with surrealism, has been the most superb attempt of Western culture to bridge the maddening distance that separates us from the truths of the Orient?

In reality, what astonishes us most is that the extremely powerful affirmation that the Universe is thought — abstraction rather than brute matter — and that there is a single source and matrix of all beings, could have led to the elaboration of the myth of the isolated artist, saint, genius, as well as to an elitist and undemocratic positioning of art. But the scientific and positivist culture of that epoch of frenzied "progress" against which they were fighting did not allow Rimbaud, Mallarmé and other avant-gardists to conclude otherwise. To understand chaos and chance while trying to decode the functioning of the universe would be, at the turn of the century, the task of the physical sciences and mathematics, an undertaking of which these artists and others were, I believe, the "prophets" — a word which means *those who speak before*.

Migration is an experience that I regard as "melogenic" — that is, generating song.

Although our way of living and thinking art is still influenced by the Romantic vision of the artist as *beacon*, *visionary*, *genius*, we must admit that, fortunately, these parameters are in the process of being completely transformed into the tangible utopia of an art that is diffused, common, panicked,[5] without aura. The waves of emigration that turned the world upside down in the twentieth century confirmed, among other things, a phenomenon that escapes statistics, and interests neither economists nor politicians: the validity of the myth of displacement and uprooting as experiences essential to artistic evolution. In other words, it must be acknowledged that the sense of being a stranger in a strange land, which characterizes the artist, is a phenomenon of the same nature as that experienced by the emigrant.

Migration is an experience that I regard as "melogenic" — that is, generating song. It is as if, in migrating, we activate a psycho-emotional device that has the power to intensify artistic potential. A single glance at the panorama of arts and letters of the last century shows us how rich is the representation of émigré artists. Such proof, however, is always ambiguous, and is less than convincing at the level of the individual. We will not explore it further, but rather leave to readers the pleasure of drawing up their own list of migrant artists. Collective cases, those concerning an entire society, have a more objective character. Of the latter, the most formidable is the Argentine tango, the nostalgic music and culture *par excellence*. More than influence, we would have to call the tango an epidemic, so much did the contribution of immigrant experience create a rich and complex poetic that acted on several generations of an entire society.

From the Museum to the Street

Through the centuries, "leading" artists have progressively become safety valves: guarantors of a very effective and longstanding alibi for the Establishment. Art, in a sense, has partially replaced religion and all the transcendences liquidated by modernity. The museums, in the words of French philosopher Régis Debray, filled up as the cathedrals emptied, which Walt Whitman had already affirmed by saying, in effect, "exit the priest, enter the poet." Today, the problems confronting art reveal a deep malaise that goes beyond the polemics among historians, critics and artists. The art of the twentieth century did not succeed in transforming society, even if production and distribution technologies resulted in profound changes on the quantitative as well as qualitative levels. All of art is at issue, not simply contemporary visual art — the most "exposed" and *scandalous* of arts — for it best reveals the common and *easy* character of artistic expression.

It is the very meaning of art, in all its forms and in all periods, that must be redefined. Faced with this inescapable necessity, perhaps before and in lieu of proposing theories, we should act. I would like to suggest an act that would signify a radical transformation in the conventional way of making and living art. An extreme, utopian gesture, which seems to me to move in a direction close to that taken by "emigrant artists" — including those participating in the exhibition **The Lands within Me** — simply, then, to challenge the stock-exchange philosophy in order to reaffirm the value of life and the *street*, the horizontal surface *par excellence*, an eminently democratic and utopian space. We also have to do everything to eliminate the old bourgeois mistrust of the street, which never stops increasing in this society of castes, of super-bourgeoisie and pariahs that is in the process of establishing itself. It is enough, for the moment, to imagine it! The movement that I foresee proceeds in a direction opposite to the one we are used to. We know that the specialists *salvage* art from the street, be it the art of graffiti painters or Fauvist writers, in order to bring that art within institutions, there to consecrate it; now we must travel in the opposite direction — from the museum to the street. The real street; but also the network, the information highway, on condition of guaranteeing to the works their public character and their freedom.

It is the very meaning of art, in all its forms and in all periods, that must be redefined.

One day someone said to me, speaking of mothers and fathers and their relationship with children, that all contradictions will be resolved, all injustices eliminated, when a toddler in tears will be able to cry out "Papa!" rather than "Mama!". In the same way, we will see the aura of art begin to fade on the day that professionals, merchants, bureaucrats, curators and artists feel the need to move their works into the street — this place *par excellence* for passing by and meeting others. Art will then take back its ancient value as therapeutic play, with profound social and political implications — at times sublime and divine, but always free-of-charge.

1 Let us recall certain facts: two world wars, several genocides, the advanced destruction of the environment, the transformation of food-consumption practices by doubtful technologies, the most savage cultural pollution by the entertainment and information industry, the reification of every aspect of life. If the last century has truly been marked by artists as we pretend, then we must end by concluding that there is something awry in the manner of making, understanding and using art. Not only contemporary art, but also modern art that was born with the Renaissance, *our* art, issued from the mercantile, aesthetic, scientific, bourgeois and industrial revolutions that succeeded each other from the fifteenth century through to the first half of the twentieth century.

2 It was Walter Benjamin who introduced this term to aesthetics in the 1930s. The German philosopher felt art to be threatened, but the power of its aura seemed to him sufficient to resist the devastation caused by merchandising. Today, this fading of the aura that he foresaw with regret and anguish, we must welcome as a potential liberation. I developed this theme in the text *Art: euthanasie de l'aura à l'ère numérique*, published in the collective work UTOPIA (Presses de l'Université de Laval, 2001).

3 In *L'art contre l'esthétique* by Antoni Tàpies, 1974. The words quoted are those of Sri Aurobindo.

4 Literal translation of the word *Mesopotamia*. The two rivers are the Euphrates and the Tigris. Iraq, the native land of Adel Alnaser, is situated in the heart of this region.

5 I use this term in the sense of "uncontrollable and of an often collective character" (*Larousse*) while referring to art rather than to terror.

THE ORIENT OR THE TRAJECTORY OF MEMORY

serge ouaknine

THE ORIENT OR THE TRAJECTORY OF MEMORY

A Canadian Premiere

Paradox is the raw material of émigré artists: on the one hand, they absorb the signs of the new world and are thus marked by the culture that receives them; on the other, they carry with them the past — emotions inscribed in the memories of everyday life. It is vital, in introducing this first and most significant exhibition by Canadian artists of Arab origin at the Canadian Museum of Civilization, to delve into the layers of meaning hidden beneath the surfaces of these works. These artworks are addressed to an intimate utopia, a world that is drawn, written and sculpted: a bridge between the signs of the old world and the faces of the new one. The importance of the past in the lives of these artists becomes a visible subtext in their work.

As though afraid that the past might disappear, the artist both itemizes the contents of yesterday and underscores the present, spinning, like an Oriental weaver, an abstract geometry.

Here we find letters, mail art, prints and collages. These are memories of ancestral brush-strokes entwined with lines that are far more recent. As though afraid that the past might disappear, the artist both itemizes the contents of yesterday and underscores the present, spinning, like an Oriental weaver, an abstract geometry. These artists are men and women who share a common calligraphy of curves and vaults, and their works re-create a labyrinth of ancient gestures. Family photographs transferred onto canvas convene the deceased. Surprising installations offer a woman's ironic perspective on a bourgeois day-to-day existence cluttered with furniture and household objects. The murals, photographs and montages, ceramics and paintings assembled by the exhibition **The Lands within Me** confront the visitor with a universe of constantly displaced references. The works require that we be both present and elsewhere simultaneously.

The strength and vulnerability of the artist is his or her simultaneous presence in two places — *here* and *there*. The artists are thus the navigators of an intimate, internal vessel sailing towards the continent of their work. These acts transcend nostalgia, and their will appropriates memory in a contemporary rewriting of trajectory and line.

The Work of and in Time

Canadian artists of Arab origin are not trapped by the production of single artifacts. Rather, their voices gather together the disparate elements of a distant vitality. The objects that result tell the stories of different ways of life (is an art possible without the fertile historical humus provided by the community?). The object is not merely skillfully deployed; it both contains and transforms lives. It is at once a memory and a project. Its creators wish it to endure, and through it they hope to contribute to the renewal of their communities. The object is thus a sign of the artist's embodied, even carnal, alliance with the multitude. If, in its negotiations with the object, the Occident privileges the marginal and the discontinuous, the Orient emphasizes the slower continuity of a longer archaic memory, rooted in an oral tradition that links every aspect of life to the voice of the community.

The Lands within Me reveals artists more concerned with re-appropriation than with transgression. These works, varying greatly from one another in style and technique, are anchored in an ancient and visceral mathematics that animates them from within. The artist's hand operates a form of algebra — an invention of Arab science that permits the transformation of quantities and the positing of imaginary objects. The one God who unifies all things juggles with the ever-mutable signs of His creation.

This knowledge is a "gymnastics of the spirit" which can be made apparent in two- and three-dimensional spaces. In this transformational vortex, all of the ingredients of memory are revisited, reworked in the *alembic* of an intimate *alchemy* (two more Arab inventions!). And if the spaces and colours are organized in a non-perspectival arrangement, it is that the Orient has partially escaped from the Occidental rhetoric that has, since the Renaissance, transformed the Eternal into a geometric reduction, in which the lines of perspective seek to invert or abolish time. The Arab vision of reality does not indicate a closed space but rather a living moment without *a priori* horizons or differentiated objects.

The Arab market is evoked — its loaded shelves, its generous accumulation of goods: fruits, spices, crafts and textiles that together comprise a unified chromatic spectrum. These accumulations are seductive, inviting the hand to touch, the body to linger. The space of these negotiations re-creates the curves of alleys and streets beneath an open sky. Here is a shady corner of green, a quarter of the city imprinted by leafy shadows. An oasis is narrated without being represented in its totality.

Colours return to white. The fragment names the whole. Form is a sensation before becoming a thing. It is a memory of the world before becoming a description of its inventory. This is how the Canadian artist of Arab origin perpetuates a knowledge that can be said to be the "breath of the mind". These artists *hear before seeing*, and the words of the Orient take form in the space where the visible and the invisible intersect. The pendulum strikes two poles: one passionate and characterized by a sensuality that longs for union with a "higher" consciousness outside of time; the other a procession of grief and wounds, of fears and revolts — the weight of the world. The *'umma*, the omnipresent community, curtails the individual's desire for independence; thus, these artists have set themselves apart from collectively convened rules and limits. But they separate themselves from reality in order to be faithful to it. One might think that the works in the exhibition, abstract and figurative, share the deconstructive preoccupations of the West. Look again: they differ in their ways of naming and rewriting memory.

Two Memories at Stake

Modern art defined itself as attempting, in Paul Klee's words, to "make visible the invisible." This short phrase contains the concentrated credo of the art of the twentieth century, and is far from innocent. In the sense given to it by its author, it means that the artist's vocation is not to illustrate but rather to show what underlies reality: a metaphorical world in which appearances mask a poetic stance, and the artist's play with form serves to expose the promises of language. The invisible occupies a central, visible role in the daily life of Arab civilizations, where the visible is assigned the role of protecting that which the eyes cannot, must not, see. Islam, like Judaism, forbids that a form be given to God. An image of the Ultimate is vanity, and thus the Arab civilizations have developed an exceptional abstract and geometric art. The interlacing motifs of a mosaic, a frieze, a pot, a platter or a carpet narrate in their variations that it is impossible for humanity to encompass infinity. Form is destined not to reveal the unknowable, but rather to keep it safe from the gazes of both mortals and the All-Powerful.

Viewing the range of works in **The Lands within Me** we realize that it is the artists' encryption of reality that has seized our interest. We are struck by an art that itemizes creation and limns human feelings and desires through the creative act. The Canadian artist of Arab origin speaks of this pathway through memory — of a recollection uprooted and recomposed in the vast spaces of modernity in which an ancient nomadic culture has been reborn. This art speaks mainly out of dispersion, but also out of silence. The Canadian artist of Arab origin is integrated into the life of the new world, and can grant his or her imagination a fertile liberty within its remembered exile. While the majority of the artists in this exhibition declare their allegiance to the modern and post-modern currents of Occidental art, one can detect, beyond the shock of first impressions, a universe that resists categorical reductions. Two levels of discourse can be detected: the visible, factual one and the one belonging to a distant memory, operating from far away.

These works are offerings made of desire: leaps of the self that attempt to repair the fracture between two worlds.

Canadian artists of Arab origin advance masked. They borrow the aesthetics of other cultures in order to preserve that which remains nameless and veiled in the intangible ferment of their inner culture. There are thus two levels to their discourse: a formal modernity and the resurgence of an intangible narrative that is lived rather than seen. At times decorative, at times dramatic, this (re)citation of the world takes up the vast history of the architecture and objects that accompany it. From the splendours of the Umayyades to the glory of Andalucia, the repetitive motifs, the iconic function of religious abstraction — in every case, what is seen demonstrates the near-metaphysical precedence of what is heard, Suras and Psalms offered to infinity. The song of these contemporary artists is at once ancient and modern. They convey a desire to integrate the urgency of the present moment with the endlessly revisited Word of eternity.

These two aspects manifest themselves in the two main ways in which the artists of this exhibition work. The first is open to the world, to narrative subjectivity, to the eloquence of the daily as expressed in private life. The second, more monumental, travels back through architectural history with majestic panels whose resplendent details communicate with one another, transforming themselves so that each single detail becomes a mirror of the whole. Paintings on canvas or paper, collages, photographs, mail art, ceramics, screens, installations and videos fuse the microcosm and macrocosm. These works are offerings made of desire: leaps of the self that attempt to repair the fracture between two worlds. Here and there, yesterday and today co-exist with the quest for a difficult present — the reminder of the "us" and the resistance of the "I" to disappearing within it.

The Lands within Me testifies to a brilliance of craft that embraces the vast fresco of disappeared worlds through an intimate, even bourgeois description of modern urban living and with the pulsing energy of the *souk*, of the desert and the *medina*. Their unique proclamations make Canadian artists of Arab origin both witnesses and members of a vast public space. On the one hand, the artist's subjectivity modestly effaces itself; on the other, the artist's majesty erects a fresco of references which objectify their sources, injecting their vitality into Canada's surging cultural spaces.

Imitation or Representation

In the West, modern art has taught us that the divine is reached through the sacrificial gesture of deconstructing appearances, by disavowing the world. In the universe of the visual arts, we are audience to either conceptual or geometric invention, or a lyrical abstraction that glorifies the subjectivity of gesture and line. From Cezanne to Rothko, the twentieth century has simultaneously simplified expression and complicated representation. Artists have dithered between one tendency or the other. Radical metamorphosis is the tool of expression (symbolism, surrealism, expressionism, tachisme), while representation relies on a process of abstractions: on the one hand, a quest for spiritual clarity; on the other, the staging of a radical materiality (ready-made, pop art, land art, wrappings, installations). Between these two poles, the world as images contradicts the world as volume. The icon denounces the reality it describes. Volume renders ironic the materiality it organizes. The Canadian artists of Arab origin follow these tendencies, but the staging of their works produces flattened images of a world whose actors are absent. Area and volume inform each other equally. Form's claim on nature's substance is not the fundamental question. Rather, in the Orient, the memory of life is of greater importance than the desire to seize it. The environment is not alien to the body; rather it is its ultimate consequence. The image does not represent — it is the word that makes us see.

In contrast to the West's radical doubts concerning the relationship of signs to the world, the Orient, implacably faithful to its transcendental wisdom, subjugates the visible world to the word. This dominance of the word in representation spreads west along the Mediterranean towards the Atlantic and eastwards to Asia and Oceania. The image is not completely absent, but it has been codified in a way that bears multiple influences. One certainty has remained: truth is beyond its worldly reflections, the "real" is shared, and this sharing bonds the community of the faithful and subjugates each member of the tribe to the One that transcends life. Thus, imitation is tainted with blasphemy. This prohibition has been avoided and ignored countless times, but from this ban on images remains an awareness of sacrifice that has been fruitfully appropriated by artists. Faced with the triumphant modernist affirmation of the West — its celebration of the tangible — the Orient reiterates, even in its democratic and secular discourses, that that which is seen is merely the antechamber of that which is heard. Beauty is not what can be stolen by the eyes, but that which has a voice to soothe the heart.

The divine and the invisible are bonded: built into the exchanges of daily life, into the interpersonal transactions of the day. This seems to be the secret of the Arab civilizations. If there is a masterful awareness of time, if there is a duration that creates meaning, it is because of an exchange — a commerce linked to the Word, and ultimately to the acceptance of a silent Presence, the source and original memory of all things. This fragile and mysterious thread links the private and public life of the Arab family. This is why, despite similarities of form, these artists speak of other things; they tell us of the countries that inhabit them, of a buried continent, of the untranslatable essence of a lost world. The schism between what is lived and how it is remembered is proper to the acts of every artist. The lived space becomes the memory of the space that is lost.

The Boatman's Knowledge

Contemporary art has legitimized the liminal zones between reality and its metaphors. We are the children of the polytheistic Greco-Roman world, as well as of the monotheistic Orient. On the one hand, imperial icons destined for the eyes and on the other, the cantillation of the sacred texts — Biblical, Koranic and Byzantine — the spiritual canticles destined for the ear. Thus these Canadian artists of Arab descent sit upon the steps of both the Orient and the Occident. They are the smugglers of complex, hybrid memories. Living in the generosity of Canadian culture, they are messengers who bring to their task a fantastic translation and elucidation of the space between two worlds. That we may better "hear" the history that **The Lands within Me** represents, they invite us to retrace their steps in order to decode the arcana of a bridge spanning two understandings of the world. The guardians of reworked memories, they knock on the door that leads to the landscapes of the future.

Can this be said of all the artists in the exhibition? Some seem more naïve than others: the images of some are more anchored in the moment, while others offer only a fleeting glimpse of the past. Some give life to the act of writing, while others evoke the daily habitat of yesterday. There are even those who offer livable spaces and visions of an entire world. If memory dominates in the Orient, it is due to its transitive and illusory quality. The essence of language is not to create with memory, but rather to be inhabited and possessed by it. Memory commandeers the subject's desire to speak. When an artist innovates, he or she reworks the world. Memory is there, mute and hidden in that metamorphosis.

Integration with reality is impossible without the return of the sensations and emotions that the artist has bartered. The first act of the immigrant is not to assimilate into the new, but to gather the scattered fragments that must be reunited. "Memory is my future," says every newcomer, "and my new home is but the trampoline of an apprenticeship — here is what I was, and I will be thus again, but differently." Memory is not a refuge for the artist. It is not the nostalgia that freezes what has been lost. Memory opens not onto the idea of remaking (that of the artisan), but that of re-creating (that of the artist). The "there" of yesterday is filtered, a dream to be interpreted "here". Thus do we come to understand the two stakes for which the immigrant artist plays — these are the responsibilities of the nomadic artist: the artists must save themselves as subjects, and also save "that land over there". This journey in two directions is the source of an initiation: an act that becomes a rite of passage, both in private and in public.

All that the Orient was, and can be remembered as, is temporarily installed in the vast spaces of Canada's cities and landscapes.

If the artists of the exhibition work from fragments, it is because it is the fragment that brings this two-headed memory to life. The figurative and representational schemes have been borrowed from the Occident, but the matrix in which they are set heralds from the "country of origin". We are witnesses to the itemization of a vast inventory: daily objects, family photos, portraits of parents, whole photo albums, daily objects from private life, calligraphies, staging of texts and objects, collages made from pieces of the past. Further, montages of architectural ruins, the broken spaces of memory, riveting photos of war, of the struggles that mark recent Arab history, and of the films that dream of their disappearance. Finally and simply, an investigation of the sensory aspect of colour, of fabric, of the brute sensuality of materials — not as a pretext for formal renderings of volume (as with the early Cubists) but as an expression of memories regenerated by the act of creation. The residue of these fragments persists, resisting its own disappearance.

These artists are the guardian angels of fused territories that together comprise the fictive continent to be revisited. All that the Orient was, and can be remembered as, is temporarily installed in the vast spaces of Canada's cities and landscapes. Thus, sand and snow, torrid heat and neverending winter, can meet and mix. The vastness of Canada and its harsh climate offers Oriental artists an enormous mirror wherein they are reflected inside-out: memory becomes the eternal present which moves forwards across the signs of the past and is transformed by its contact with newer stories. The contemporary accumulations carry the same loads as the antique caravans, moving from the infinitely large into intimacy, transferring the architecture of the covered market and the closed garden into the microcosm of the home, where they lose their "official" functions, becoming traces of a vast heritage from lands deceased.

The Nomad Mind

The mind of the nomad can still be seen in Arab cities, where the ebb and flow of movement slowly rounds every contour. It is time and not space that strengthens the heraldic figures of memory. The nomad mind is sinuous, meandering and tangled. An ideology of the unrepresentable is superimposed upon one of excess: this accumulation signifies the abundance and pleasure of the ultimate Source.

The objects amassed by the nomad return as story, as narration. These forms declare only that they have a past, that they were once in movement. Hence the genius of Arab arts for variations within symmetrical structures, creating a subtle equivalence between the world of song and dance. Paint, hammered copper, stucco, leatherwork, curving feathers — these elements appear as though against a white background, lines that justify the space that surrounds them. Arab art is not a form that encloses a single space, but a line that can contain a whole life.

What is to become of the artist's vision in a sedentary world? Like all displaced ideas, it must re-create the past through a syncretic balance between memory and life in the new world. Arab art is inhabited by countries living in time, by vital impulses that do not require an Occidental-style deconstruction but a detour within the sensation of immobility. What will be the fate of this accumulation of signs in the contemporary world? A smile at that which arrives, an elegant silence at that which is built. The Canadian artists of Arab origin are, here especially, the ambassadors of their own independence. They have made a break with the coercive hold of their socio-cultural universe, where their role is not always recognized and validated. This, perhaps, explains the tender irony of these works.

Translated by Daniel Mroz — Montreal, February 2003

PART TWO

PART TWO

2

Adel Alnaser

"I wanted a country to belong to, a place to establish myself, a country that would recognize my presence and my rights. It was proposed to me that I emigrate to Canada. I had no idea; I only knew that it was a country covered with snow, an industrialized and democratic country that welcomes people coming from all over the world. So I accepted. . . .

"I arrived in Canada on February 7, 1989."

(Extract from an interview with the artist)

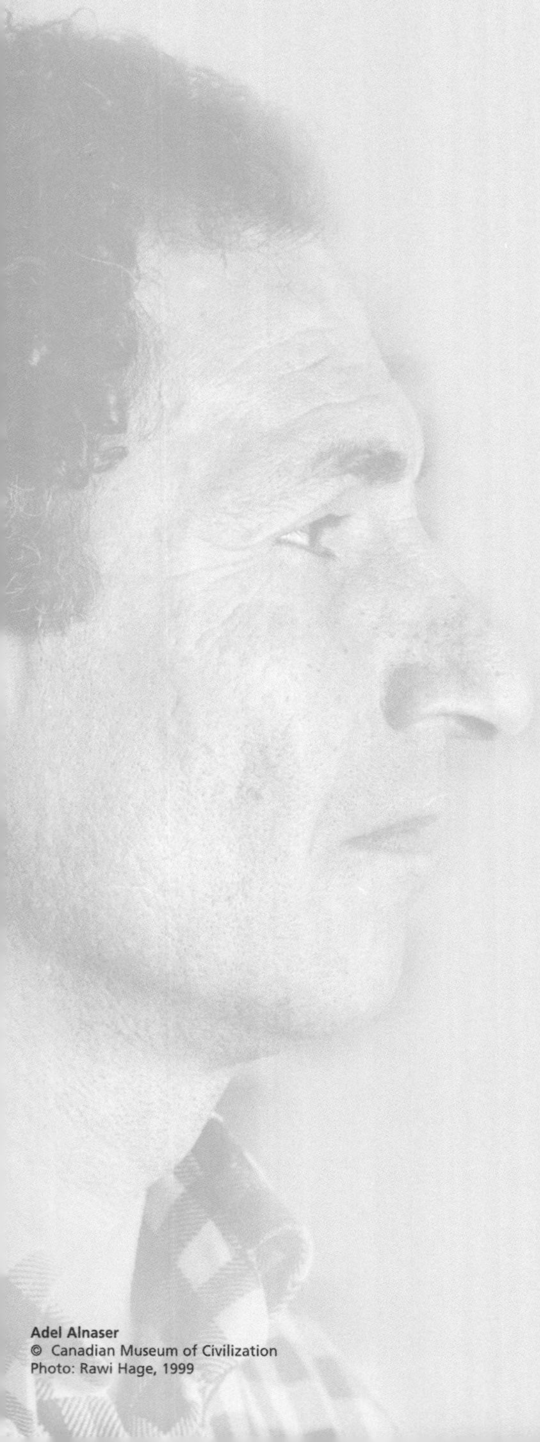

Adel Alnaser

Photo: Rawi Hage, 1999

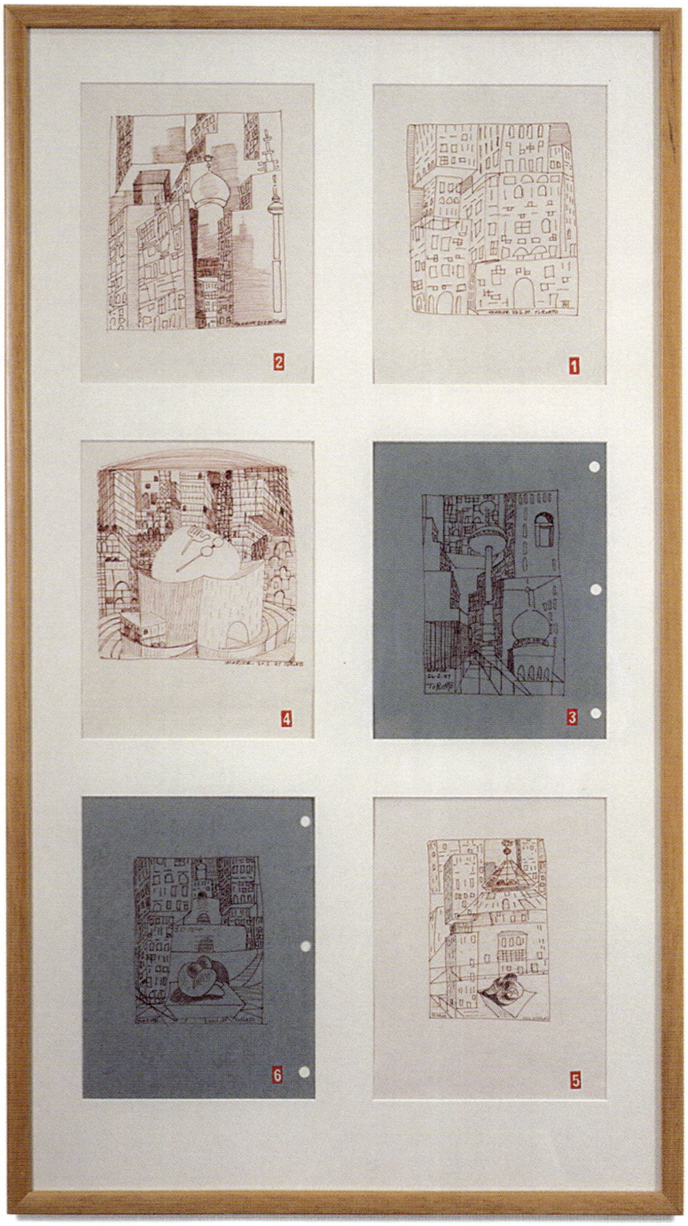

Drawings and texts from *A Great Country Welcomes You*, 1989

Pencil and ink on paper

Collection of the Canadian Museum of Civilization
Photo: H. Foster, © Canadian Museum of Civilization
T2002-46

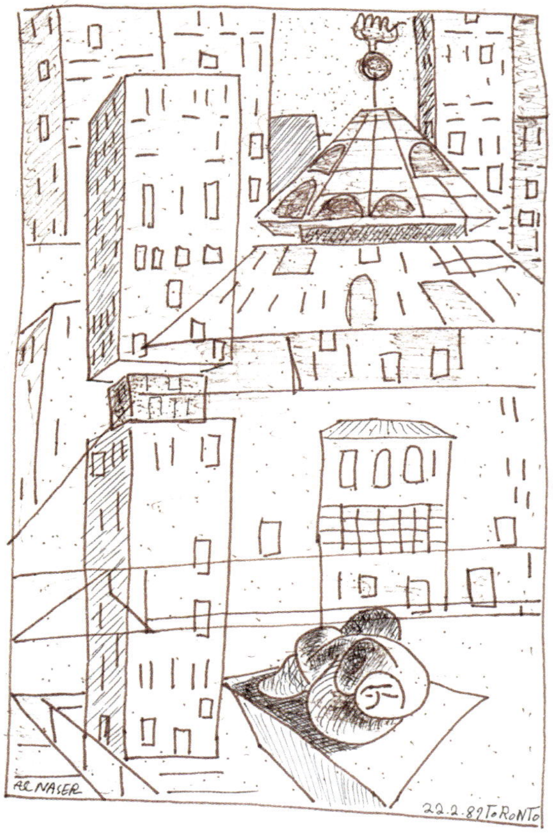

Drawing from *A Great Country Welcomes You*, 1989

Pencil and ink on paper

Collection of the Canadian Museum of Civilization
Photo: H. Foster, © Canadian Museum of Civilization
T2002-47

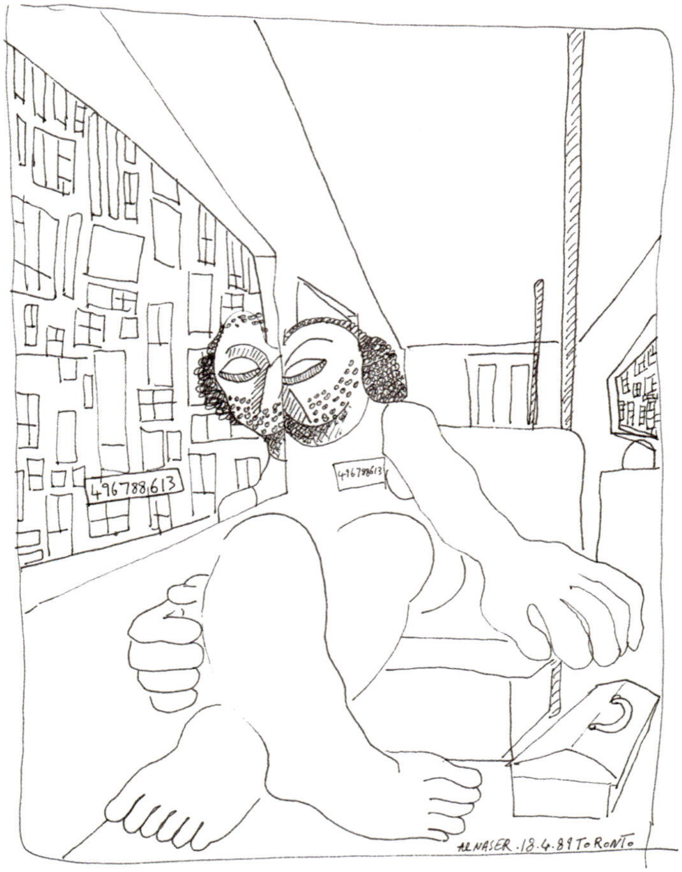

Drawing from *A Great Country Welcomes You*, 1989

Pencil and ink on paper

Collection of the Canadian Museum of Civilization
Photo: H. Foster, © Canadian Museum of Civilization
T2002-48

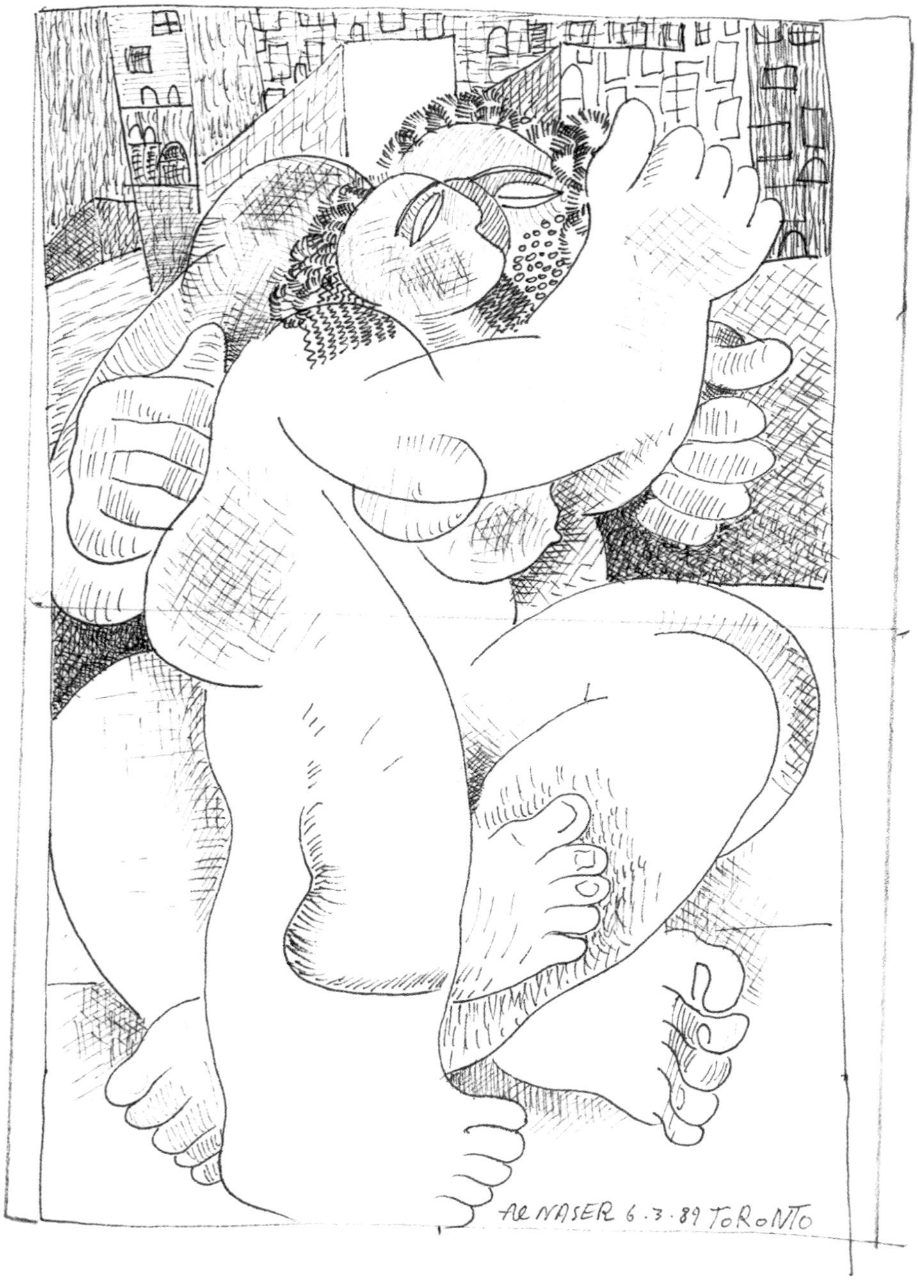

Drawing from *A Great Country Welcomes You*, 1989

Pencil and ink on paper

Collection of the Canadian Museum of Civilization
Photo: H. Foster, © Canadian Museum of Civilization
T2002-49

Hannah Alpha

"It was a winter evening and we were watching television. The programme was interrupted by a news bulletin. The Gulf War had started. I had lived in Saudi Arabia for nine years, and it was a shock to see the bombs falling. Wars had become like video games. They even looked pretty and very artistic on TV . . .

"We were watching a video game, but with real people being hurt. That's when I started A series of events 1991.*"*

(Excerpt from the artist's statement)

Hannah Alpha
© Canadian Museum of Civilization
Photo: Rawi Hage, 1999

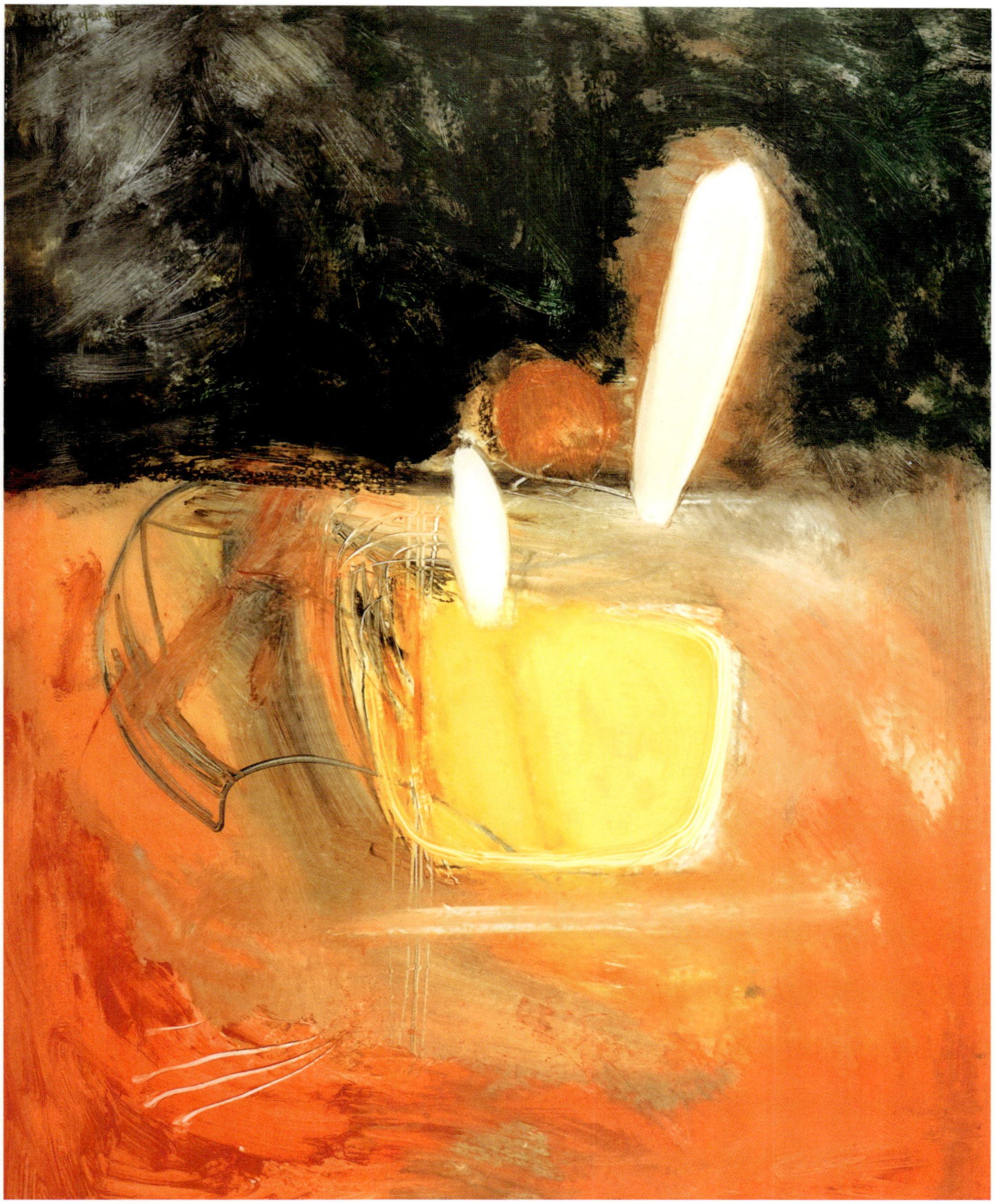

The Fires of Kuwait (From *A series of events 1991*), 1991

Oil on acetate • 121.9 x 143.5 cm

Collection of the Artist
Photo: H. Foster, © Canadian Museum of Civilization
T2002-39

Mirella Aprahamian

"I have lived in so many countries that I have not yet found my home; I search for it still. I say that I have found it, that it is my cabin in Canada. But I still don't know if I have found it. I don't know."

"There was nothing but snow and I remember one thing — I painted the basement of my house apple green. Green because I thought the snow would never melt."

(Extracts from an interview with the artist)

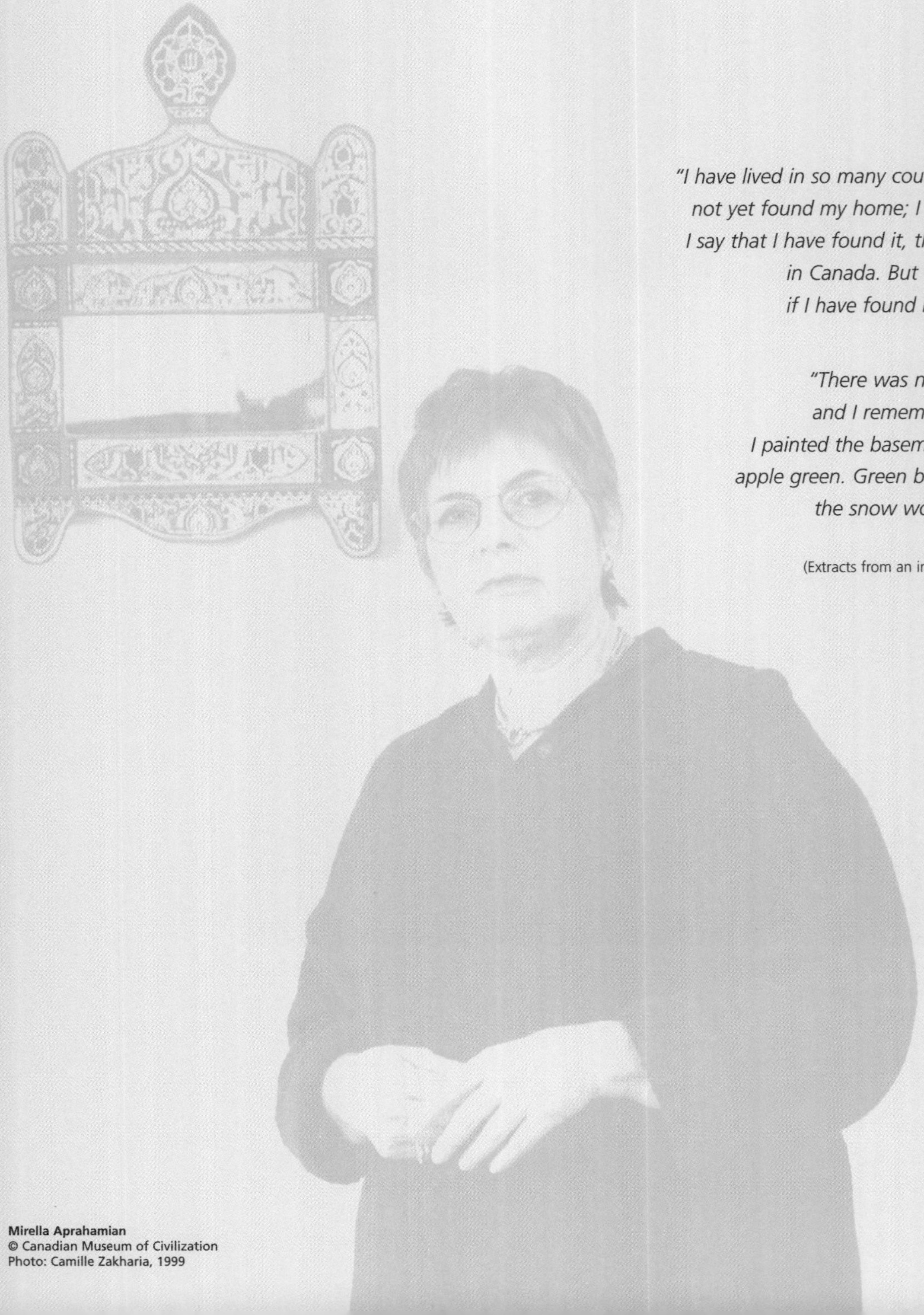

Mirella Aprahamian

Photo: Camille Zakharia, 1999

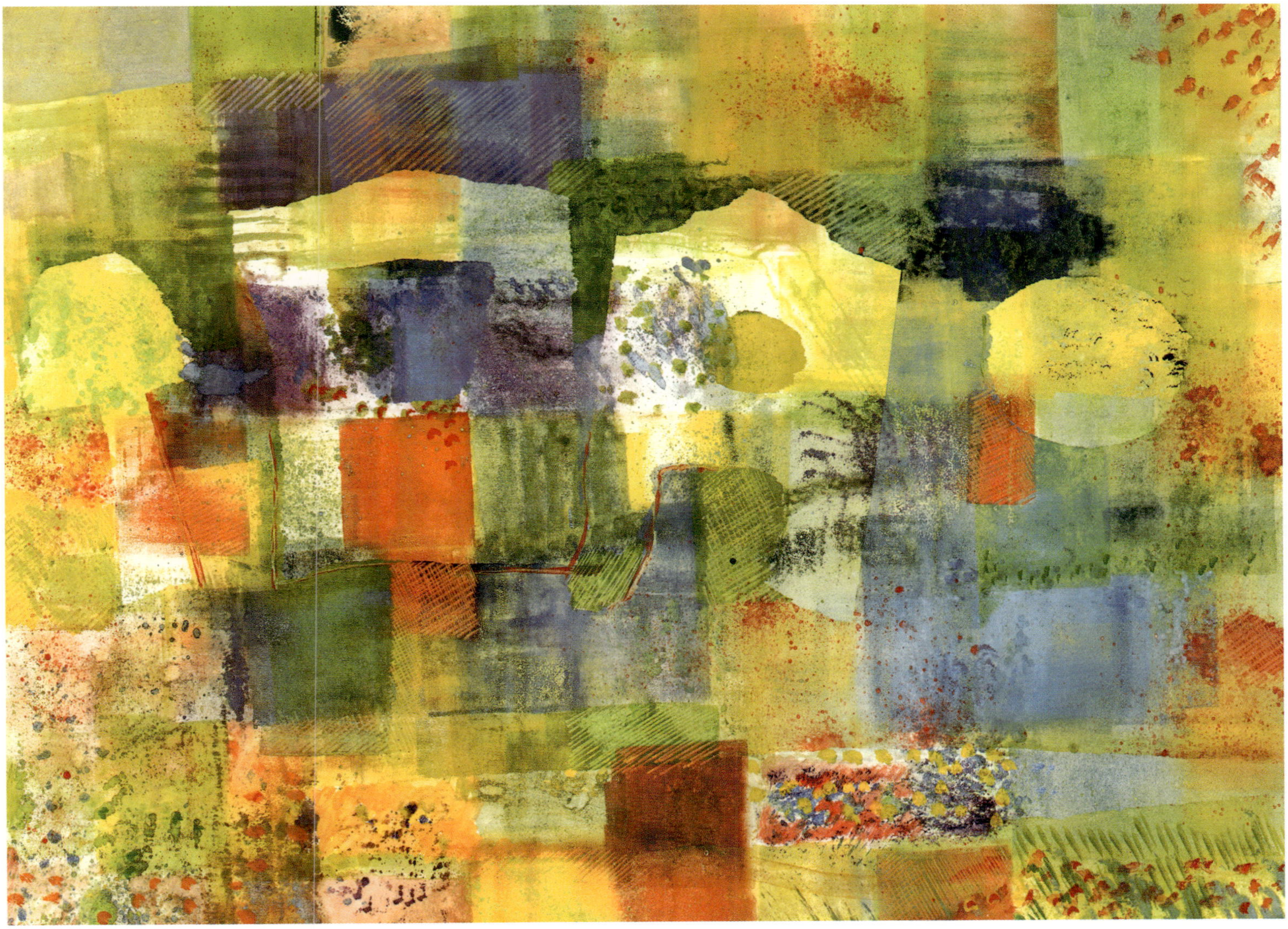

Once upon a time I, 1990

Monoprint on paper • 50 x 38.5 cm

Collection of the Artist
Photo: H. Foster, © Canadian Museum of Civilization
T2002-14

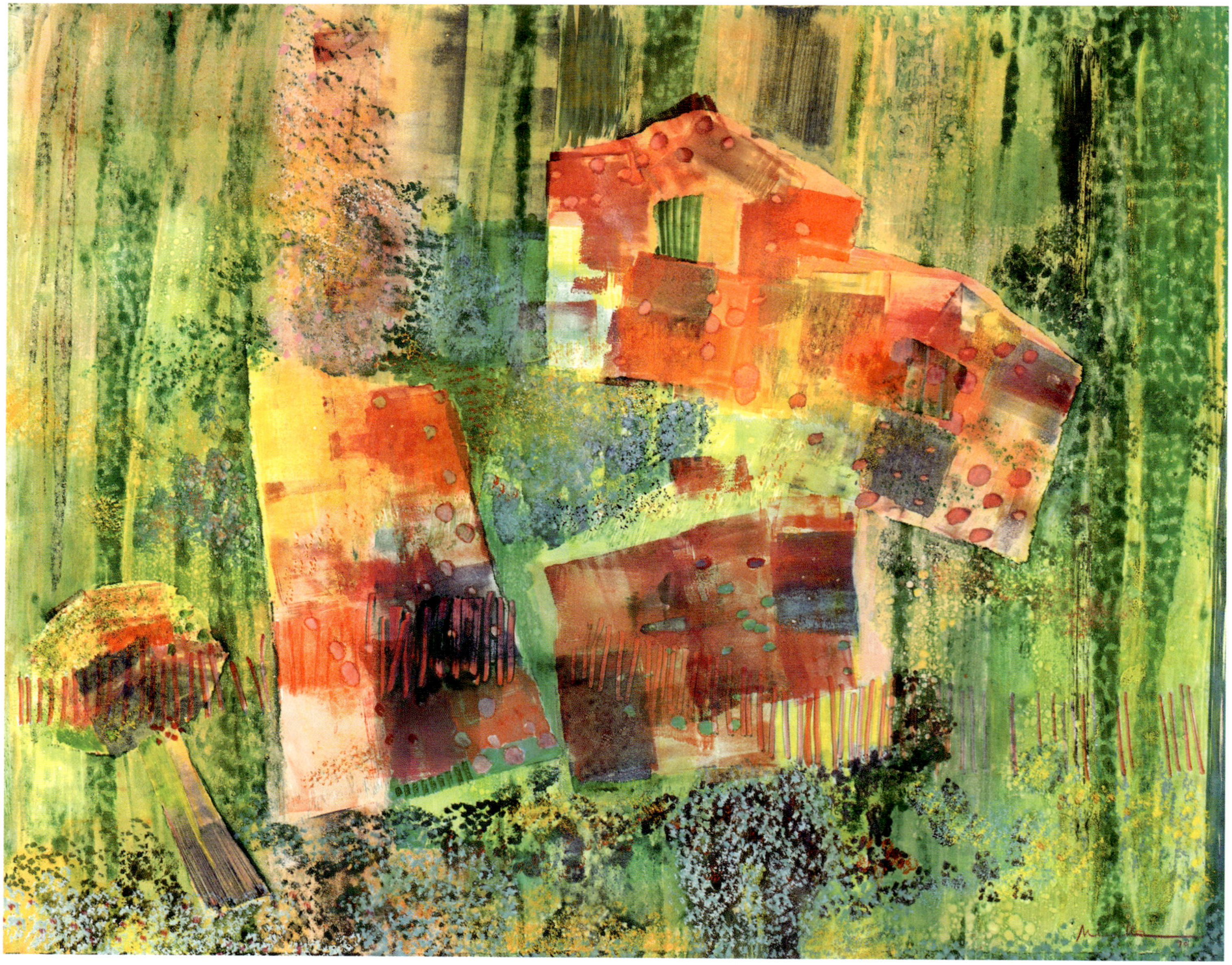

Once upon a time II, 1990

Monoprint on paper • 50 x 38.5 cm

Collection of the Artist
Photo: H. Foster, © Canadian Museum of Civilization
T2002-15

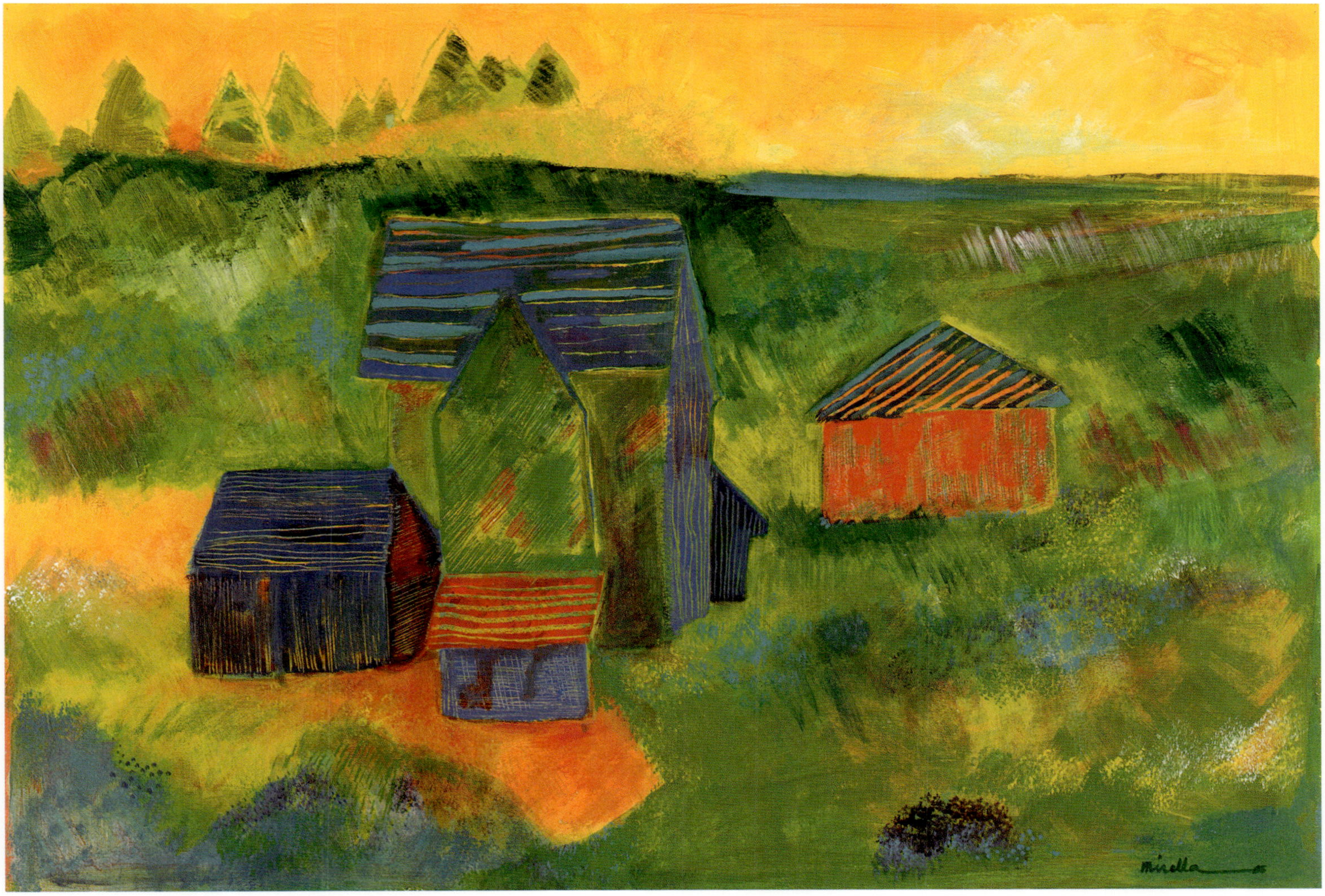

Ma cabane au Canada (My House in Canada), 1987

Acrylic on Arches paper • 50 x 38.5 cm

Collection of Nayiri Tchakmakian and Vatche Tchakmakian
Photo: H. Foster, © Canadian Museum of Civilization
T2002-16

Yasser Badreddine

*"Calligraphy is like every other art:
you cannot master it nor subjugate it
nor train it the way you would train a horse
or tame a wild animal. In fact, it is the poem
that writes you, not you who writes
the poem. And beautiful music is the music
that seduces you and soothes you.
In the same way, beautiful calligraphy
is the calligraphy that woos your pen
and enters, through its sinuosity, during your
moments of inspiration and creation . . .*

*"Dr. Dahesh, my teacher, used to say,
'Calligraphy is a visual music.'"*

(Excerpt from a text by the artist, *La Calligraphie et moi*)

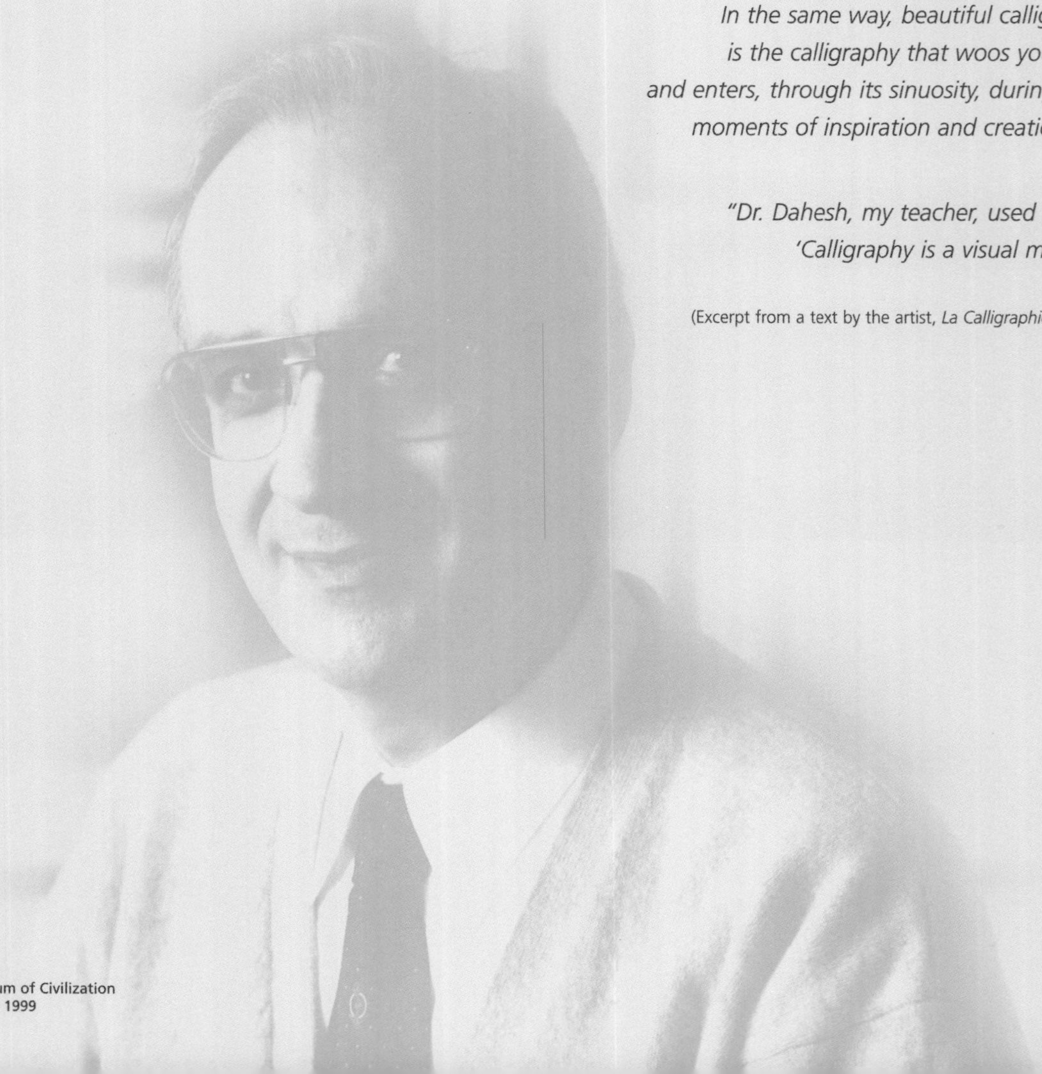

Yasser Badreddine

Photo: Rawi Hage, 1999

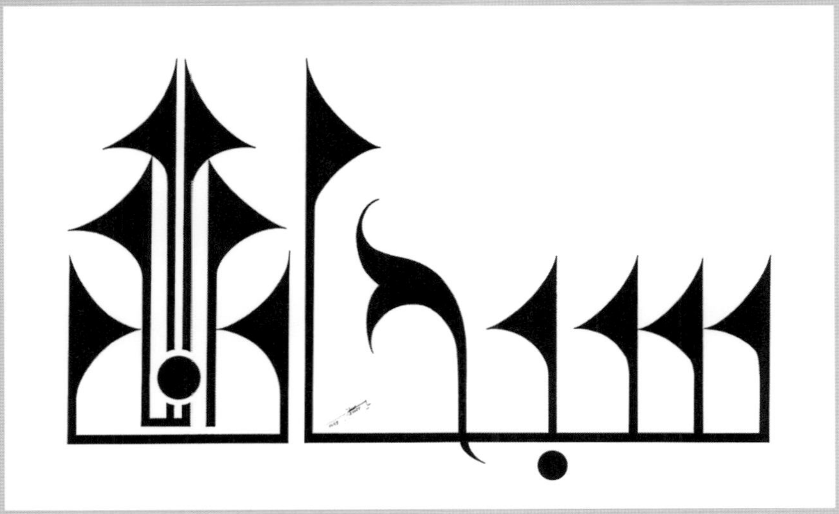

"Glory to God", 1997
Calligraphy in modern free Kufic style

China ink on white paperboard • 51 x 31.5 cm

Collection of the Artist
Photo: H. Foster, © Canadian Museum of Civilization
T2002-31

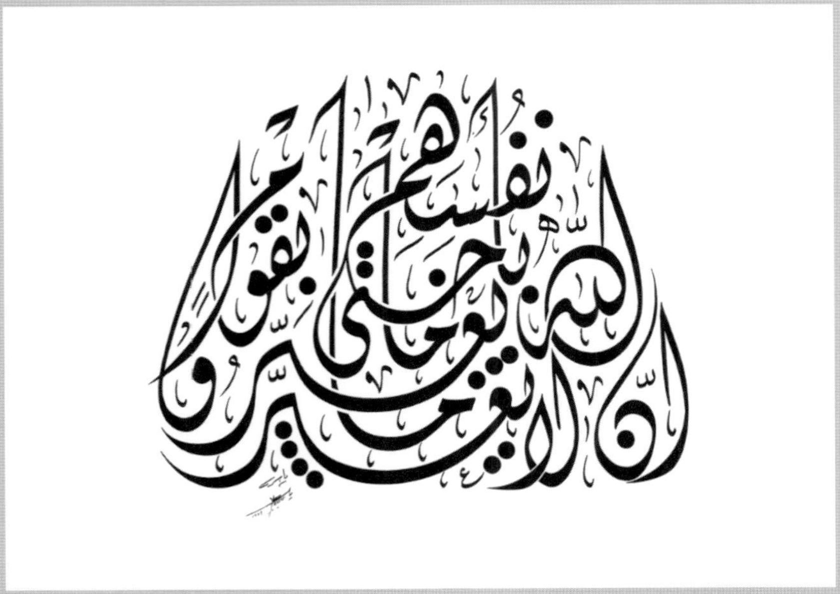

"God does not alter the state of a people, insofar as the individuals who compose it do not alter what is in themselves.", 1997
Calligraphy in Diwani style

China ink on white paperboard • 47 x 32 cm

Collection of the Artist
Photo: H. Foster, © Canadian Museum of Civilization
T2002-32

Laila Binbrek

". . . I trace and explore my own identity as I delve into societal rituals that deal with intimate, and often taboo, body issues.

"Mirror, Mirror *is a piece that explores outer identity — the facade that we put on to face the world. I find that the facade I choose to wear depends on the society I mingle in.* Mirror, Mirror *exposes the identities that are within me. . .*

"I purposely left the mirror frame empty to show the flow from one side to the other."

(Excerpt from the artist's statement)

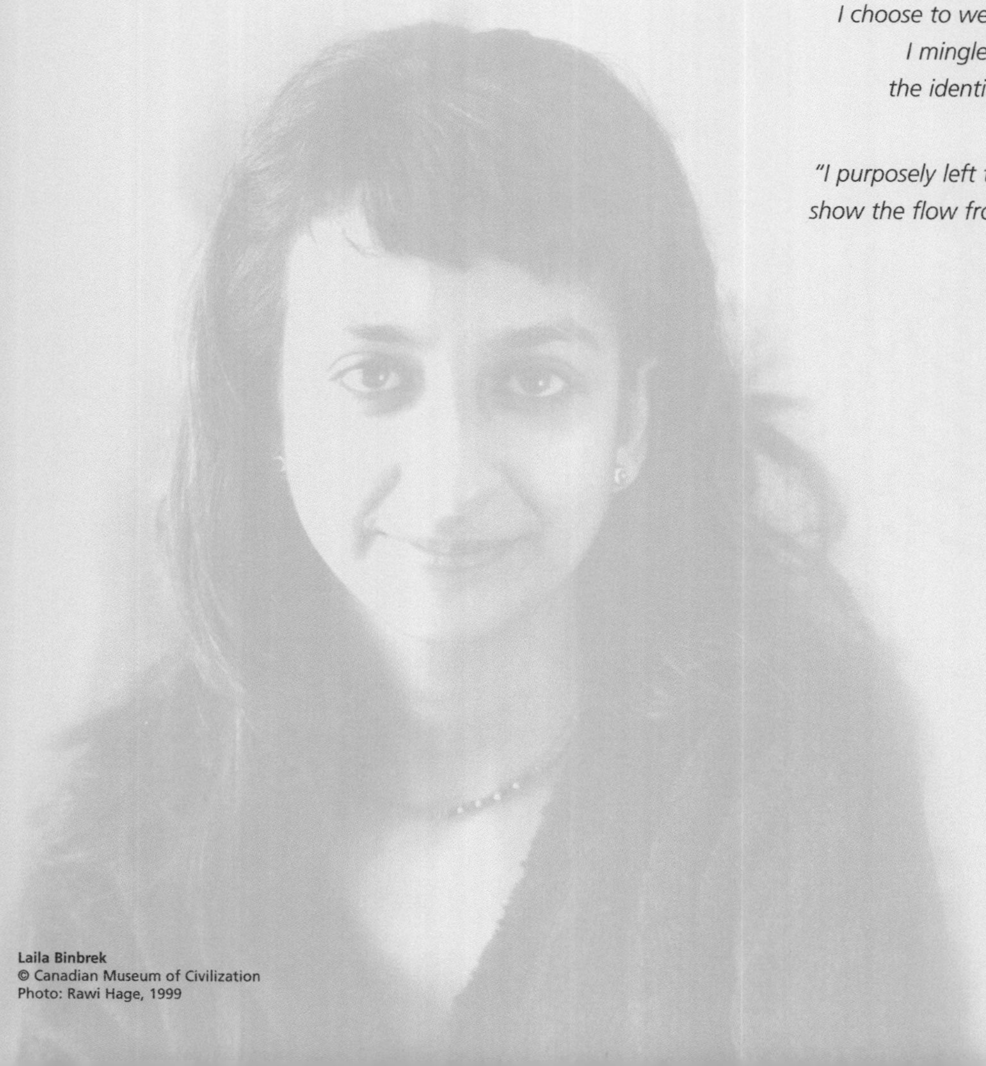

Laila Binbrek

Photo: Rawi Hage, 1999

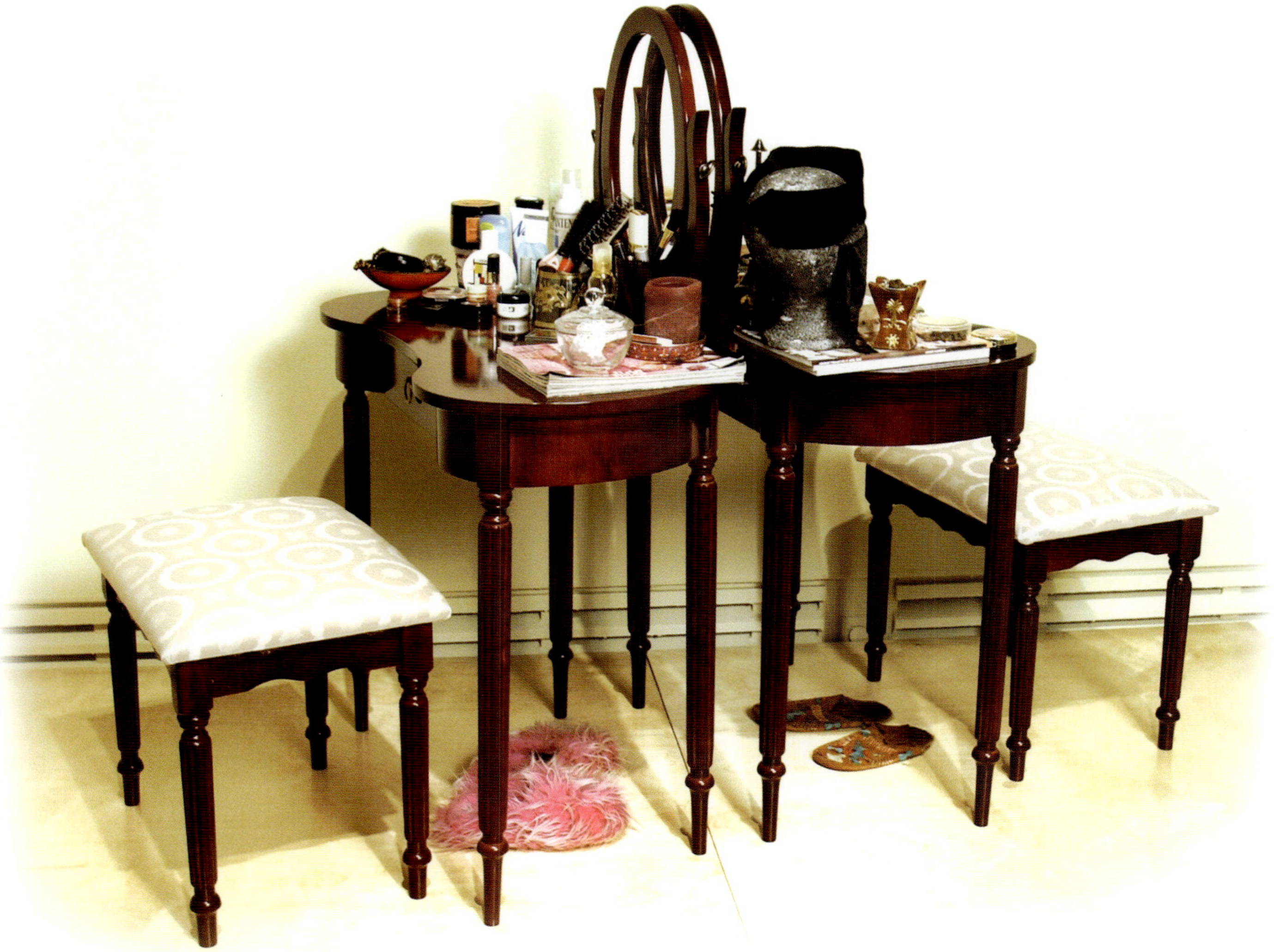

Mirror, Mirror, 2000

Installation: two dressing tables with stools, miscellaneous objects
152 x 78 x 120 cm

Collection of the Artist
Photo: H. Foster, © Canadian Museum of Civilization
D2002-16086

Marc Eliany

*"When I was walking
through the markets and artisans' quarters,
I was delighted
by the sight of cotton and wool
dyed in bright colours.
Suspended above my head,
they were dancing
to the rhythm of a light breeze,
bringing to mind
an enigmatic Berber custom
where women line up for dancing
and choose a husband
for a marriage that will last only seven days!"*

(Excerpt from a text by the artist, *Gates of Welcome*)

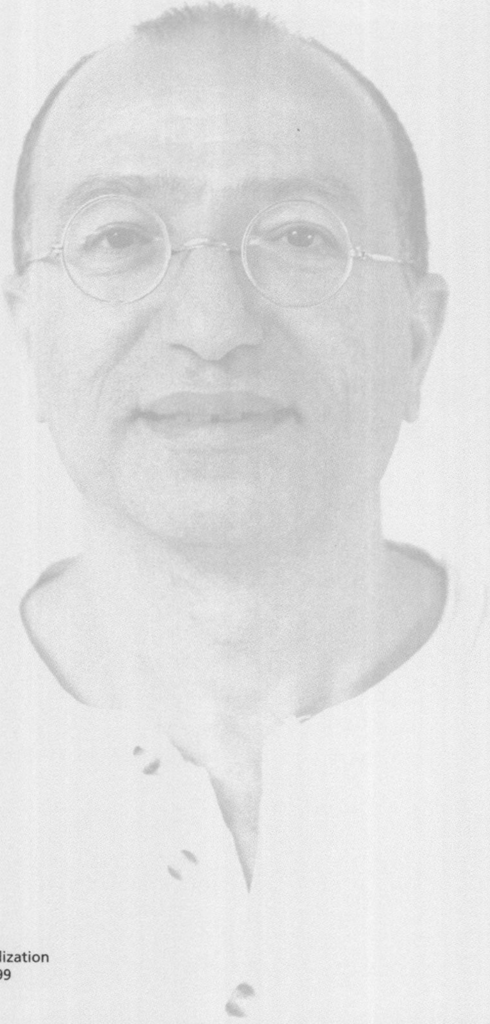

Marc Eliany

Photo: Camille Zakharia, 1999

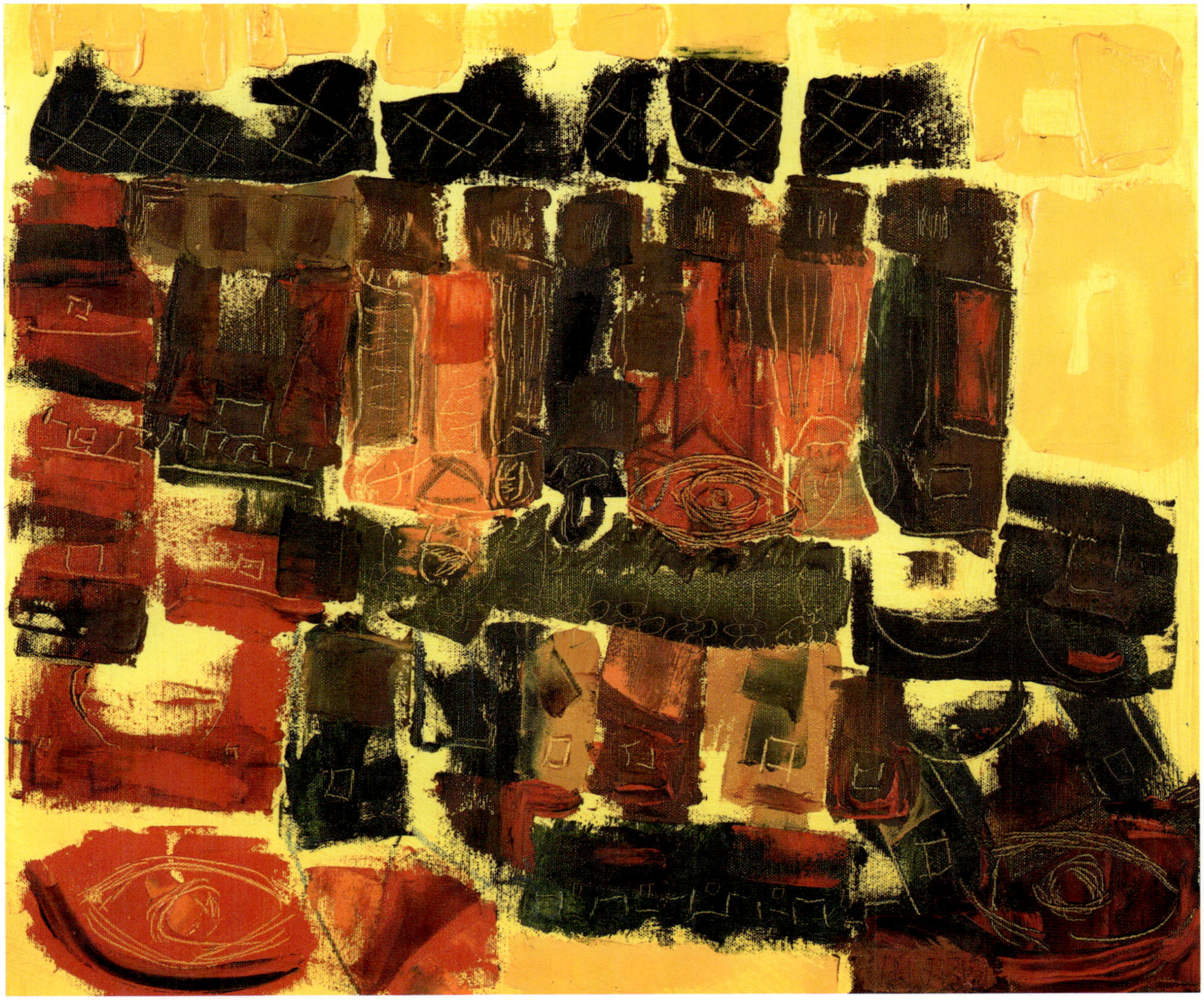

In the market on a bright sunny day, 1993

Oil on canvas • 60 x 50 cm

Collection of Cécile Dujardin
Photo: H. Foster, © Canadian Museum of Civilization
T2002-8

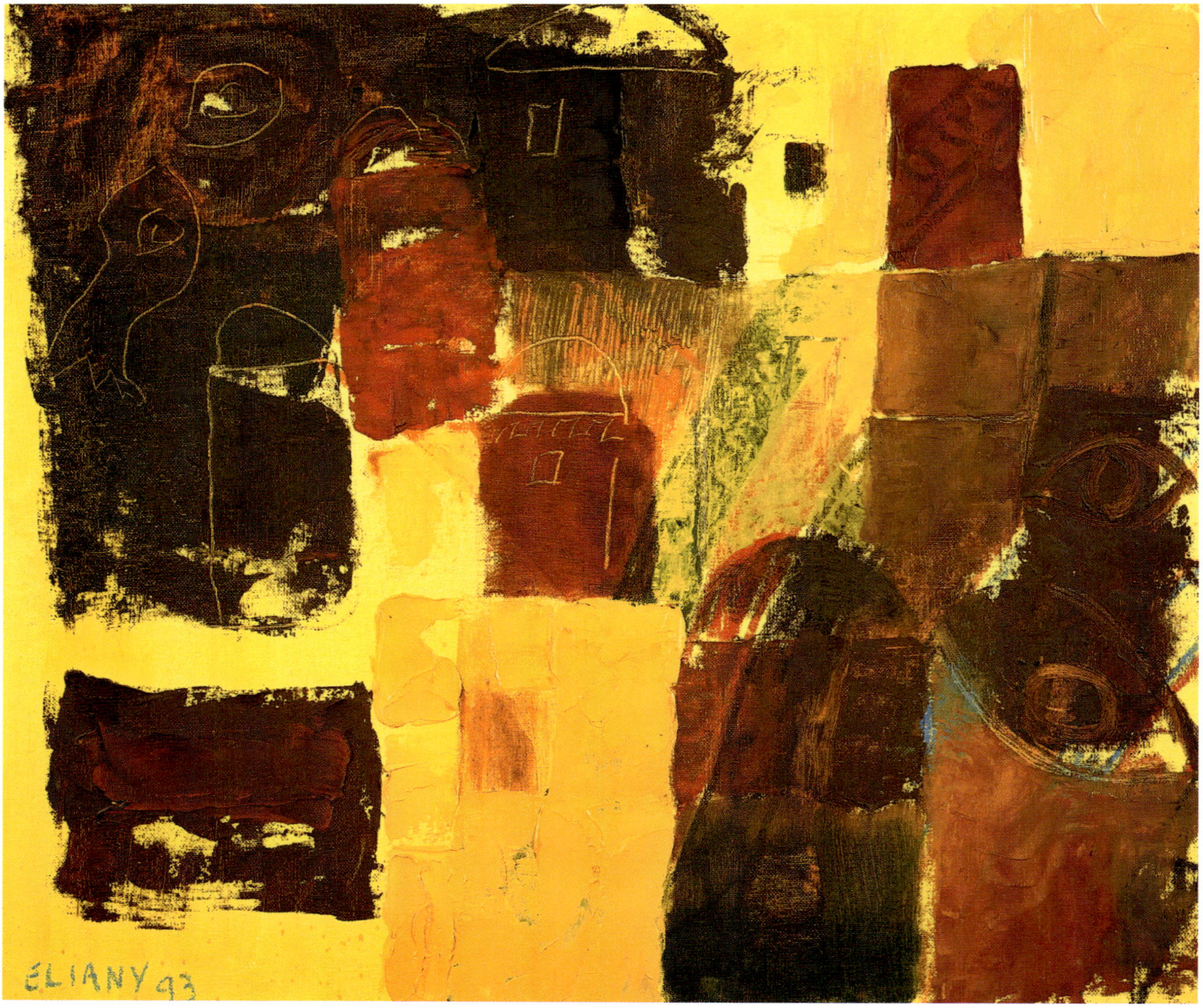

After the market on a bright sunny day, 1993

Oil on canvas board • 60 x 50 cm

Collection of Cécile Dujardin
Photo: H. Foster, © Canadian Museum of Civilization
T2002-9

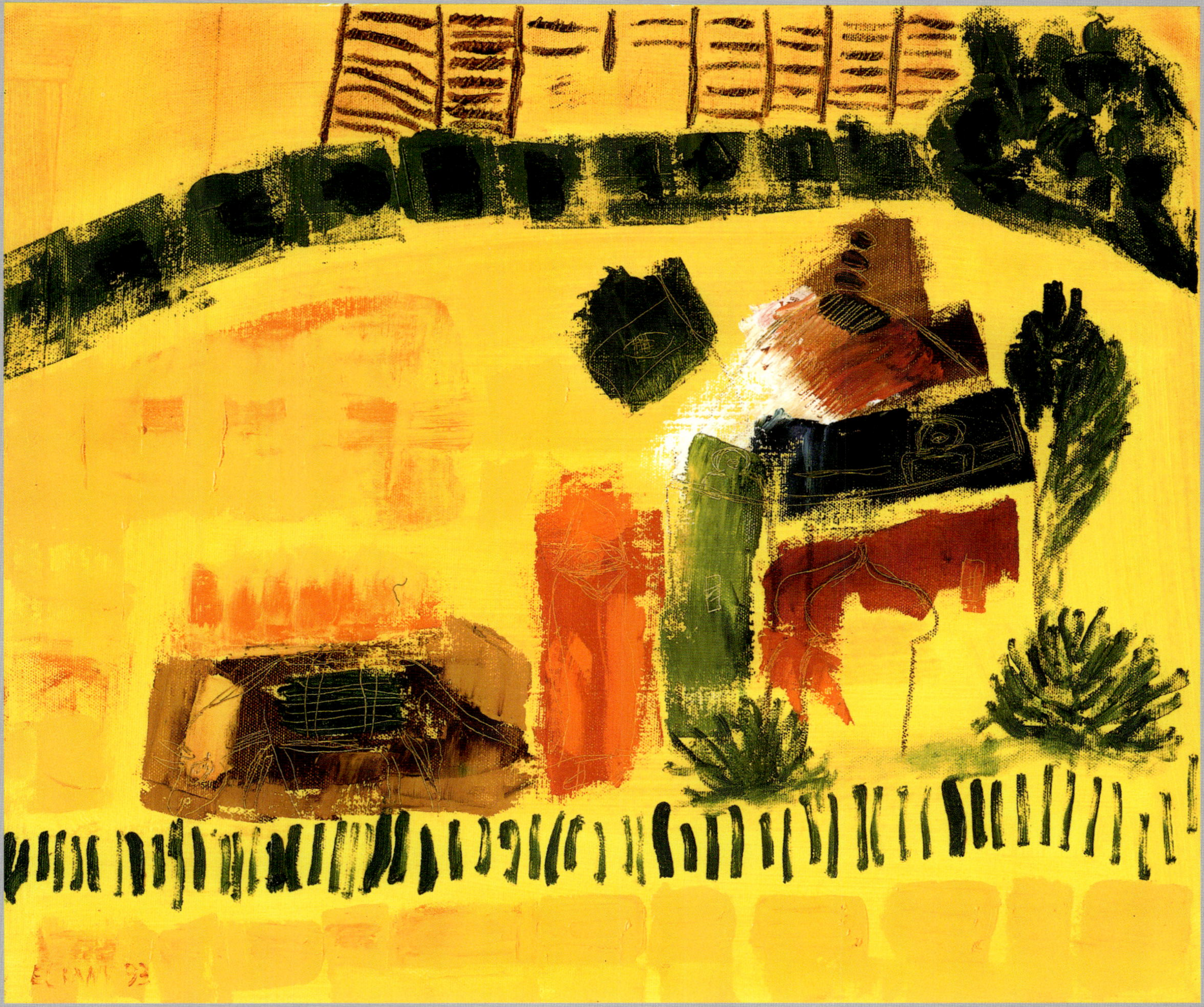

Going to the market on a bright sunny day, 1993

Oil on canvas • 60 x 50 cm

Collection of Cécile Dujardin
Photo: H. Foster, © Canadian Museum of Civilization
T2002-7

Rawi Hage

"I had wanted to tell a story,
almost a biography. . .

"Postcards are what people send when they visit a place. I think that all immigrants feel that sense of transience. Sometimes people don't accept the idea of being here permanently; they deny it. Their denial is a form of hope, the hope of having the choice to return."

(Extract from an interview with the artist)

Rawi Hage

Photo: Camille Zakharia, 1999

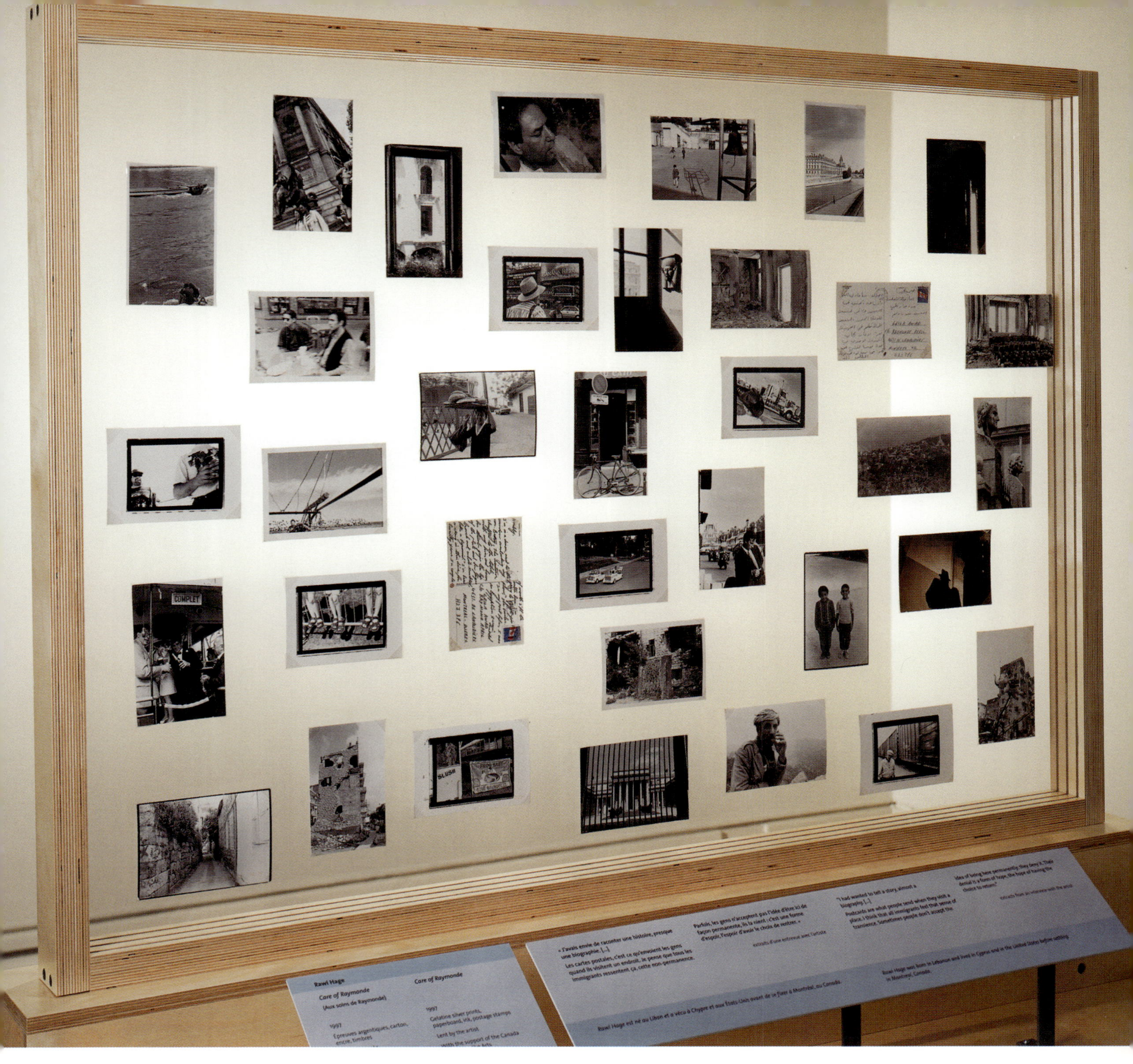

Care of Raymonde, 1997

Silver gelatin prints, paperboard
35 postcards under plexiglass • 20 x 25.4 cm
1 box measuring 51 x 51 x 76 cm

With the support of the Canada Council of the Arts

Collection of the Artist
Photo: H. Foster, © Canadian Museum of Civilization
T2002-45

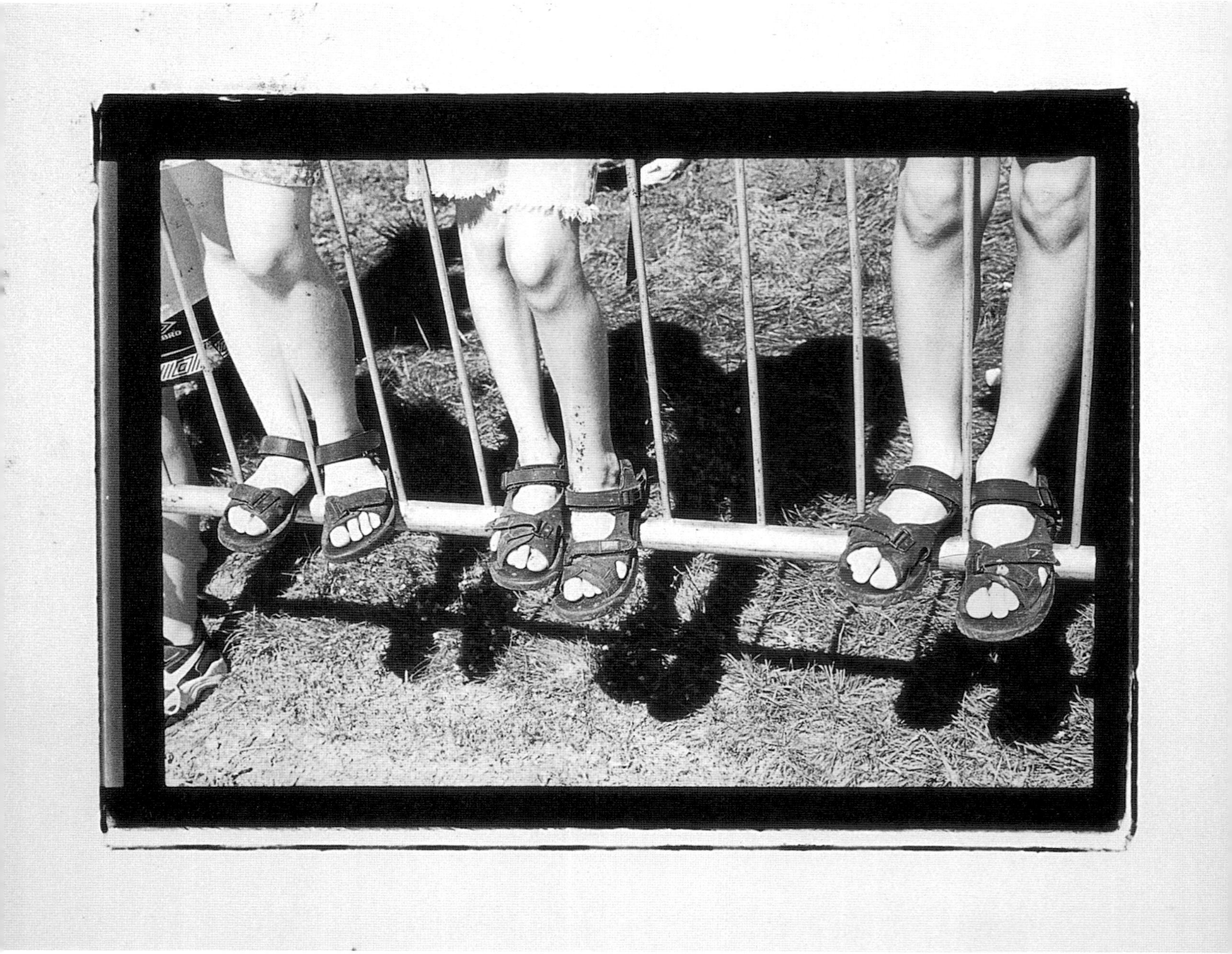

Care of Raymonde (detail), 1997

Silver gelatin prints, paperboard

With the support of the Canada Council of the Arts

Collection of the Artist
Photo: H. Foster, © Canadian Museum of Civilization
S2002-4612

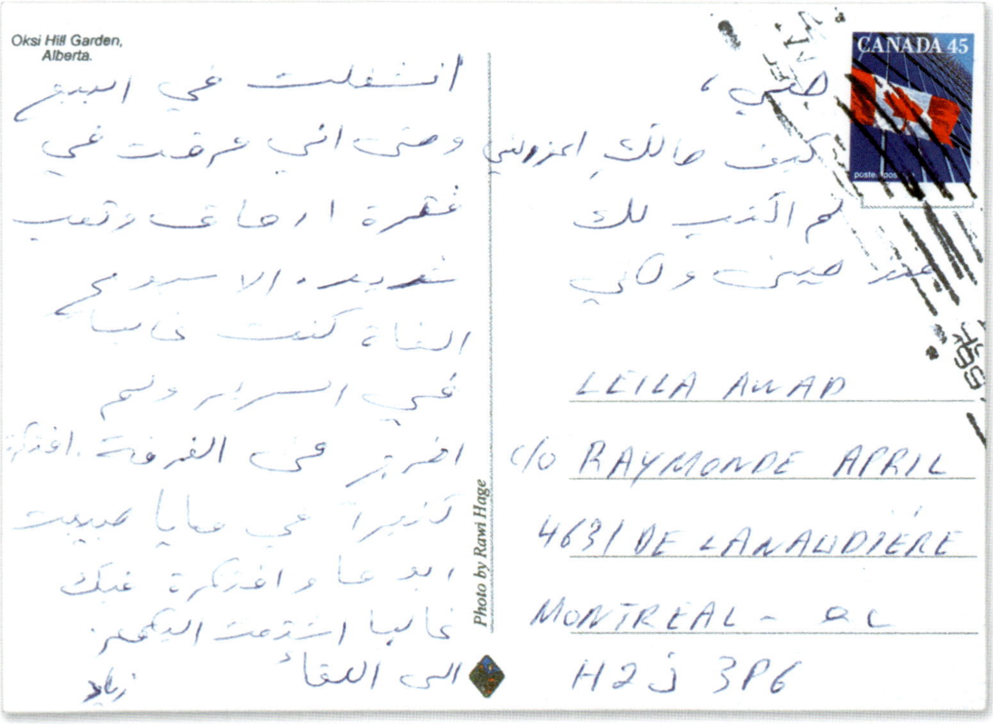

Care of Raymonde (detail), 1997

Silver gelatin prints, paperboard, ink, postage stamp

With the support of the Canada Council of the Arts

Collection of the Artist
Photo: H. Foster, © Canadian Museum of Civilization
S2002-4613

Abd Hanafi

"My work is full of people so that I may feel surrounded by them, and also because they enrich the scene. The characters are there so that I may feel good, to make me happy and to please themselves. . . . These are my children; I bring them into the world as one would deliver babies. . .

"At home, for example, the souks are very crowded. And when a place is very crowded, very animated . . . there is much more life."

(Extract from an interview with the artist)

Abd Hanafi
© Abd Hanafi
Photo: Abd Hanafi, 2002

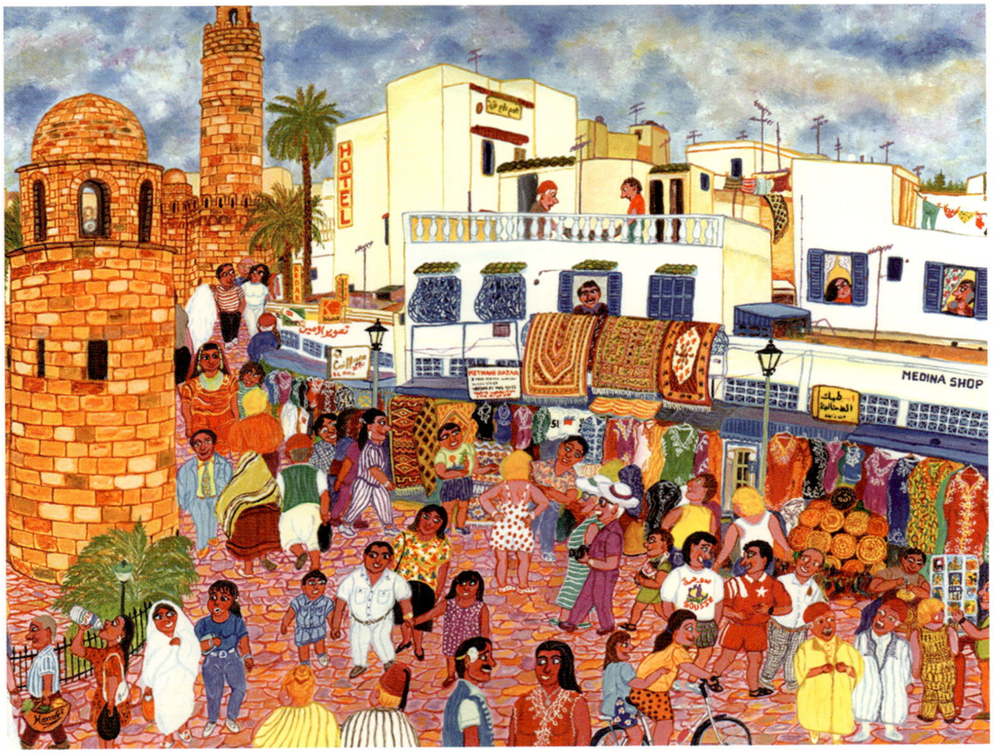

Variétés de la Médina, Sousse
(The Diversity of the Medina, Sousse), 1995

Oil on canvas • 45.7 x 61 cm

Collection of Darra Lang and Malcolm Pesner
Photo: H. Foster, © Canadian Museum of Civilization
T2002-10

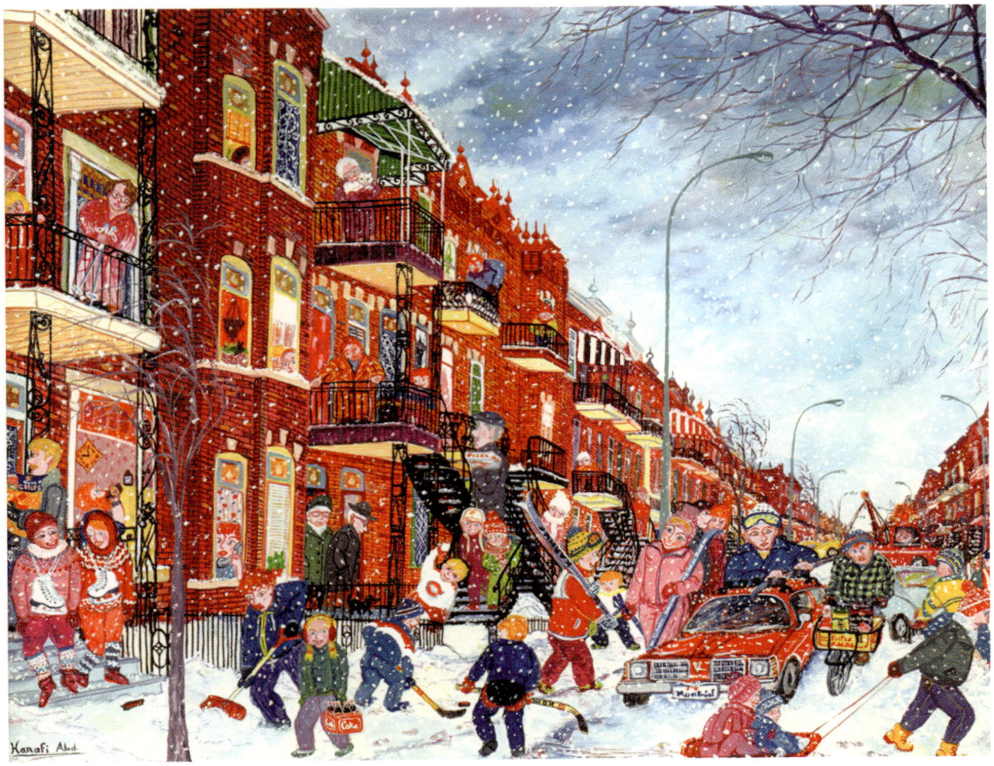

Rue St-Denis, Montréal (St. Denis Street, Montreal), 1991

Oil on canvas • 45.7 x 61 cm

Collection of Susan Frank and Max Haberkorn
Photo: H. Foster, © Canadian Museum of Civilization
T2002-11

Jamelie Hassan

"L'espace de l'alphabet – II (The Space of the Alphabet — II) *is a version of an earlier larger installation titled* L'espace de l'alphabet. *It presents various cultural artifacts in a replica bookshelf, which would have originally been designed to hold rare books. The installation includes two videos; in them, two children are filmed over a two-year period. In* Topsy Turvy, *the children investigate their relationship to Arabic geography, history and language, and discuss their efforts to learn Arabic as they move through familiar sites. In* Les langues du monde, *the setting is the library, and a third person reads in French a text on the Arabic language.*

"Moving between fragments of English, French and Arabic, L'espace de l'alphabet – II *asks the viewer to question definitions of identity as belonging exclusively to the realm of language."*

(Excerpt from the artist's statement)

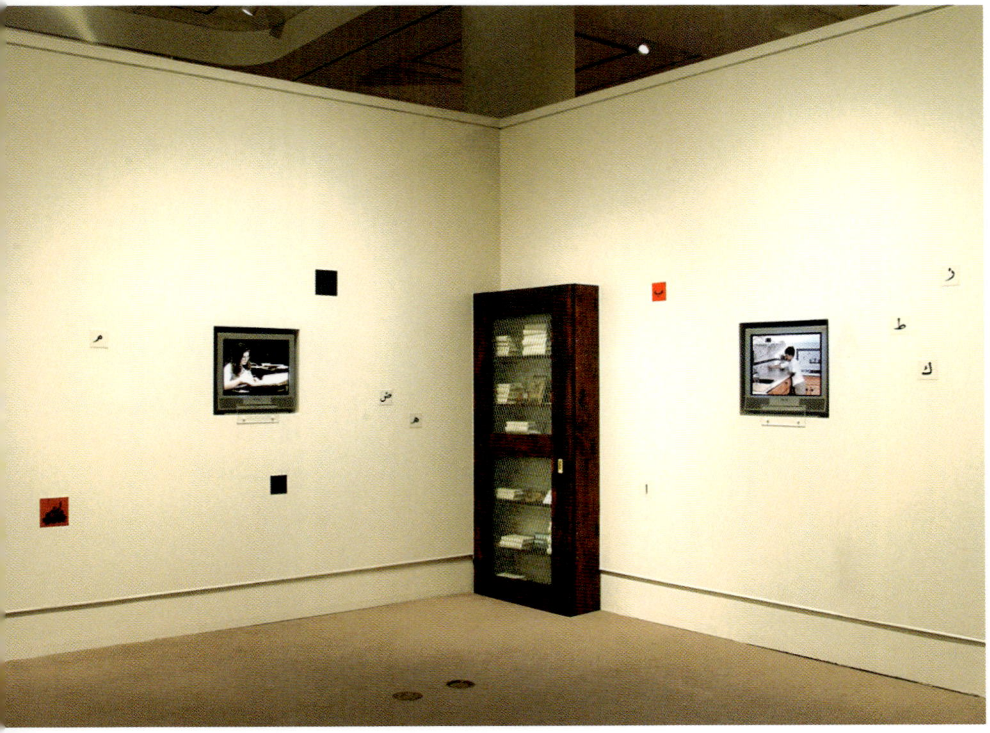

L'espace de l'alphabet – II (The Space of Alphabet — II), 1999–2001

Video Installation: two videos
(*Topsy Turvy Land*, 1999; *Les langues du monde*, 2000),
wooden bookshelf, glazed ceramic tiles, miscellaneous objects

Bookshelf built by Ron Benner, based on a design of bookshleves
in the Special Collections Library, D.B. Weldon Library,
University of Western Ontario, London, Canada.

Collection of the Artist
Photo: H. Foster, © Canadian Museum of Civilization
D2002-16091

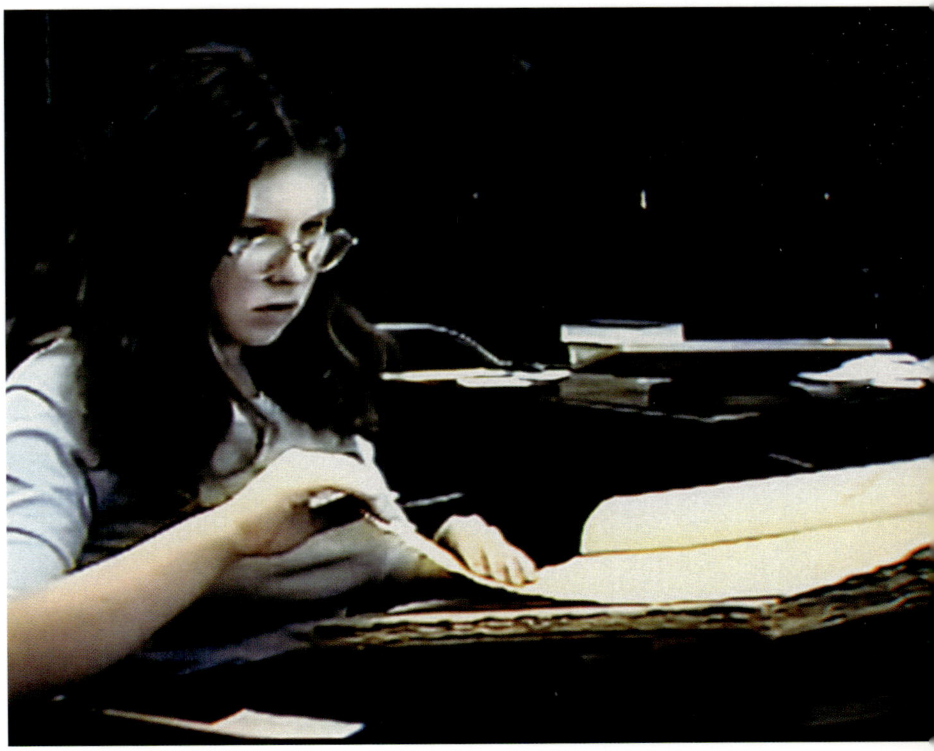

L'espace de l'alphabet – II (The Space of Alphabet — II)
(detail), 1999–2001

Video Installation: two videos
(*Topsy Turvy Land*, 1999; *Les langues du monde*, 2000),
wooden bookshelf, glazed ceramic tiles, miscellaneous objects

Bookshelf built by Ron Benner, based upon a design of bookshleves
in the Special Collections Library, D.B. Weldon Library,
University of Western Ontario, London, Canada.

Collection of the Artist
Photo: H. Foster, © Canadian Museum of Civilization
T2002-91

Liliane Karnouk

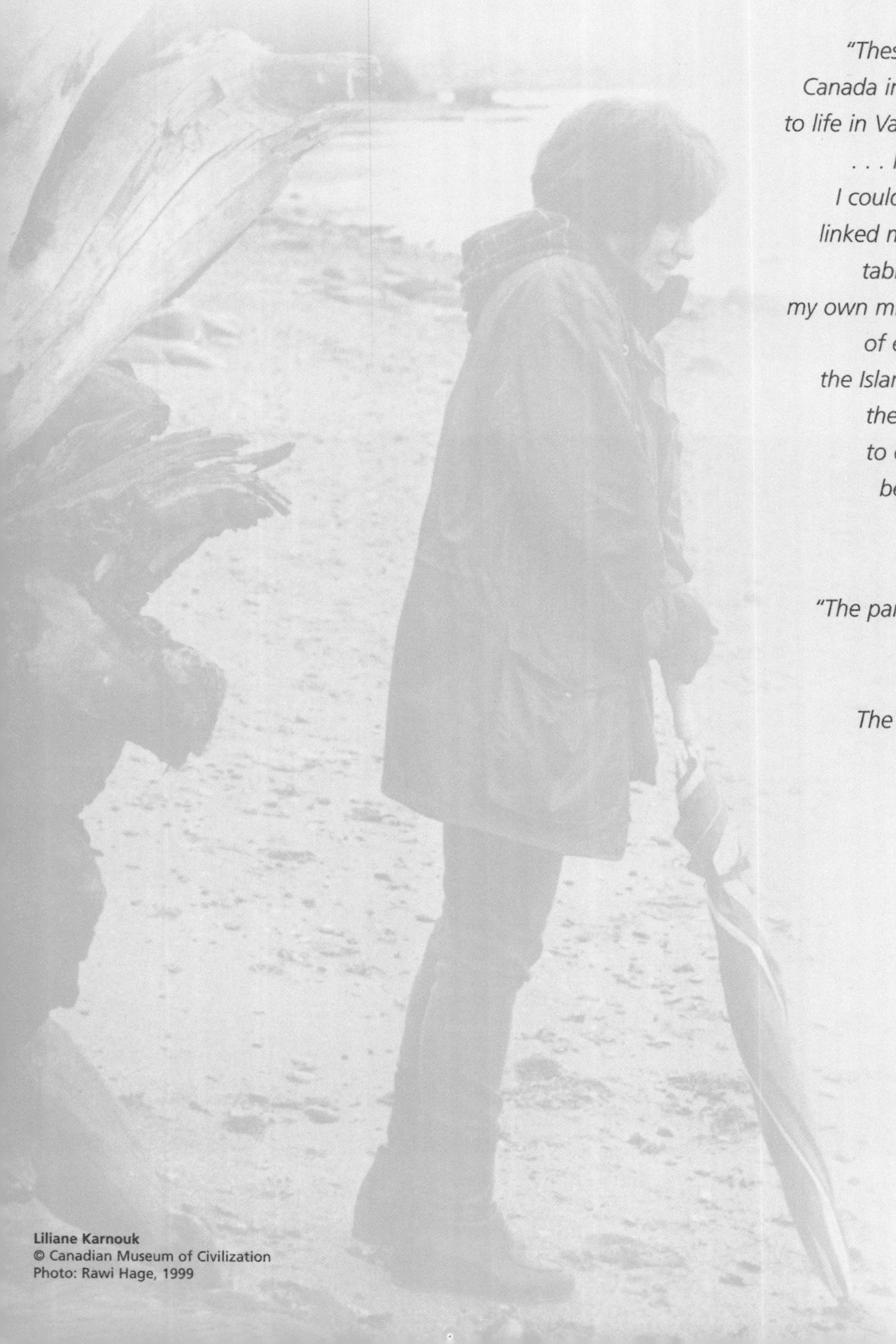

Liliane Karnouk

Photo: Rawi Hage, 1999

"These works, dating from my return to Canada in 1997, represent my readjustment to life in Vancouver after a very long absence. . . . I chose to design furniture because I could not find contemporary items that linked my Islamic carpet and my computer table, nor could I find passages within my own mind that connected the two worlds of experience. It made sense to adopt the Islamic philosophy of art, which unites the functional with the aesthetic, and to explore plain geometry and colour, because I needed time to remember and time to forget.

"The panels were painted by hand in what felt like an eternity, but they were cut by machine in moments. The ritual of transition was complete."

(Excerpt from the artist's statement)

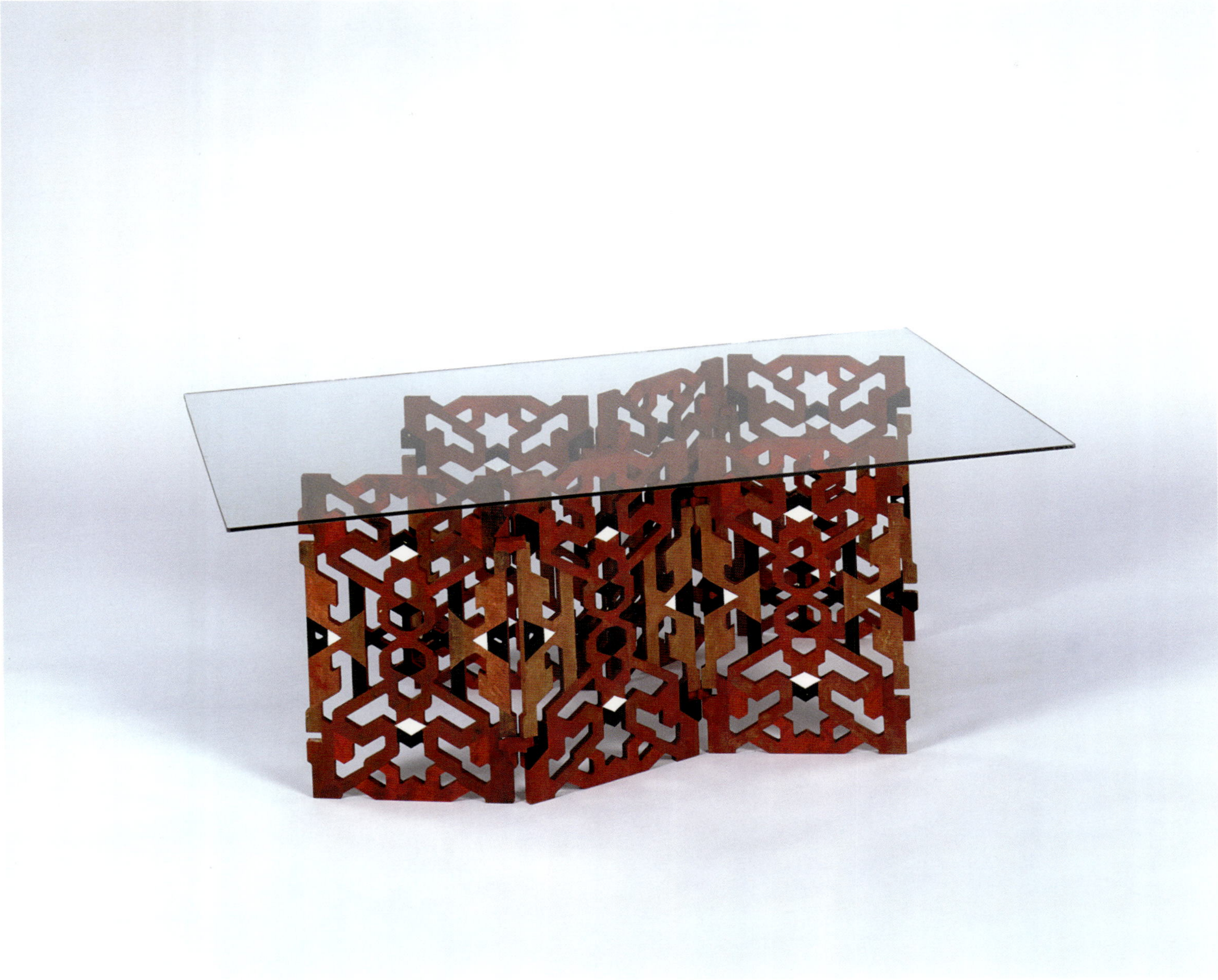

Coffee Table, 1997

Acrylic on fibreboard, glass • 122 x 73.7 x 45.7 cm

Collection of the Artist
Photo: H. Foster, © Canadian Museum of Civilization
T2002-23

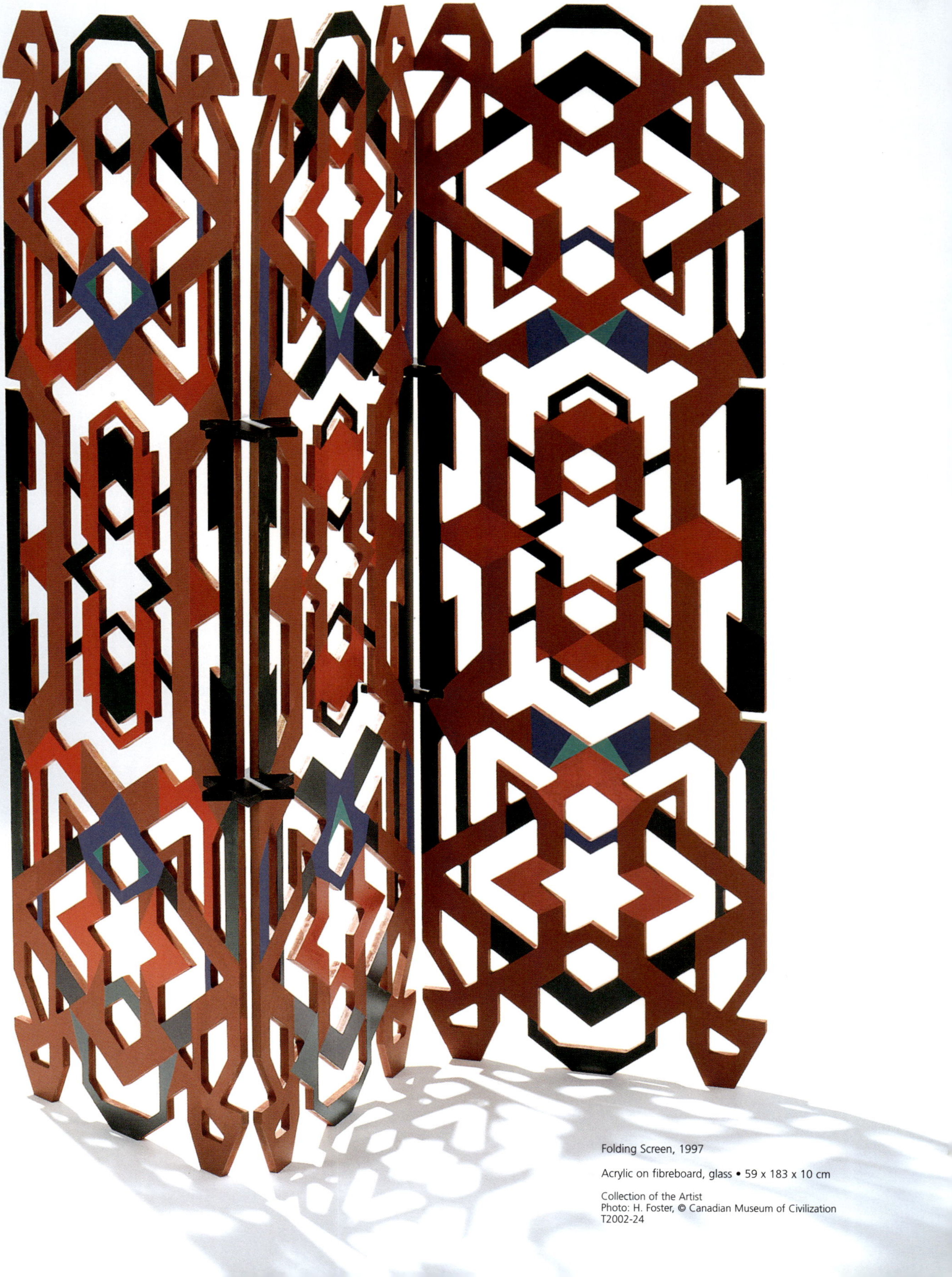

Folding Screen, 1997

Acrylic on fibreboard, glass • 59 x 183 x 10 cm

Collection of the Artist
Photo: H. Foster, © Canadian Museum of Civilization
T2002-24

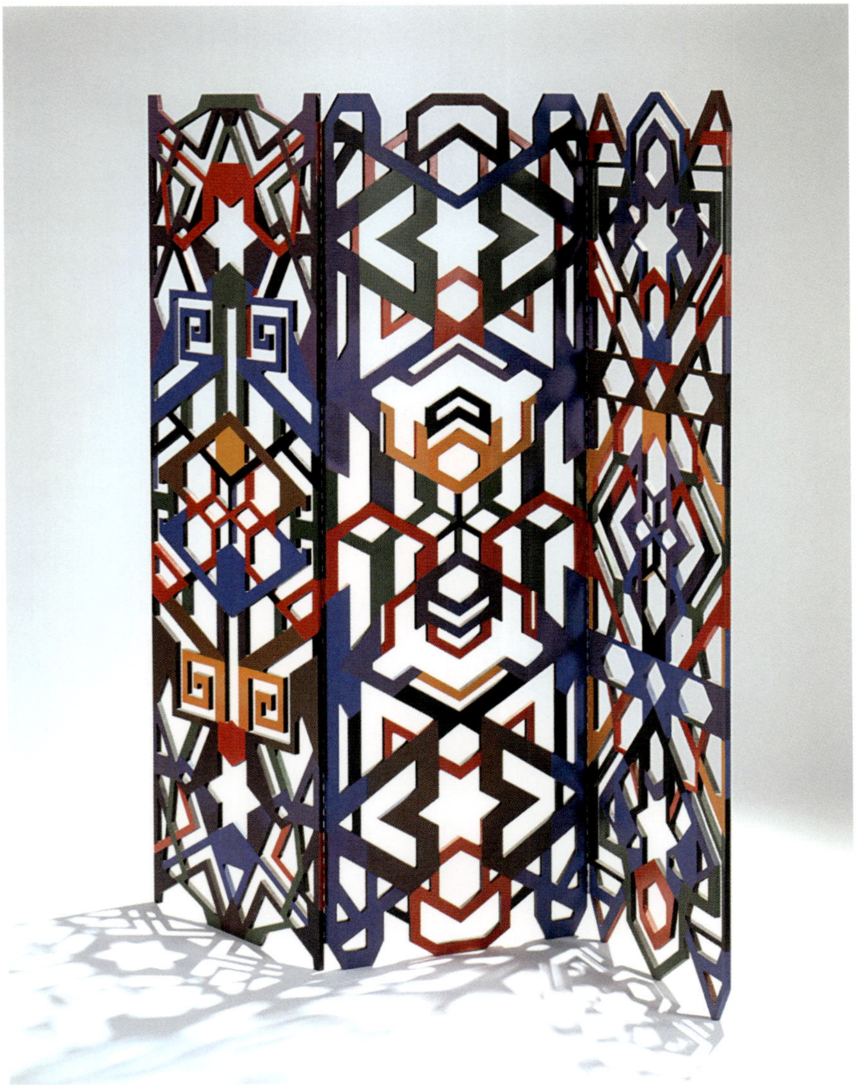

Folding Screen, 1997

Acrylic on fibreboard, glass • 51 x 152 x 10 cm

Collection of the Artist
Photo: H. Foster, © Canadian Museum of Civilization
T2002-25

farouk kaspaules

"I define my cultural identity in the context of the practice of art, employing iconography of mixed cultural origins (Sumerian, Chaldean, Arab).

"I address culture, displacement, and the definition of one's identity in the context of exile . . . Thus, I strive in my work to refer the circumstances around me to broader geopolitical and social questions — affirming both culture and identity, on the one hand, and my artistic position vis-à-vis the political and the aesthetic, on the other hand."

(Excerpt from the artist's statement)

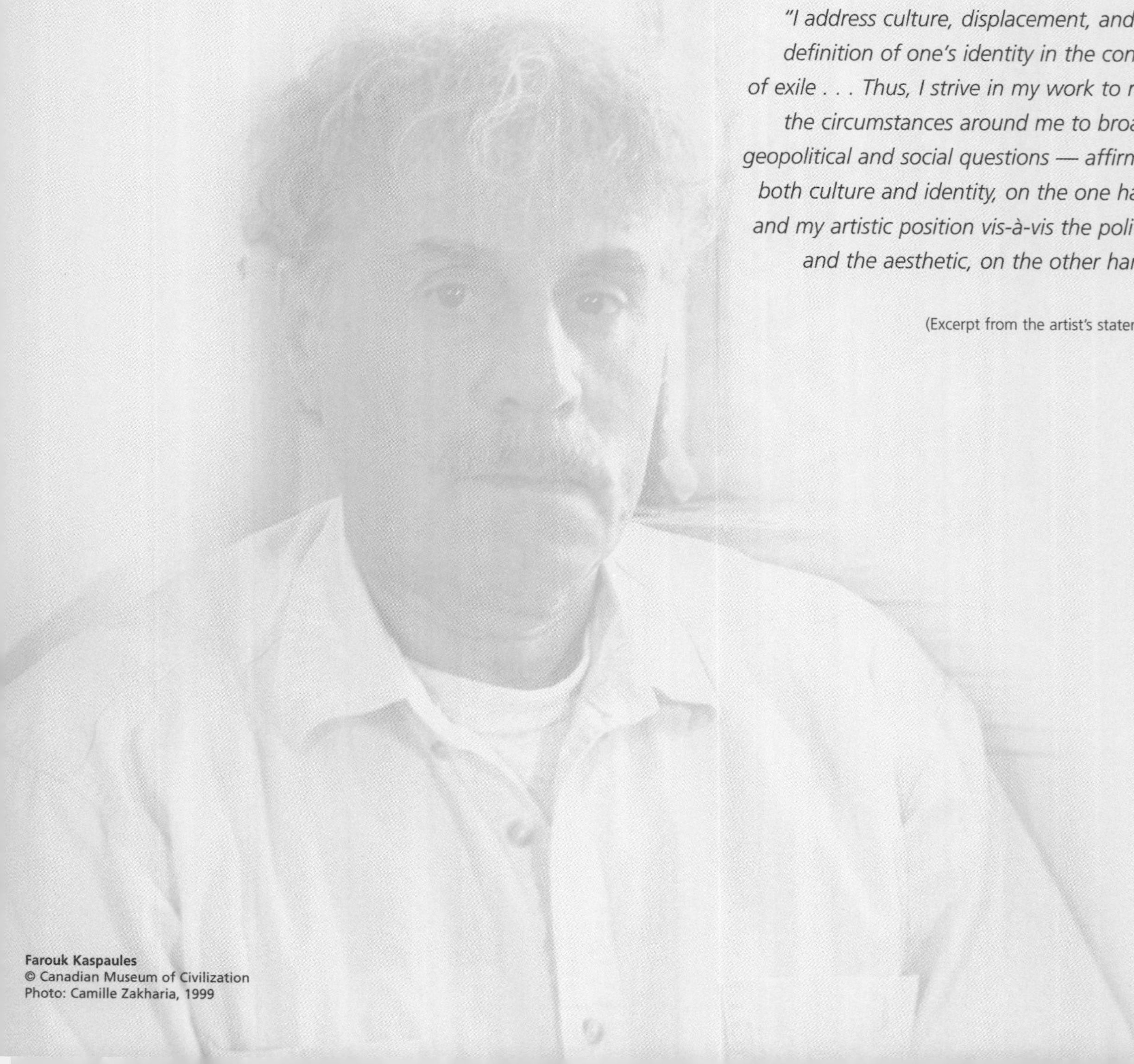

Farouk Kaspaules

Photo: Camille Zakharia, 1999

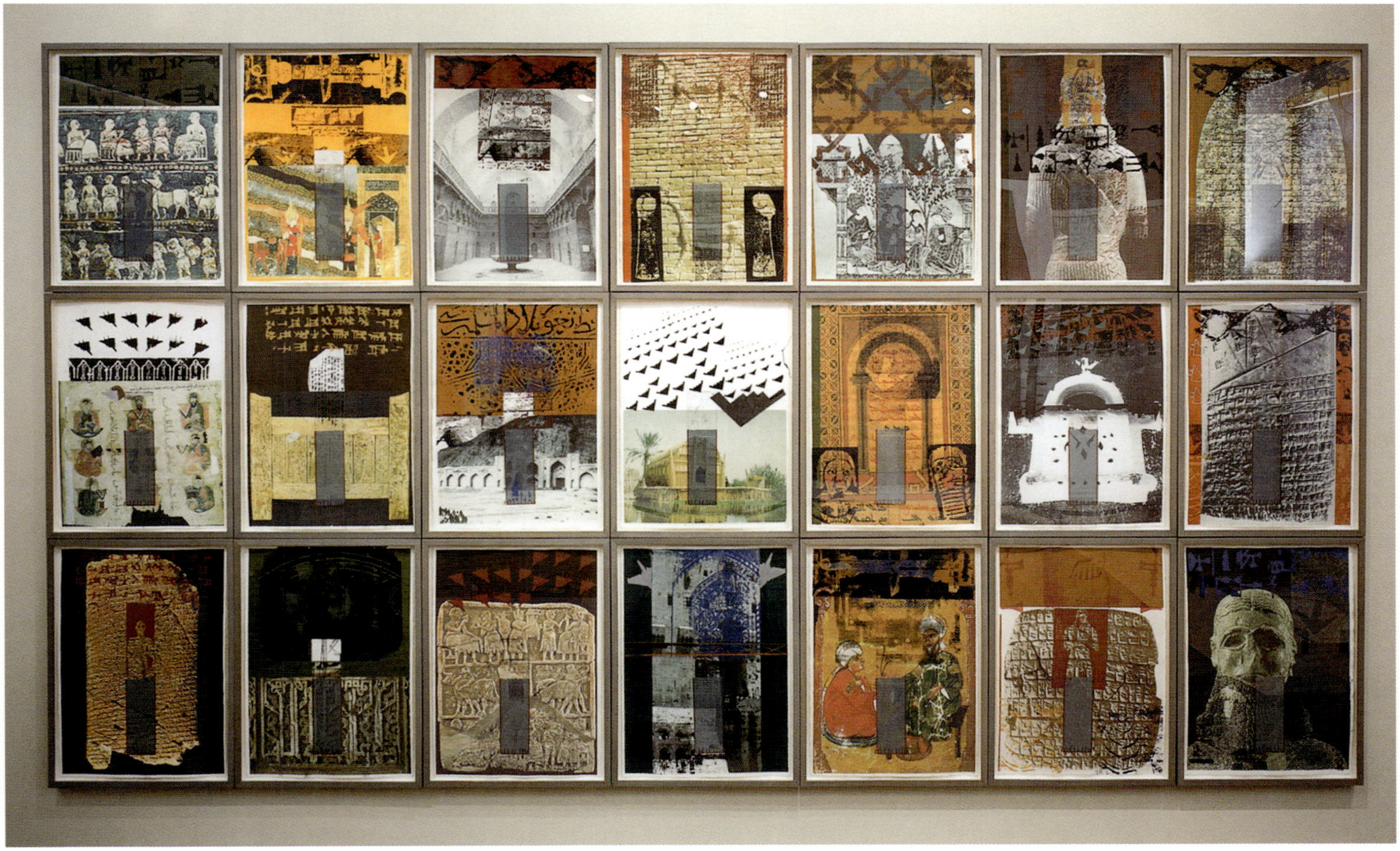

. . . and at night we leave our dreams
on the window sill, memory of a place, 2000

Wall Installation: mixed media on BFK Rives paper • 444.5 x 287 cm

Collection of the Artist
Photo: H. Foster, © Canadian Museum of Civilization
T2002-42

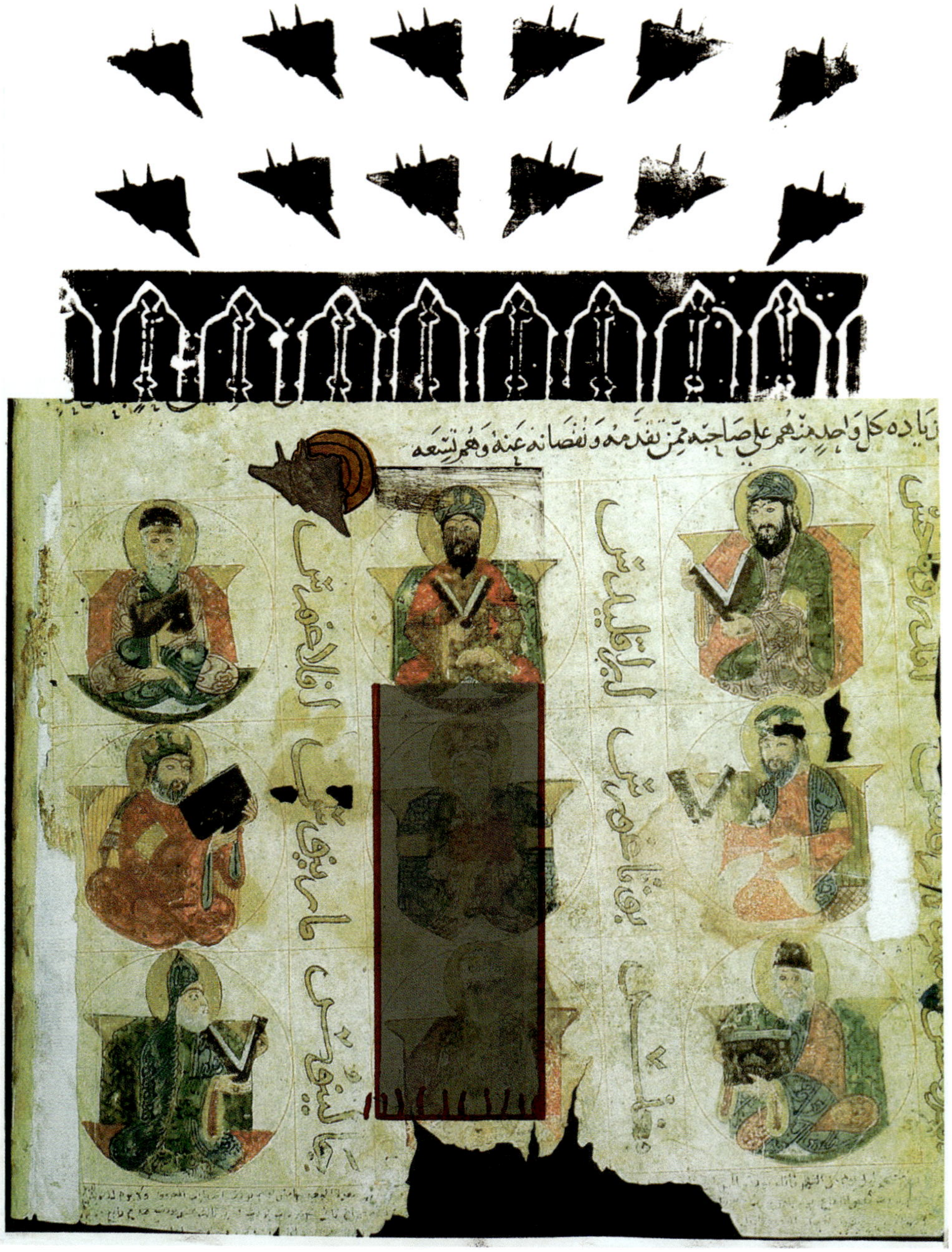

. . . and at night we leave our dreams
on the window sill, memory of a place (detail), 2000

Wall Installation: mixed media on BFK Rives paper

Collection of the Artist
Photo: H. Foster, © Canadian Museum of Civilization
T2002-43

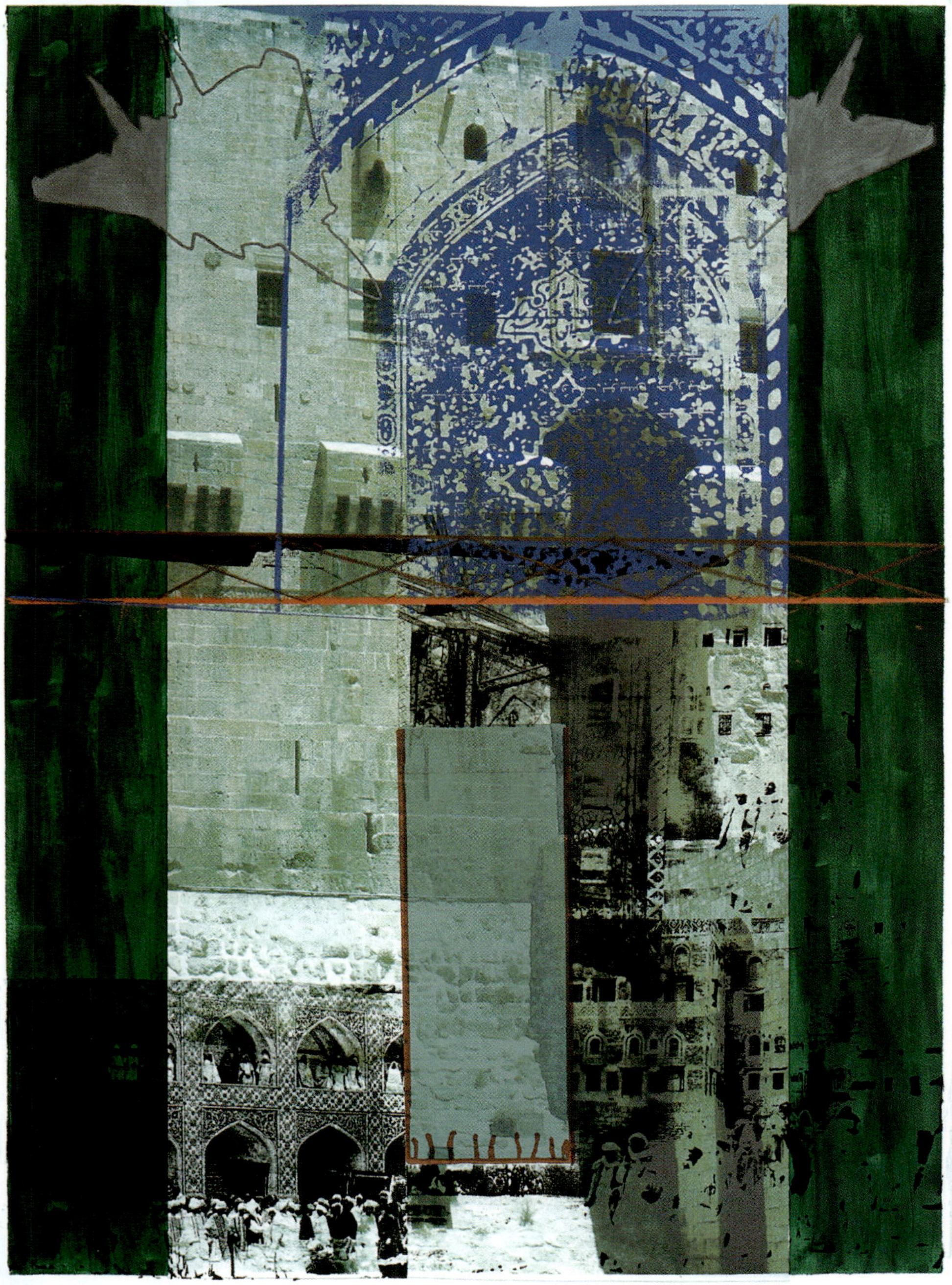

. . . and at night we leave our dreams on the window sill, memory of a place (detail), 2000

Wall Installation: mixed media on BFK Rives paper

Collection of the Artist
Photo: H. Foster, © Canadian Museum of Civilization
T2002-44

Ali Kichou

"Once upon a time, in a village lived a man who had a wife and two children. The mother owned a cow. But one day she fell ill. When she felt herself near death, she called her husband and said to him, 'Promise me that you will not sell the cow, that you will keep it always for the little orphans. . .'

"With this extract from the tale The Orphans' Cow, *I want the orphans to represent the people, left to their own devices, and the cow to represent the country.*

"In a sense, the theme is a pretext for artistic and technical confrontations. . .

"In terms of form, my aesthetic and cultural inspirations and peregrinations lead me — or rather, essentially, bring me back — to primitive art, to the Kabyle homes of Algeria, decorated with a profound emotional mastery by women. To African masks, to those Berber carpets and signs . . . as well as to the M'zab and its admirable architecture."

(Excerpt from the artist's statement)

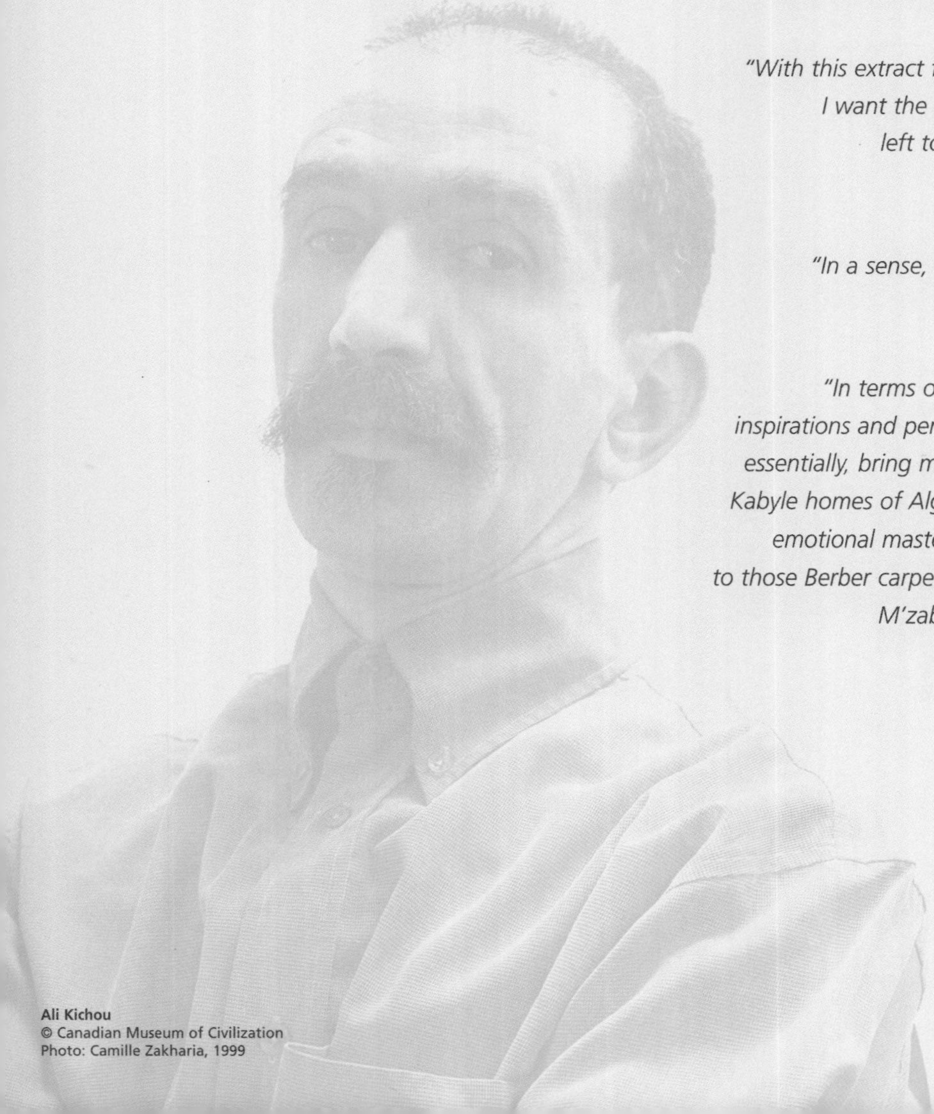

Ali Kichou

Photo: Camille Zakharia, 1999

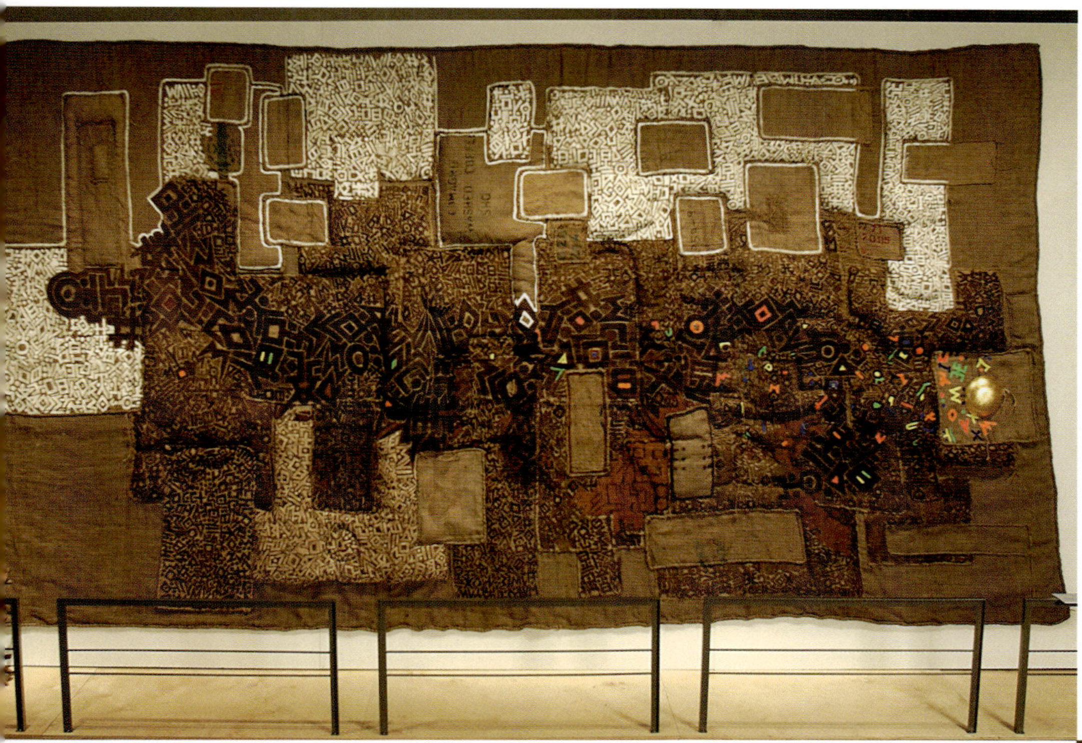

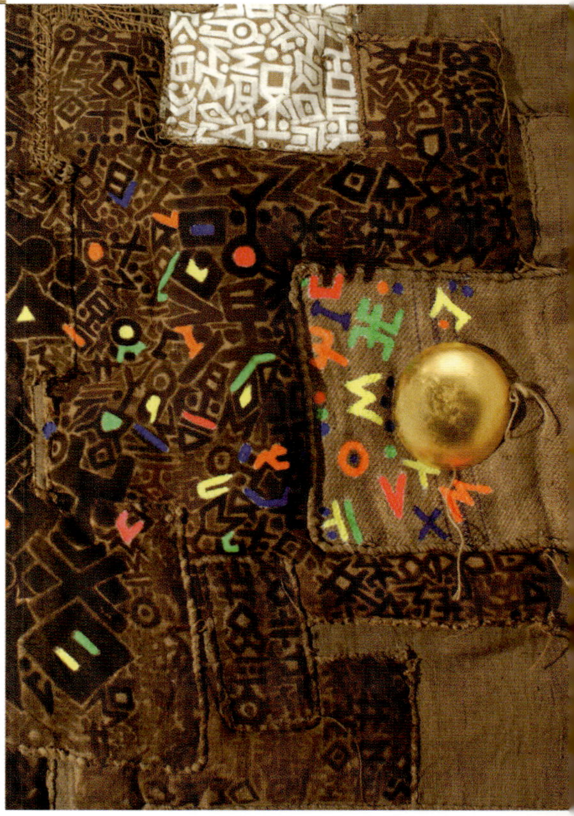

La vache des orphelins (The Orphans' Cow), 2000

Installation: pigments on woven and stuffed jute canvas, wood
61 x 43 x 232.4 cm (chair)
541 x 310 cm (canvas)

Collection of the Artist
Photo: H. Foster, © Canadian Museum of Civilization
D2002-16092

La vache des orphelins (The Orphans' Cow — detail), 2000

Installation: pigments on woven
and stuffed jute canvas, wood

Collection of the Artist
Photo: H. Foster, © Canadian Museum of Civilization
D2002-16089

Bernice Lutfie Sorge

"What is it like to be born of a place, to stay and live there, to know that you are of it *(Edward Said)* . . . *and of another place, a fantasy place, born of a mother's memory?"*

"We were compensated in our most difficult times by our mother's stories that transported us to Syria, to her childhood. Her village near Damascus became an ideal place in my mind . . .

"This dichotomy of the two villages, mine and hers, reality and myth, provided an in-between world for me, a world which consisted of both places. My imagination was stimulated by a desire to make everything one, to find wholeness, to solve the mystery of difference. How can these two worlds meet, what is the same about them? My quest became existential."

"The large wooden frame that surrounds the prints was created by one of my Syrian mother's grandsons . . . This view, within a frame, gives perspective and distance and brings us back to the here and now."

(Excerpts from the artist's statement and from a text by the artist)

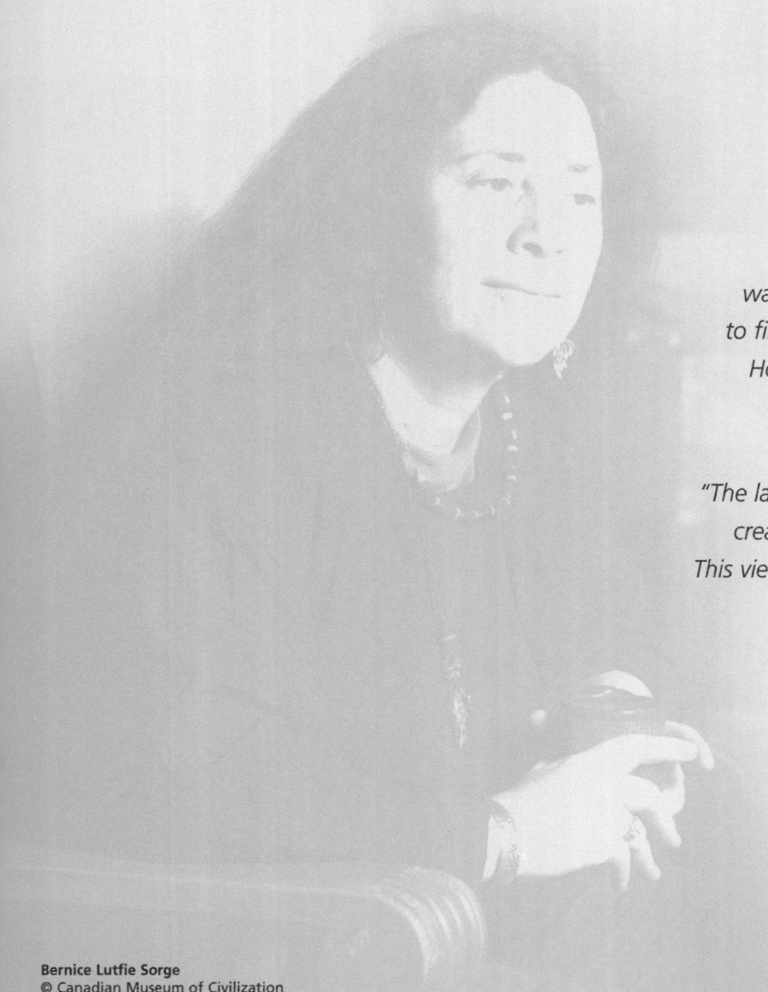

Bernice Lutfie Sorge

Photo: Rawi Hage, 1999

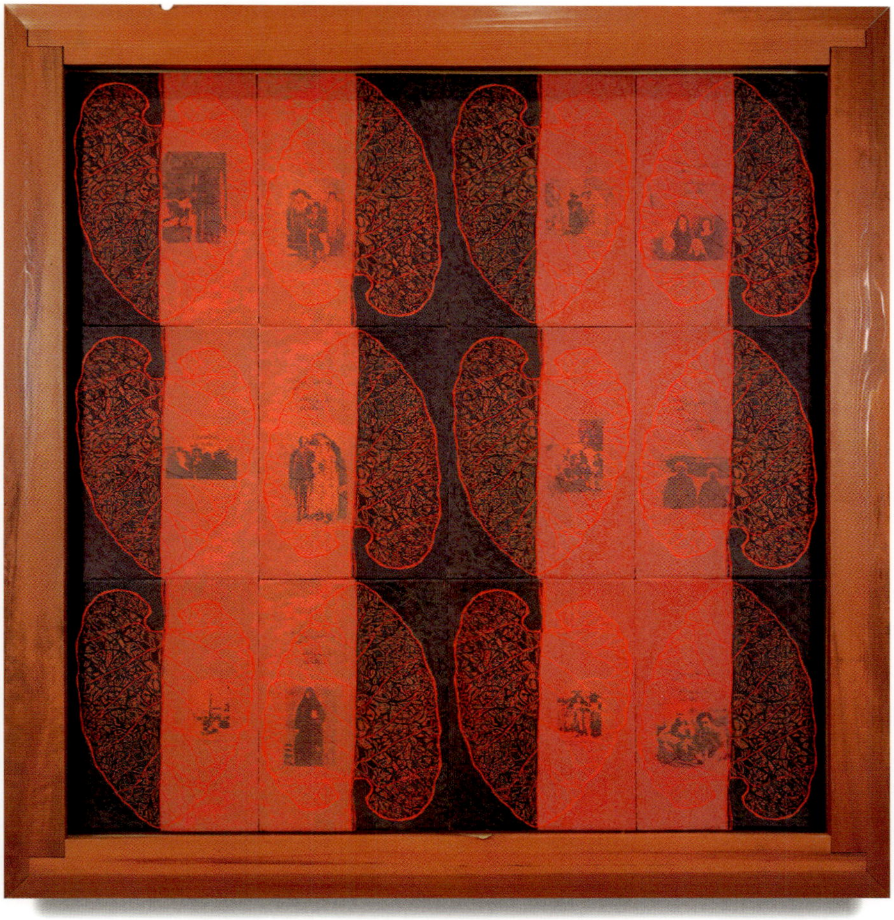

A Place for Rose, 2000–2001

Produced in collaboration with Julien Sorge Geoffroy and Gloria Sorge

Mural work with sound: intaglio, silkscreen printing on Arches vellum, frame of California redwood, audio component (recorded narration)

16.5 x 267 x 267 cm

Collection of the Artist
Photo: H. Foster, © Canadian Museum of Civilization
T2002-50

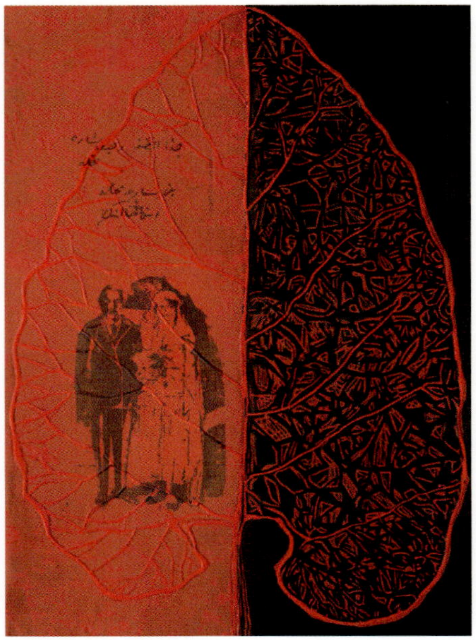

A Place for Rose (detail), 2000–2001

Produced in collaboration with Julien Sorge Geoffroy and Gloria Sorge

Mural work with sound: intaglio, silkscreen printing on Arches vellum, frame of California redwood, audio component (recorded narration)

16.5 x 267 x 267 cm

Collection of the Artist
Photo: H. Foster, © Canadian Museum of Civilization
T2002-51

See Appendix II for audio narrative text

nihal Mazloum

"As for the jewellery, the ones I like to create resemble ancient amulets and talismans. These are objects that have, as in antiquity, a sacred character, and are inspired by traditional and symbolic motifs."

(Excerpt from a text by the artist)

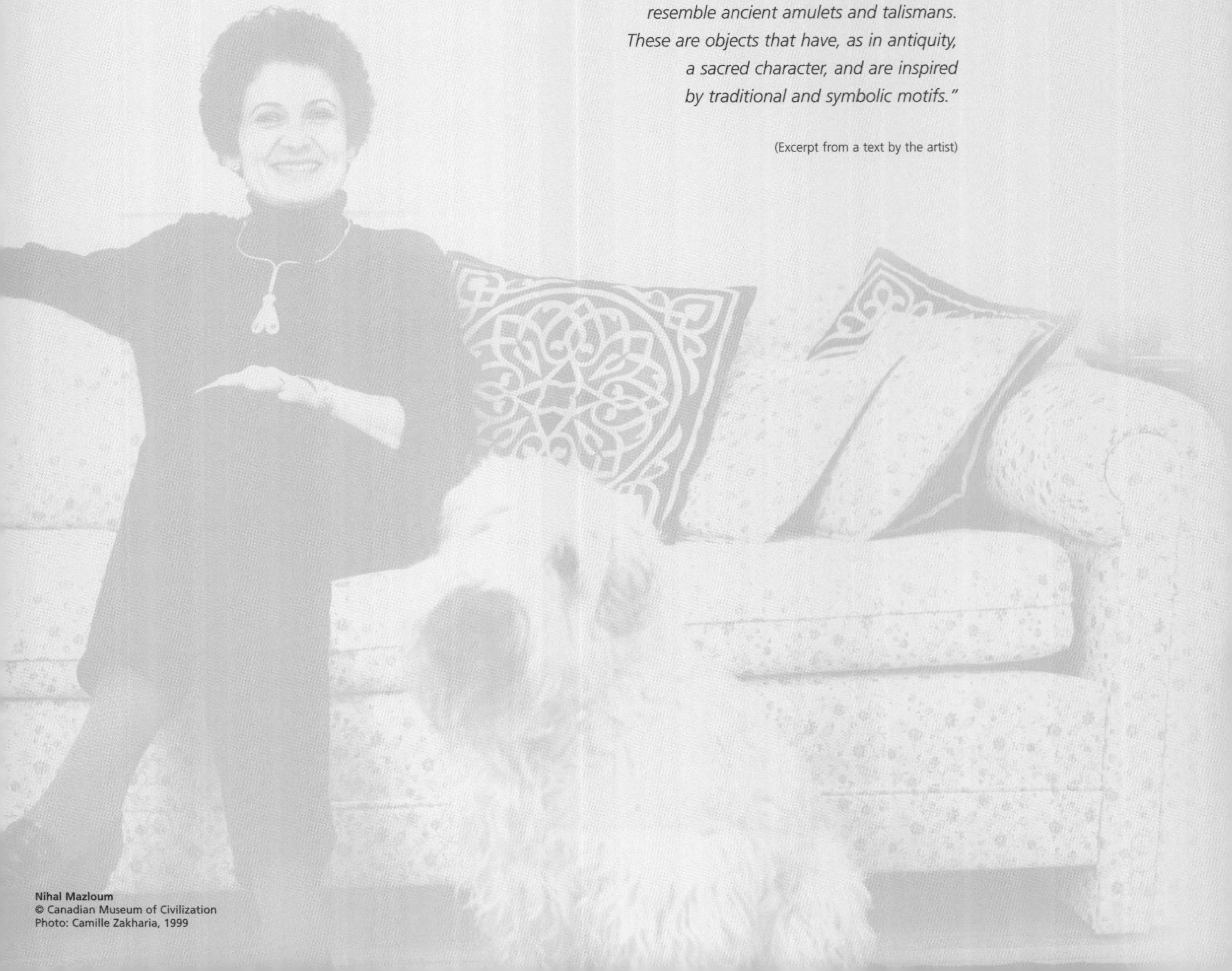

Nihal Mazloum

Photo: Camille Zakharia, 1999

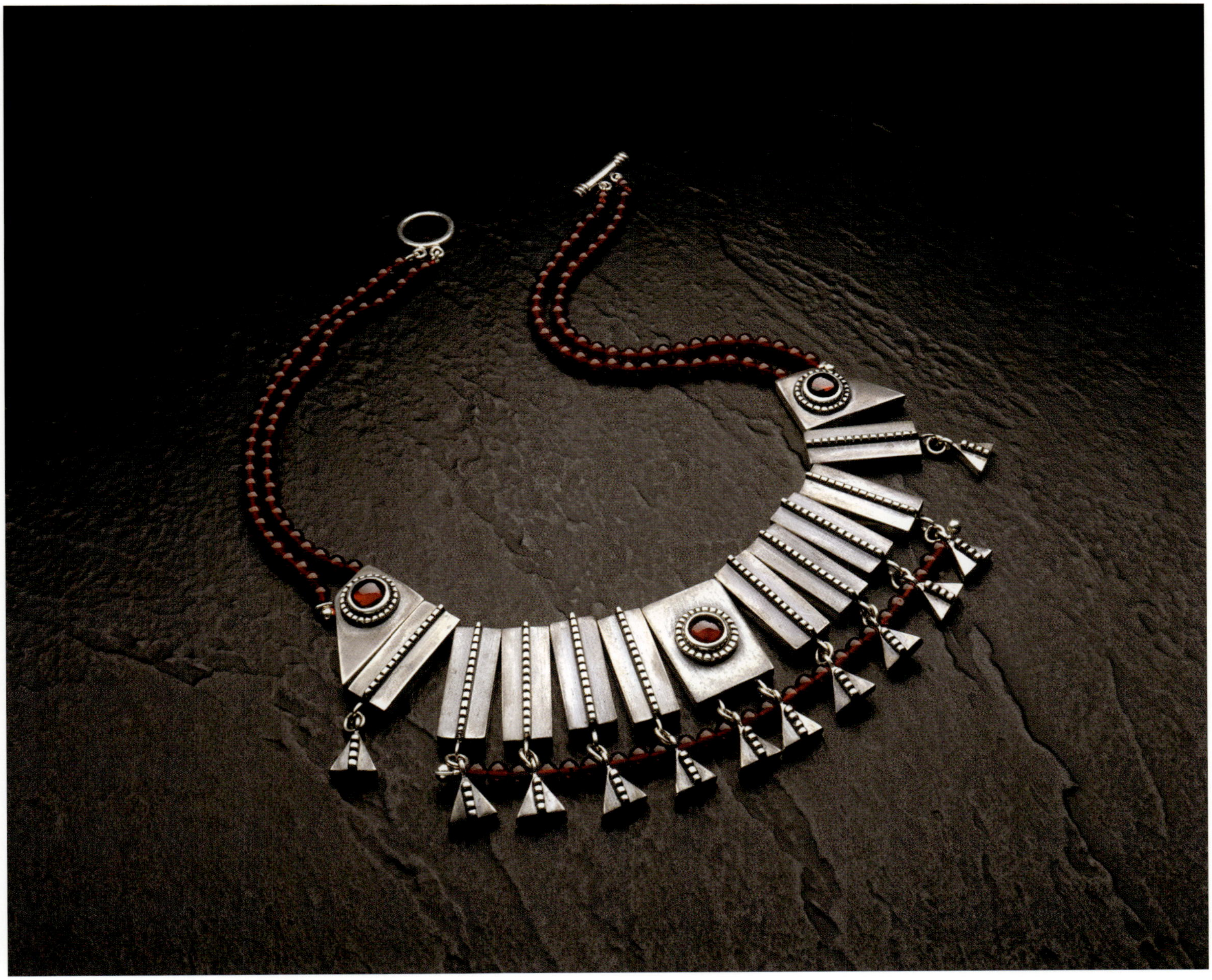

Necklace, 2000

Sterling silver, cornelian • 19 x 14 cm

Collection of the Artist
Photo: H. Foster, © Canadian Museum of Civilization
T2002-20

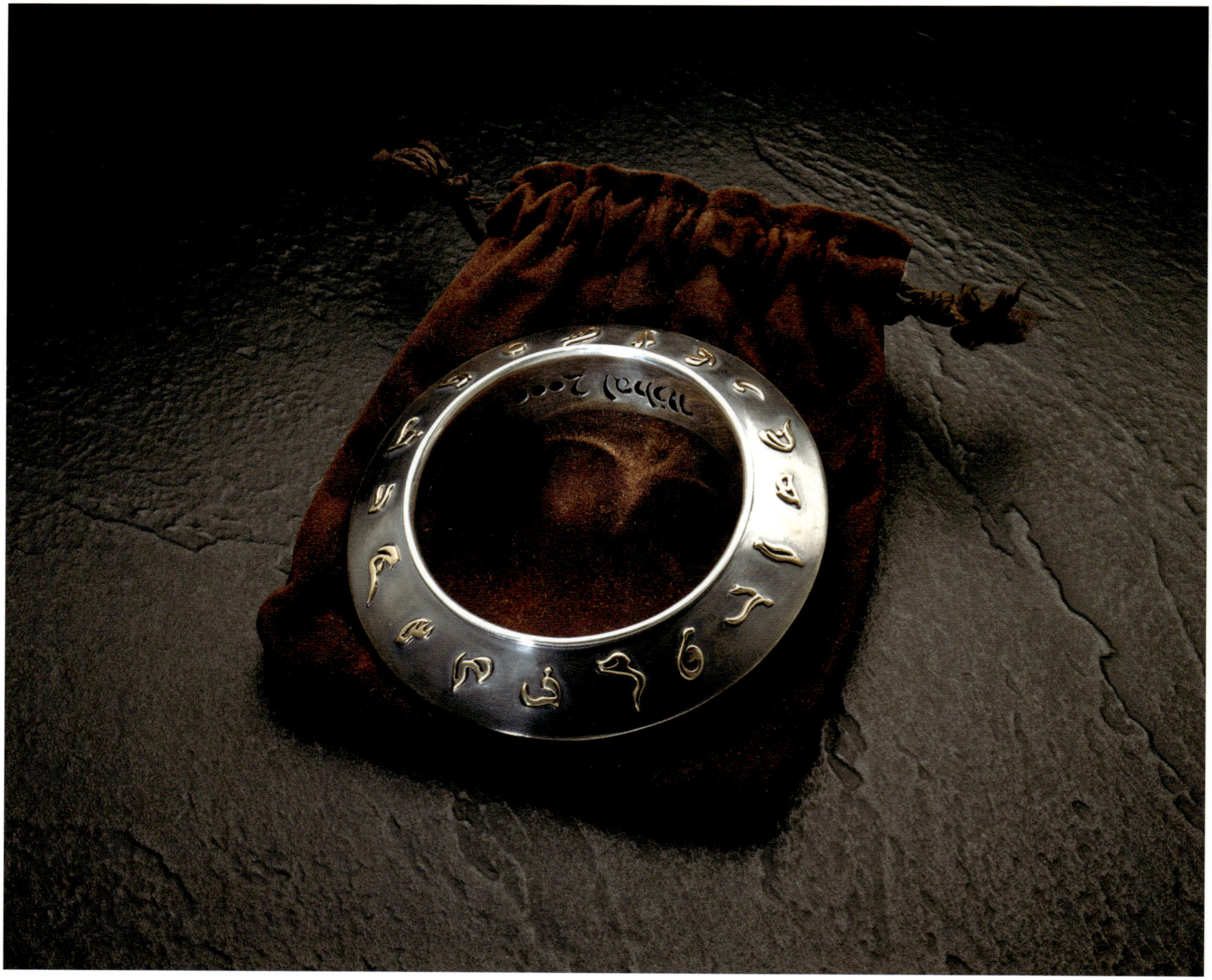

Bracelet, 2000

Sterling silver, 18-karat gold • 9.5 cm (outside diameter)

Collection of the Artist
Photo: H. Foster, © Canadian Museum of Civilization
T2002-21

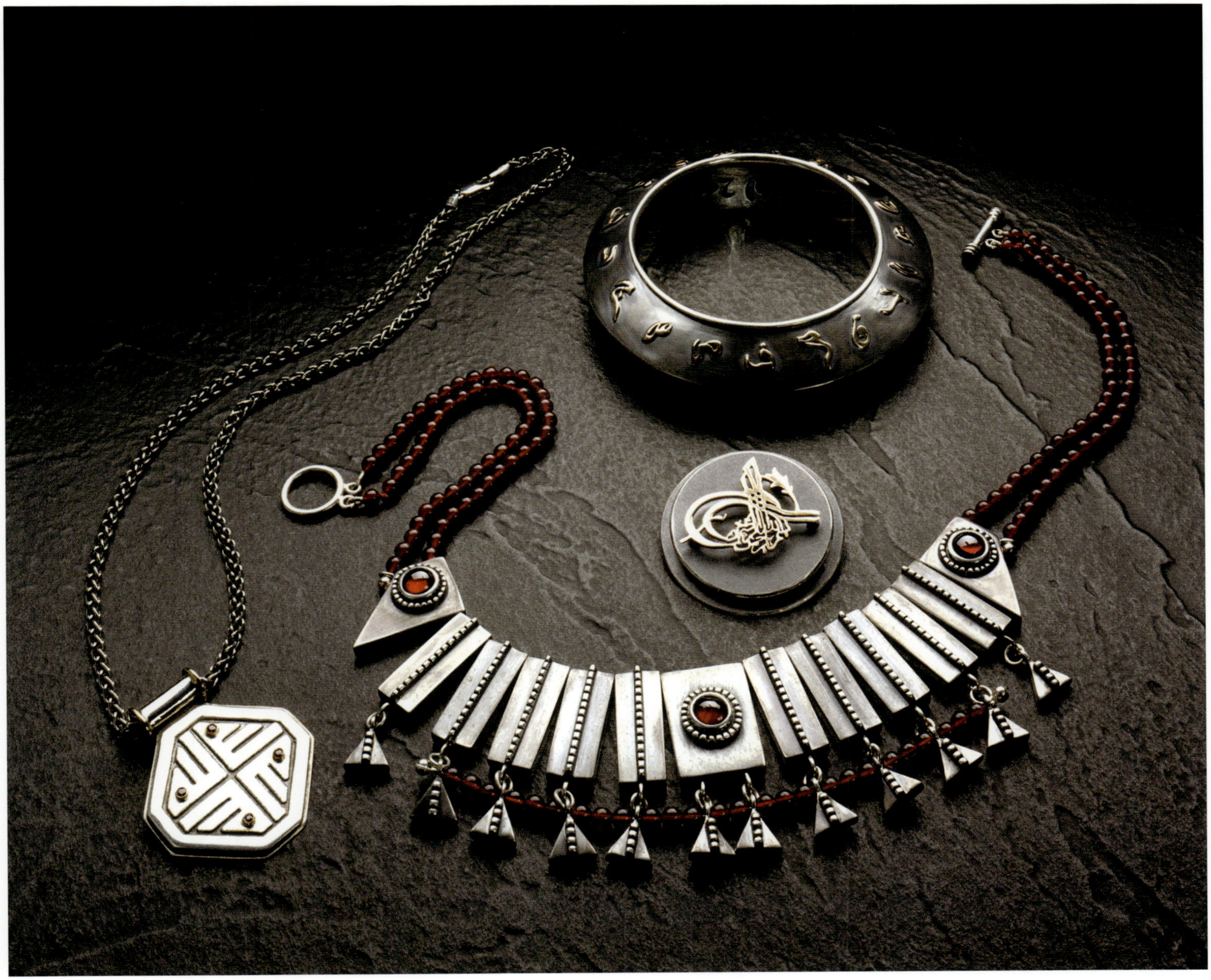

Jewels, 2000

Sterling silver, 18-karat gold, 14-karat gold, cornelian and rubies

Collection of the Artist
Photo: H. Foster, © Canadian Museum of Civilization
T2002-22

Joseph Moukhtar

"All my life, I have lived among many cultures. Syria is a country of several cultures: there are Bedouins, Kurds, Assyrians, Armenians, Circassians and still others . . .

"I love the blending of immigrant cultures with Canadian and Quebec cultures. In time, we shall see the birth of a new culture . . .

"Because I live, I must change.
Every day, I see new things.
We must change incessantly,
each of us, until the end of our life."

(Extract from an interview with the artist)

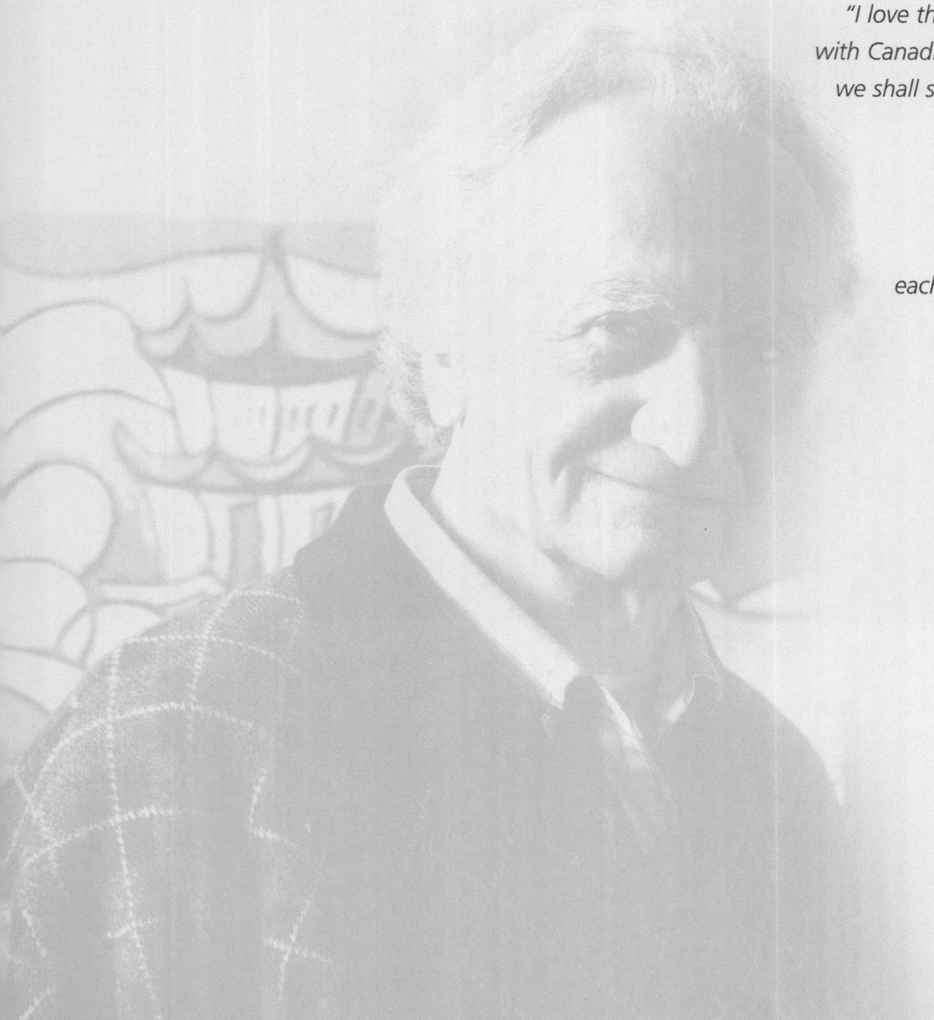

Joseph Moukhtar

Photo: Rawi Hage, 1999

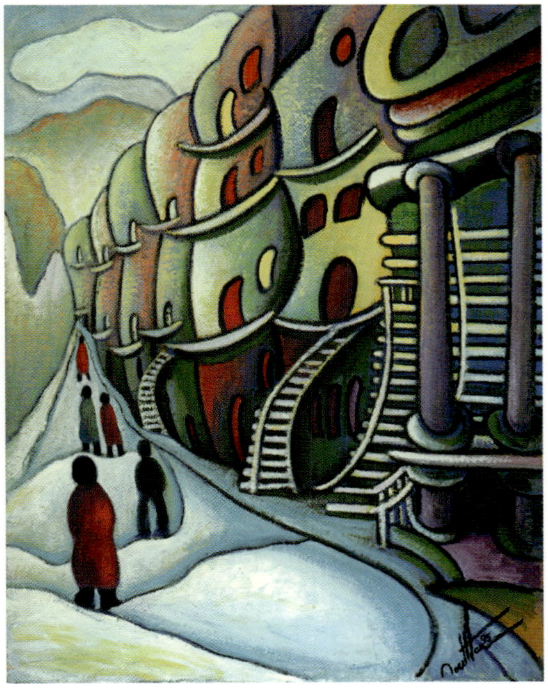

Montréal, St-Denis en hiver (Montreal, St. Denis Street in Winter), 1995

Oil on canvas • 60.7 x 76 cm

Collection of the Artist
Photo: H. Foster, © Canadian Museum of Civilization
T2002-12

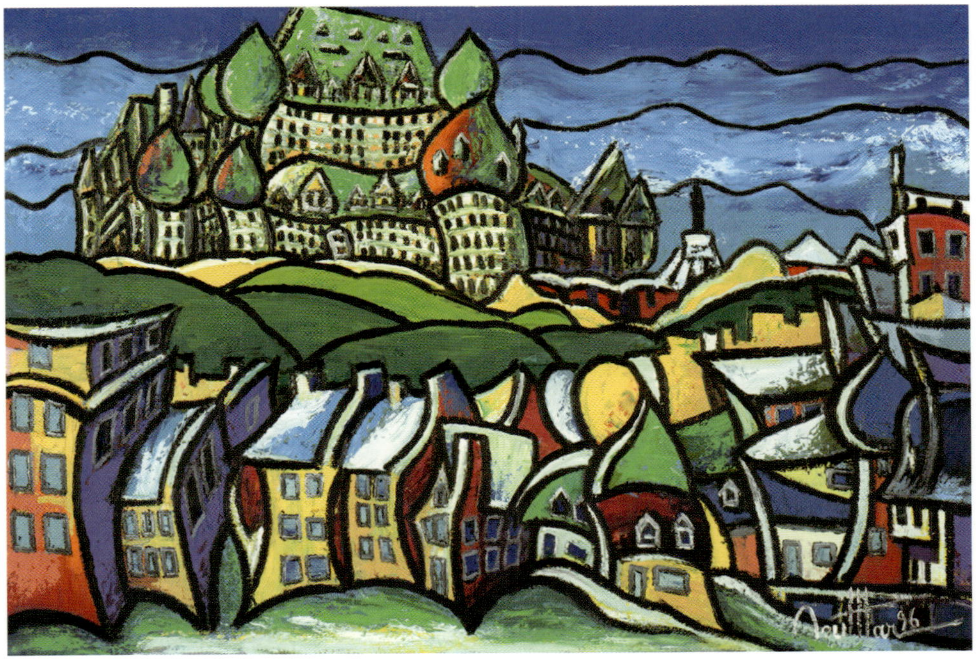

Québec, la cinquième saison (Quebec City, the Fifth Season), 1996

Oil on canvas • 91.2 x 61 cm

Collection of the Artist
Photo: H. Foster, © Canadian Museum of Civilization
T2002-13

Hadjira Preure

"Red ochre, burned earth, scent of my land,
I am a prisoner.
My hand, my eyes, my heart search for you.
I will find you again.
The child who was born cried out — a cry of liberty?
Forgive me, my mother, I have left you, but my heart is there, very close to you.
I hold you tight in my arms.

"To my Mother"

"I do not think that another country
can bring me solace, not so long as the problem
in my own country still exists.
But I am thinking above all
of stability for my children . . .

"For me, the most beautiful thing is hope,
and light."

(Extracts from a text by the artist and an interview)

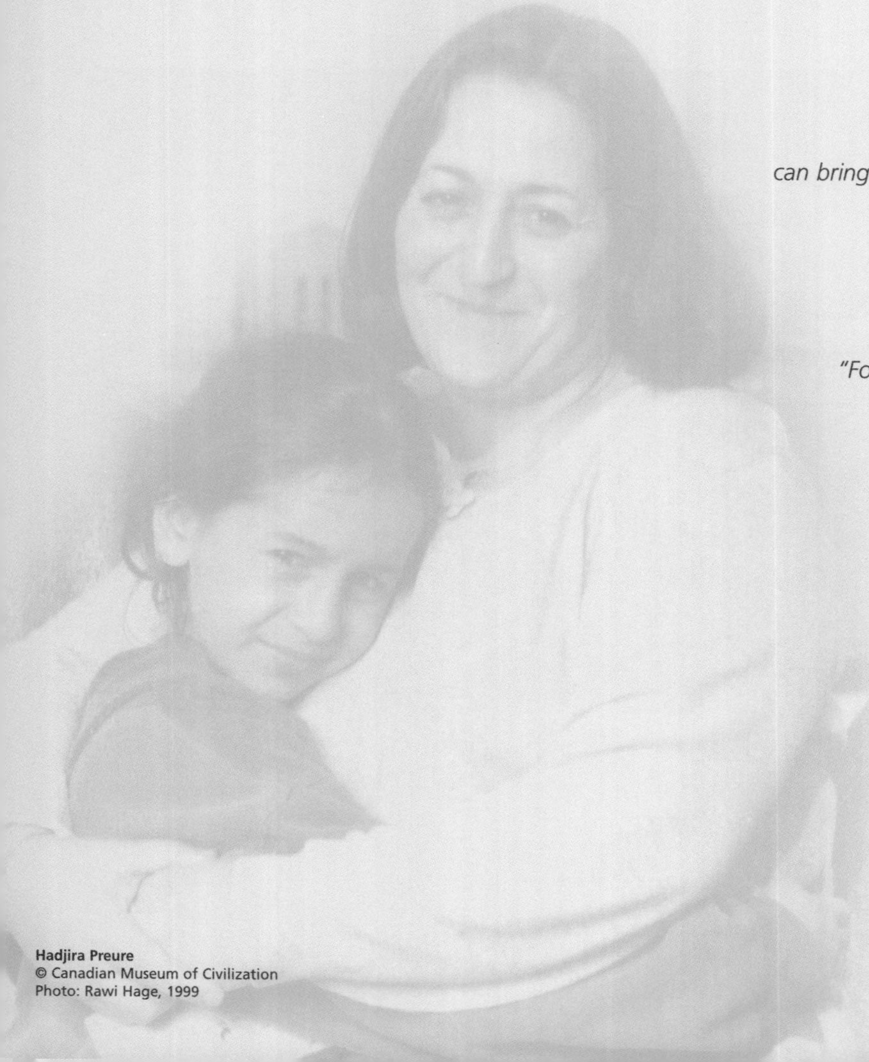

Hadjira Preure

Photo: Rawi Hage, 1999

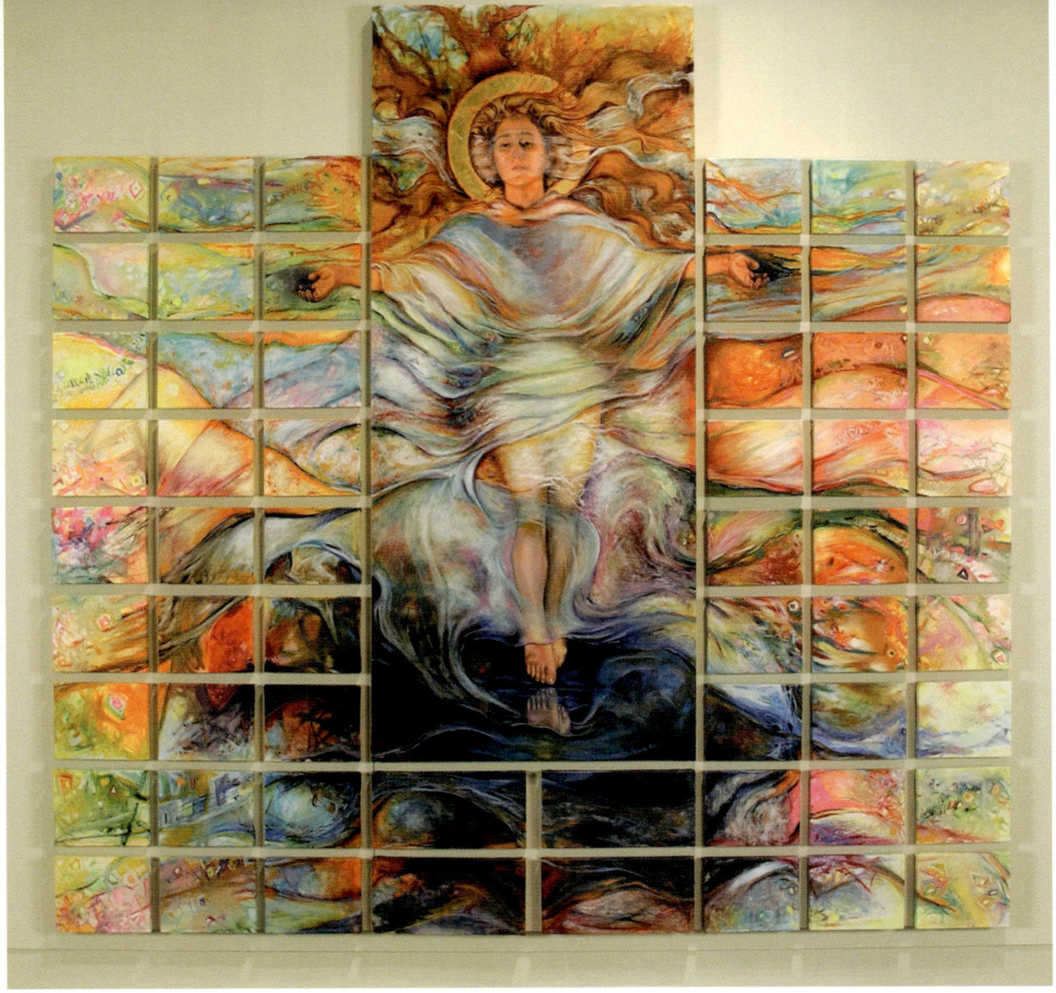

Houria, 2000

Oil, acrylic and gold leaf on cotton duck • 83.8 x 200.7 cm

"Houria" is a first name which was frequently
given to girls in Algeria during the 1950s.
For the artist, *Houria* symbolizes the women of Algeria.

Collection of the Artist
Photo: H. Foster, © Canadian Museum of Civilization
D2002-16087

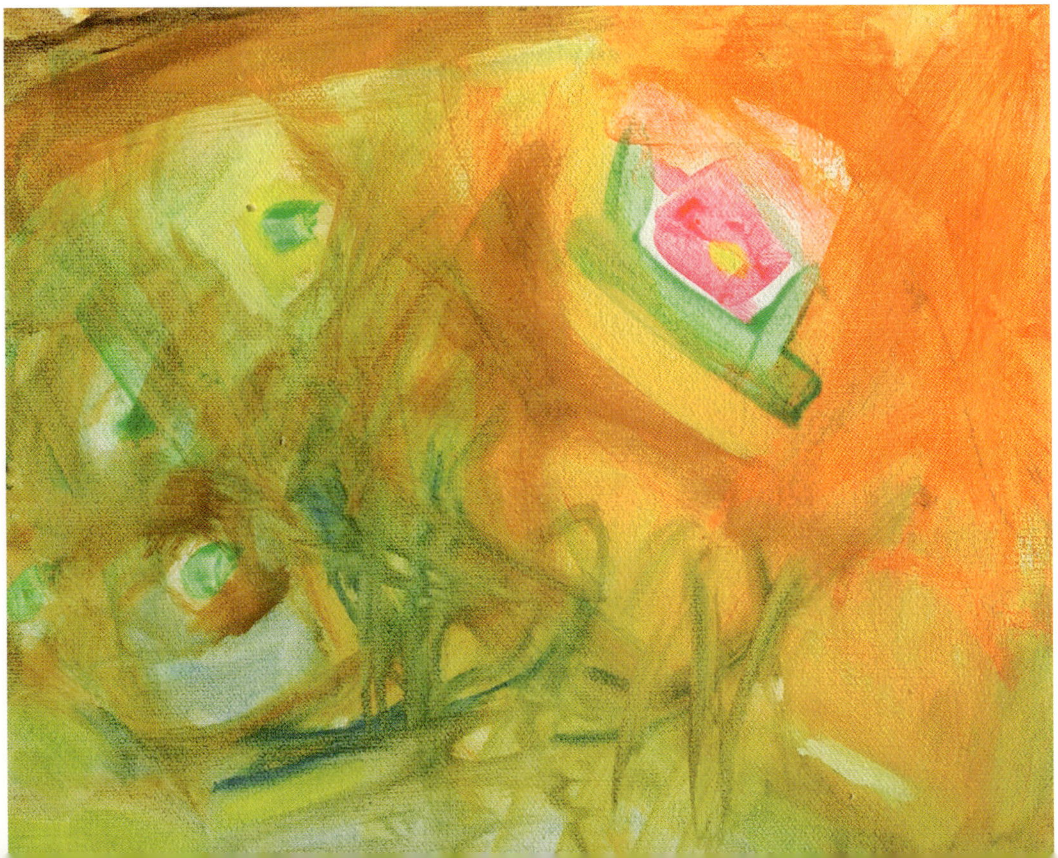

Houria (detail), 2000

Oil, acrylic and gold leaf on cotton duck

Collection of the Artist
Photo: H. Foster, © Canadian Museum of Civilization
D2002-16088

Aldin Rashid

"My work is the expression of my life story and the stories of millions of people. It is the representation of who I am in a foreign land. It gives me peace and tranquility, while at the same time passing on to present and future generations the good words of my ancestors, in the form of calligraphy and ornaments that, in turn, represent the many schools of writing."

(Excerpt from the artist's statement)

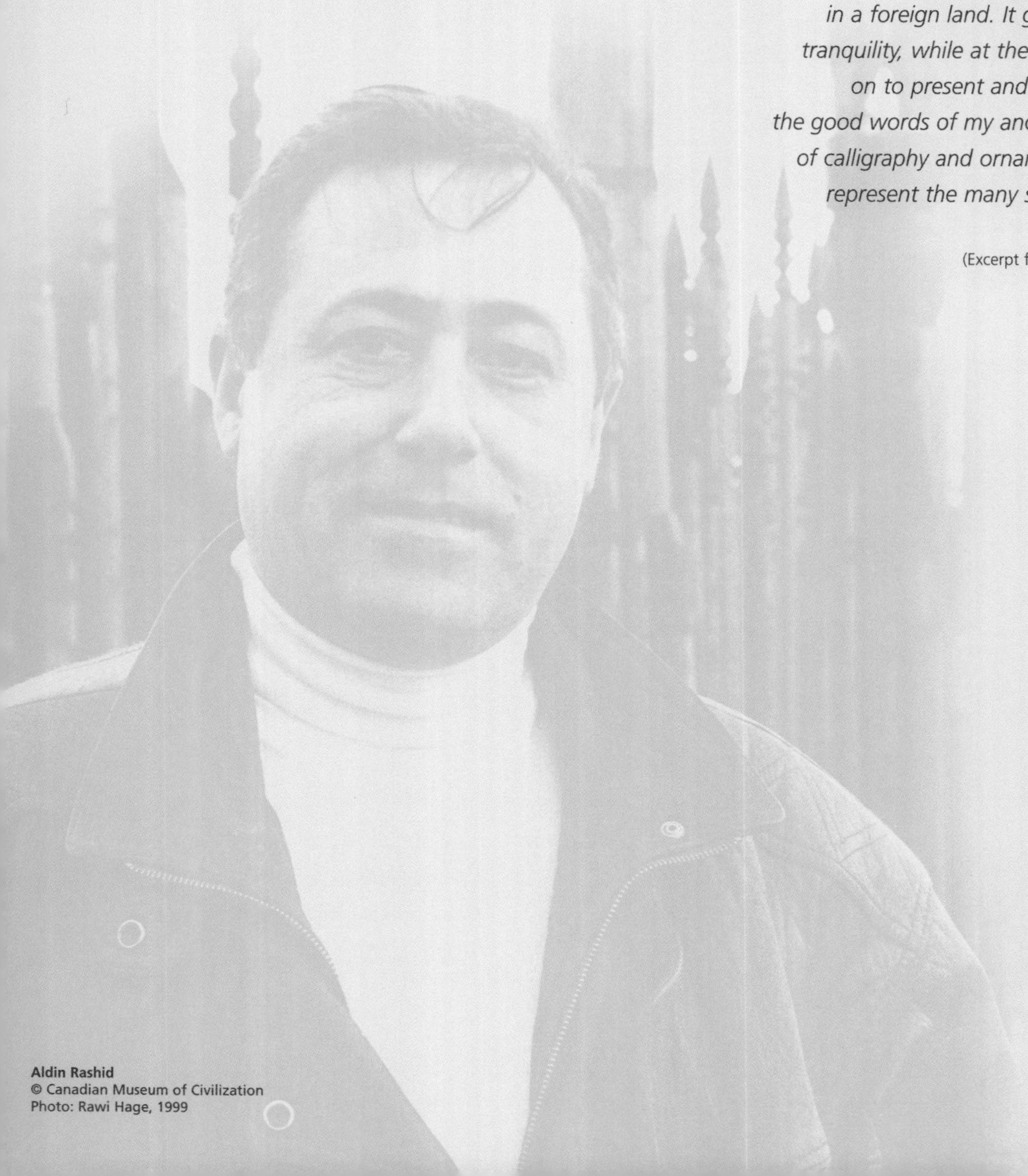

Aldin Rashid
© Canadian Museum of Civilization
Photo: Rawi Hage, 1999

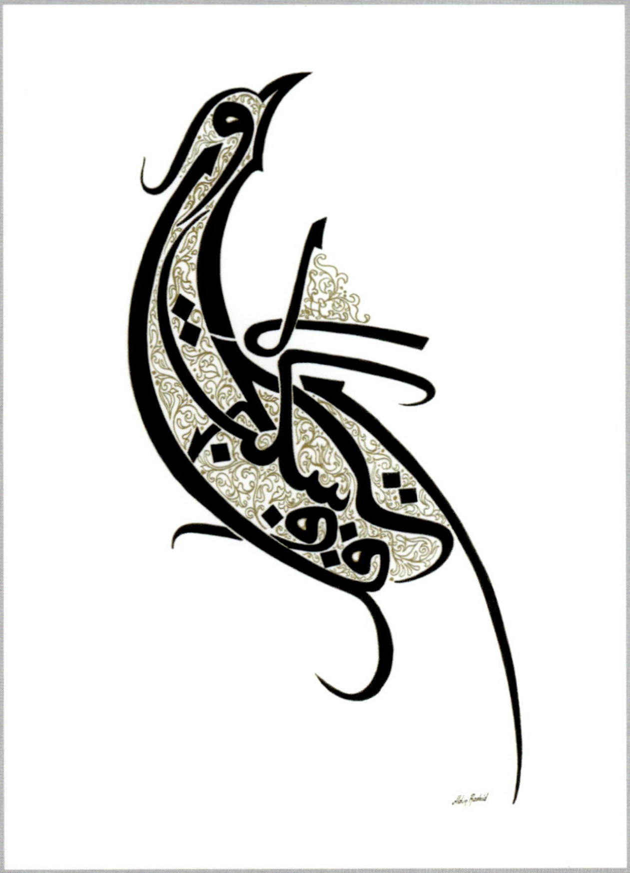

"If you can't say a good word, keep silent.", 1990
Calligraphy in Thuluth style

Ink and gold leaf on paper • 76 x 57 cm

Collection of the Artist
Photo: H. Foster, © Canadian Museum of Civilization
T2002-29

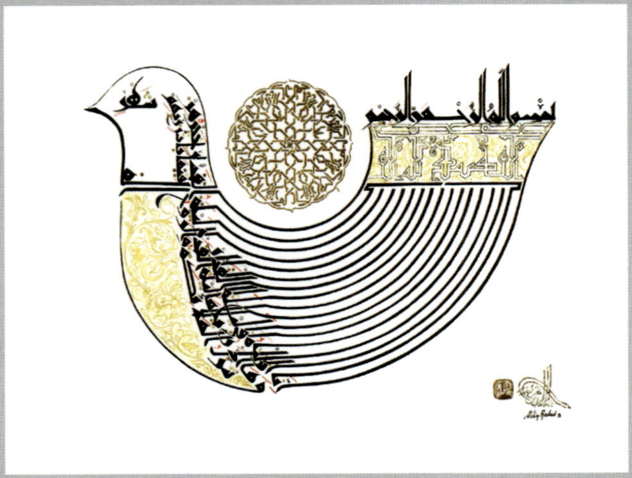

Sûrat Al-Qadr (Surat "The Night of Decree" from The Koran), 1996
Calligraphy in Nisaburi Kufic style

Ink and gold leaf on paper • 76 x 57 cm

Collection of the Artist
Photo: H. Foster, © Canadian Museum of Civilization
T2002-31

Karim Rholem

Karim Rholem
© Canadian Museum of Civilization
Photo: Karim Rholem, 1999

"This bond of trust that is established between me and the person I am photographing, before the picture is taken, is a moment that is dear to me."

"For me, photography is a door that lets me go towards other people, other places, 'elsewhere', the unfamiliar, towards all that is unknown to me."

(Extracts from the artist's statement and an interview)

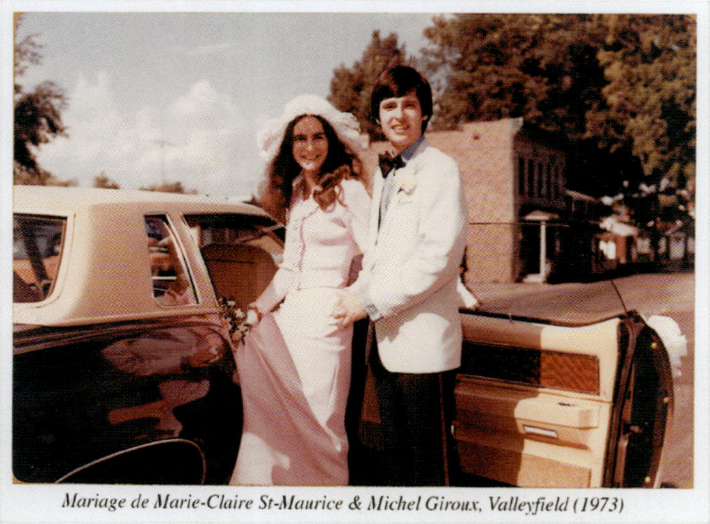

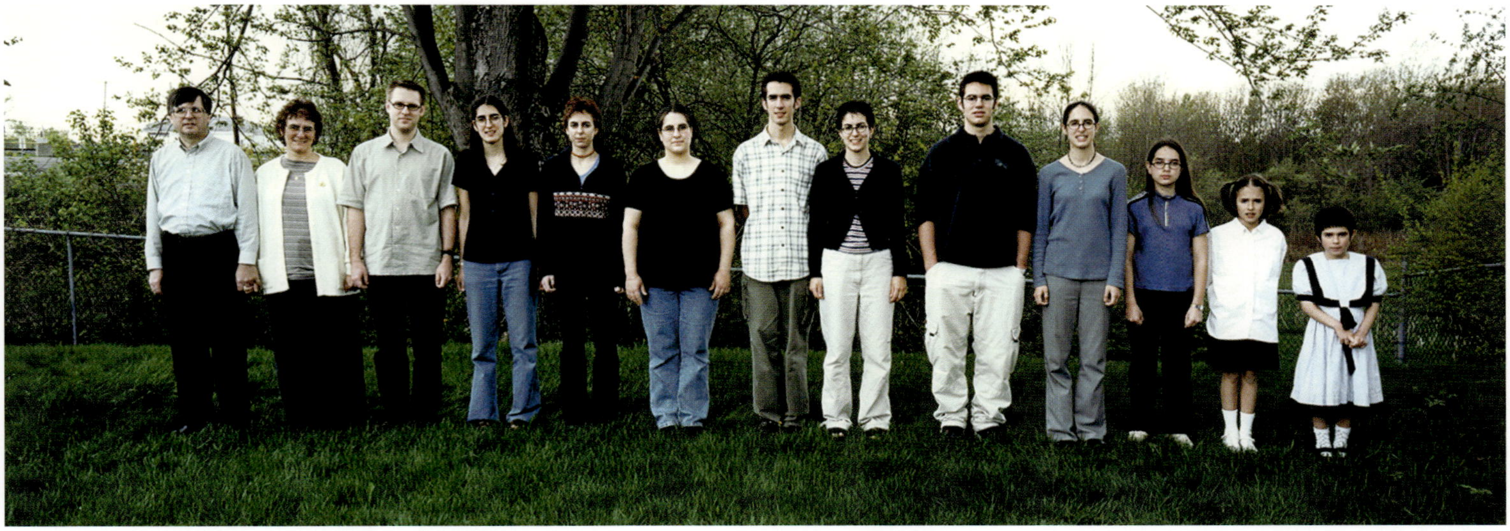

Les Giroux (The Giroux Family)
Marie-Claire, 46 years old; Michel, 52 years old;
11 children: 7 to 24 years old
Sainte-Rose de Laval (Quebec), May 2000

From the series *Un air de famille 2000 (A Family Likeness)*
Colour print • 138 x 64 cm

With the support of the Comité
des célébrations du Canada

Collection of the Artist
Photo: H. Foster, © Canadian Museum of Civilization
T2002-53

Marie-Claire and Michel Giroux, wedding photograph
Valleyfield, 1973

Digitized archival photograph

T2002-54

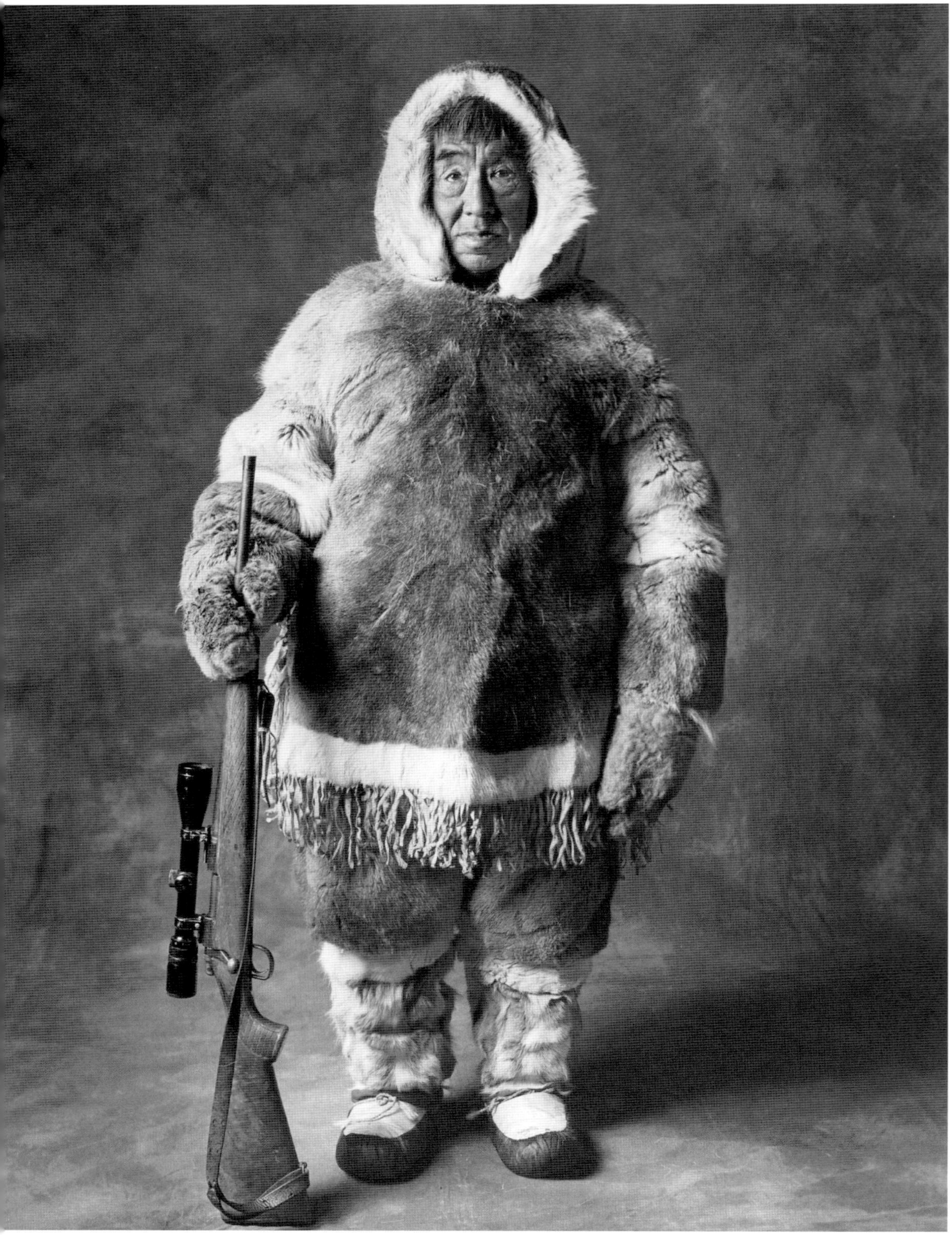

Gamilie Akeeagok, 66 years old, died in 1997
Aujuittuuq (Grise Fiord), N.W.T., July 1996

From the series *Uvagut : Portrait d'un peuple (Uvagut: Portrait of a People)* 1996
Silver gelatin print • 64 x 74 cm

With the support of the Canada Council for the Arts

Collection of the Artist
Photo: H. Foster, © Canadian Museum of Civilization
T2002-52

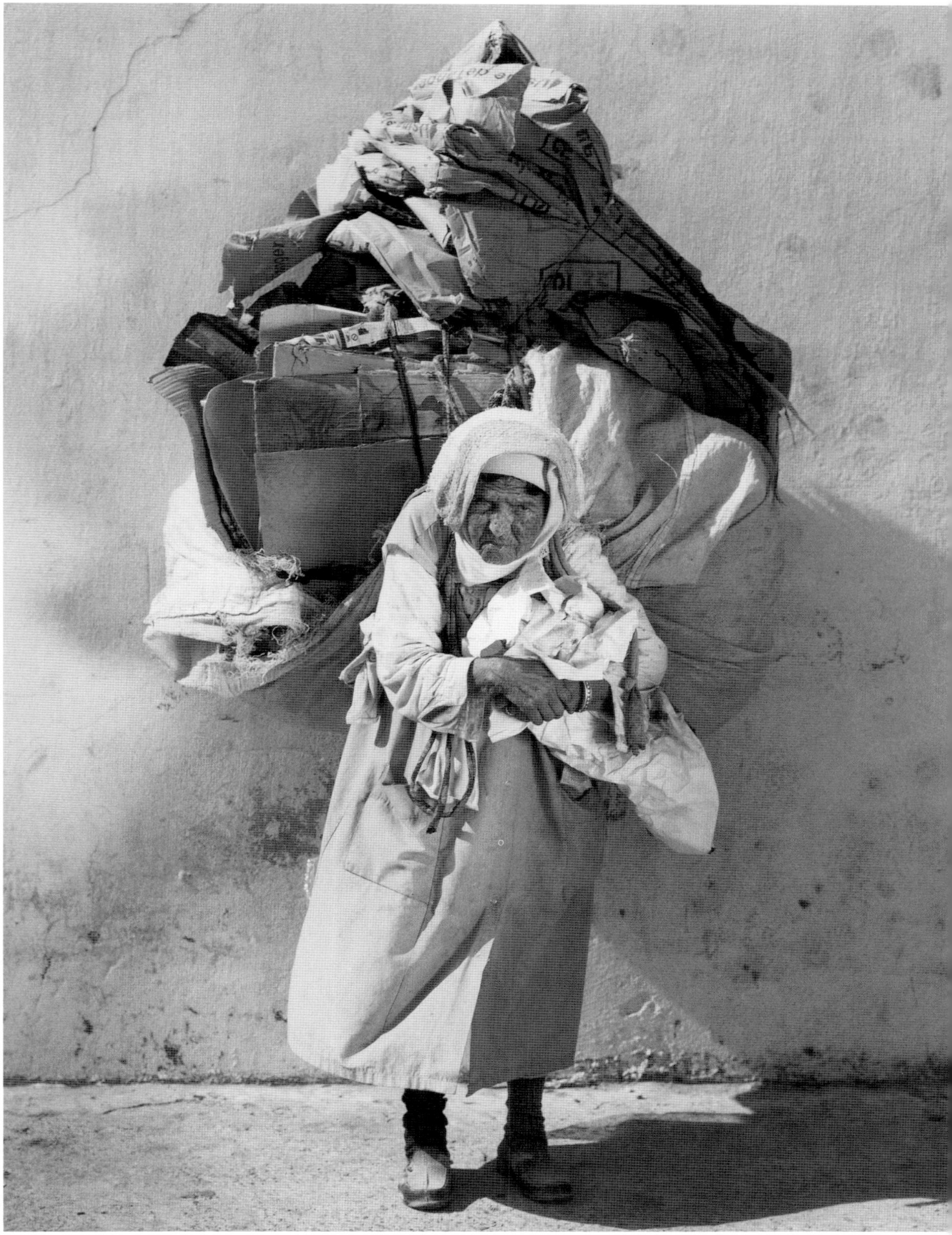

Yamma El Fellah, 76 years old,
Tangiers, Morocco, August 2000

From the series *Le poids du destin (The Weight of Destiny)*, 1996
Silver gelatin print

Lent by the Artist

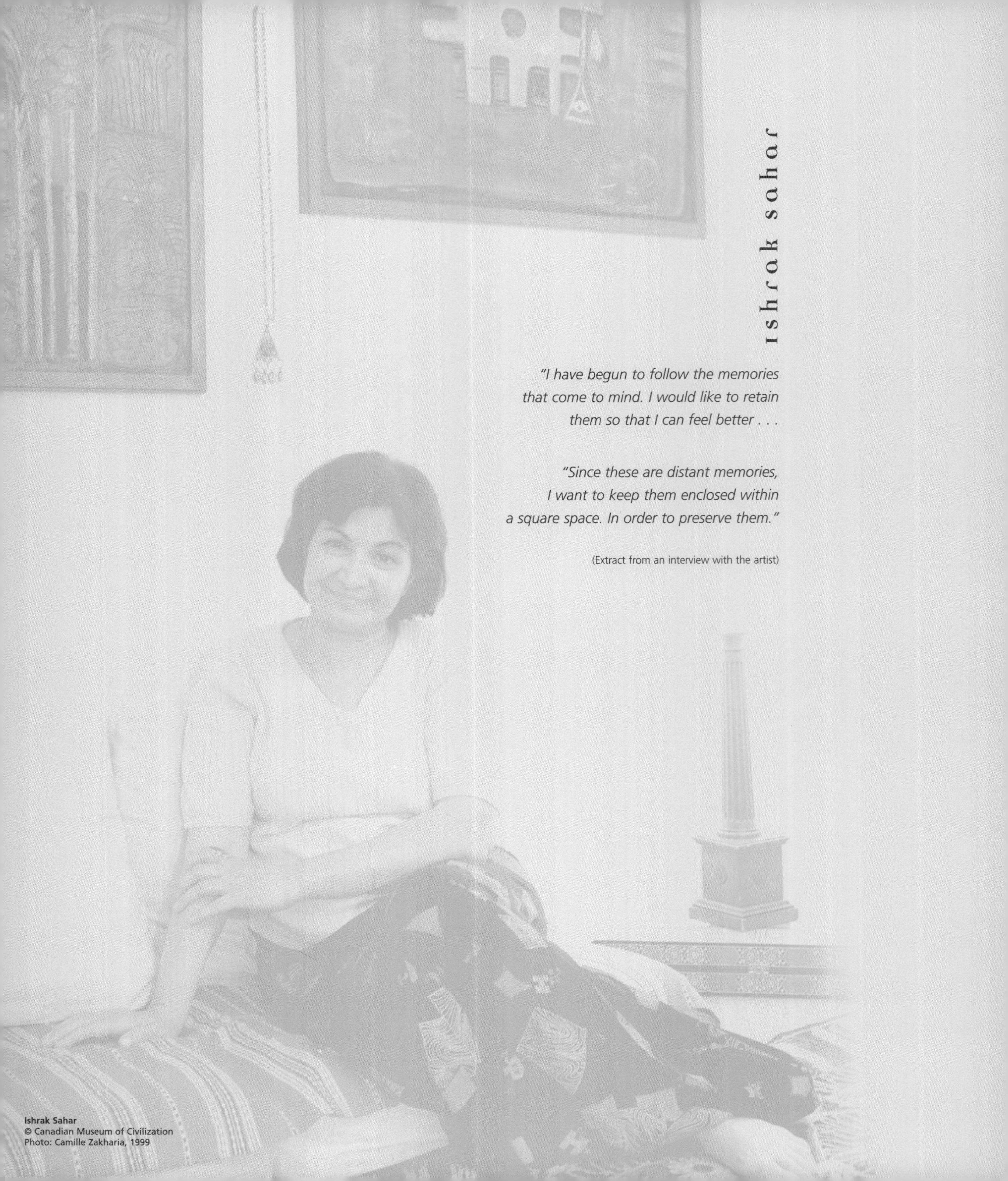

ishrak sahar

"I have begun to follow the memories that come to mind. I would like to retain them so that I can feel better . . .

"Since these are distant memories, I want to keep them enclosed within a square space. In order to preserve them."

(Extract from an interview with the artist)

Ishrak Sahar

Photo: Camille Zakharia, 1999

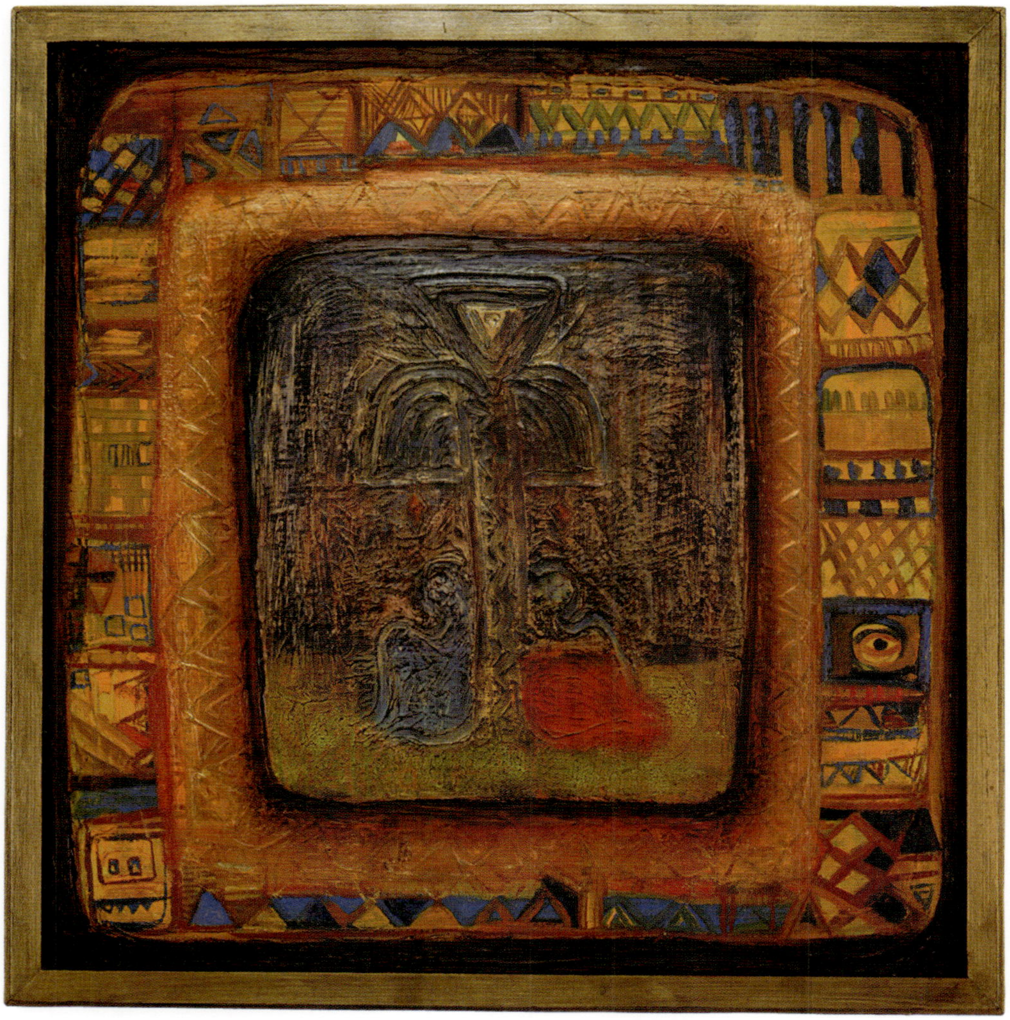

Shadow, 1995

Mixed media on wood • 64.5 x 64.5 cm

Collection of the Artist
Photo: H. Foster, © Canadian Museum of Civilization
T2002-4

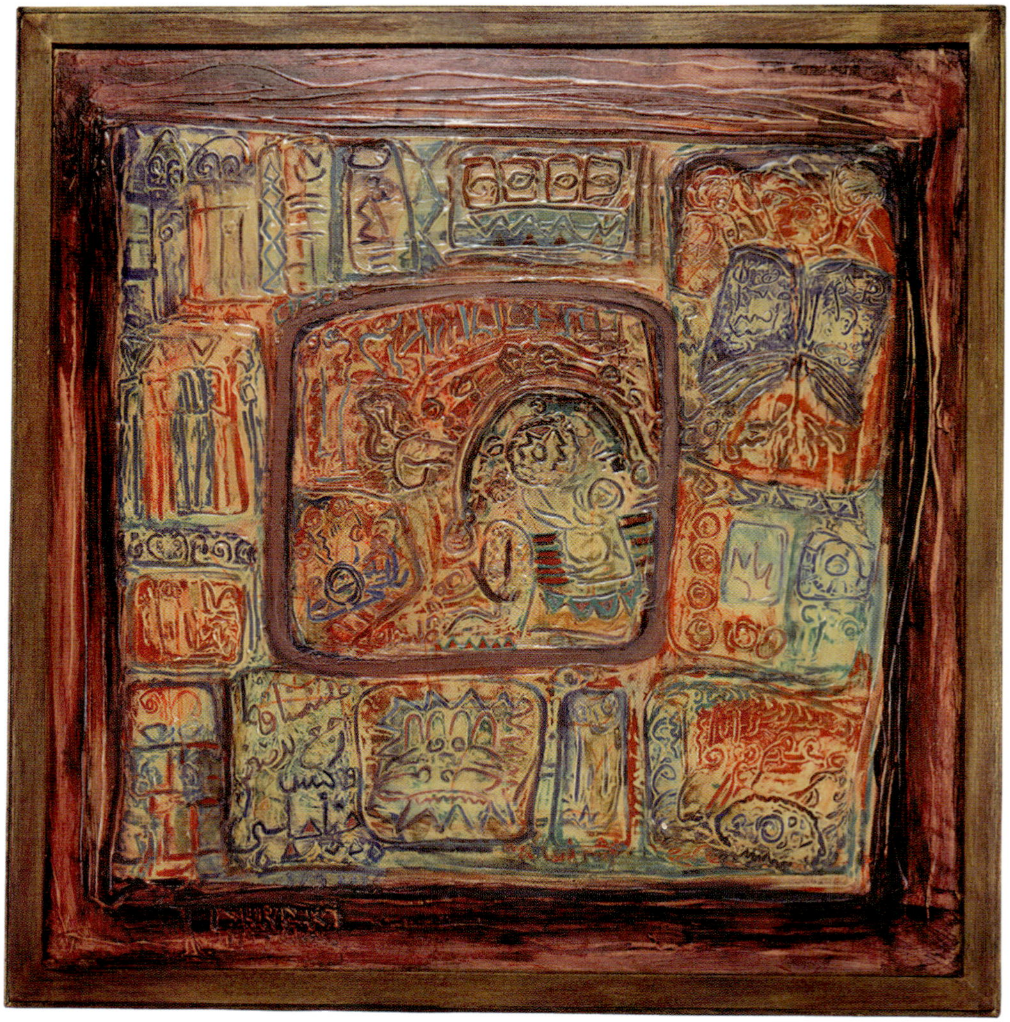

Djanadjil (child's bangle), 1997

Mixed media on wood • 64.5 x 64.5 cm

Collection of the Artist
Photo: H. Foster, © Canadian Museum of Civilization
T2002-5

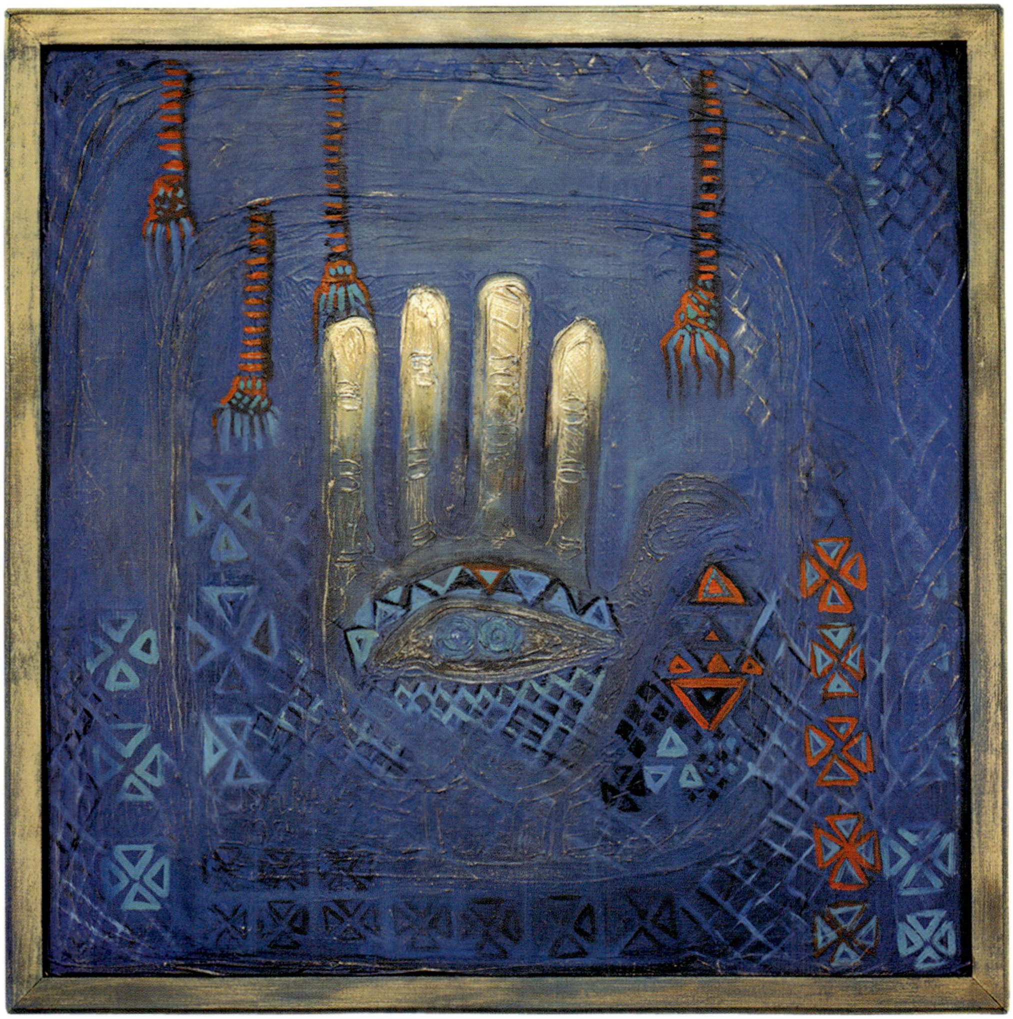

Voice, 1996

Mixed media on wood • 64.5 x 64.5 cm

Collection of the Artist
Photo: H. Foster, © Canadian Museum of Civilization
T2002-6

Jayce salloum

"Continuing my series of projects (1979–1999) addressing cultural-political manifestations, ethnographic representation and states of being, this installation focuses on borders, nationalism, movement (shifts, transitions and interstitial space/time) and subjectivity, and the conditions of moving and living cross-culturally and trans-culturally . . .

"I am interested in creating a collision between the intensely personal space of the dialogue moment and the context of the intrinsic social and political site, different with each subject but with overlapping and overarching points of contention/ correspondence: sense of place, notions of community, disenfranchisement and transnational ties."

(Excerpt from the artist's statement)

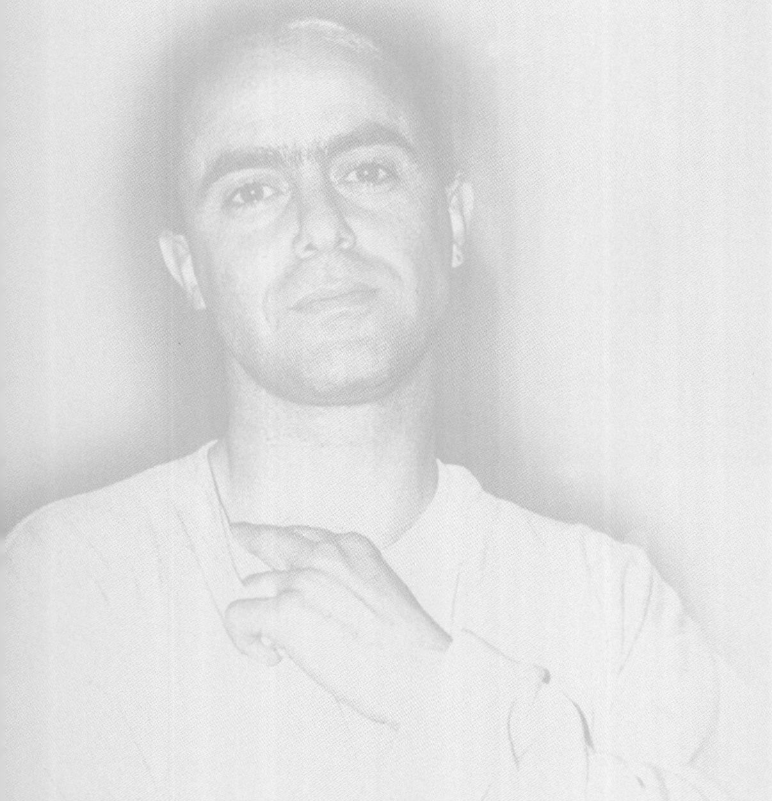

Jayce Salloum
© Jayce Salloum
Photo: Moukhtar Kokache, 1996

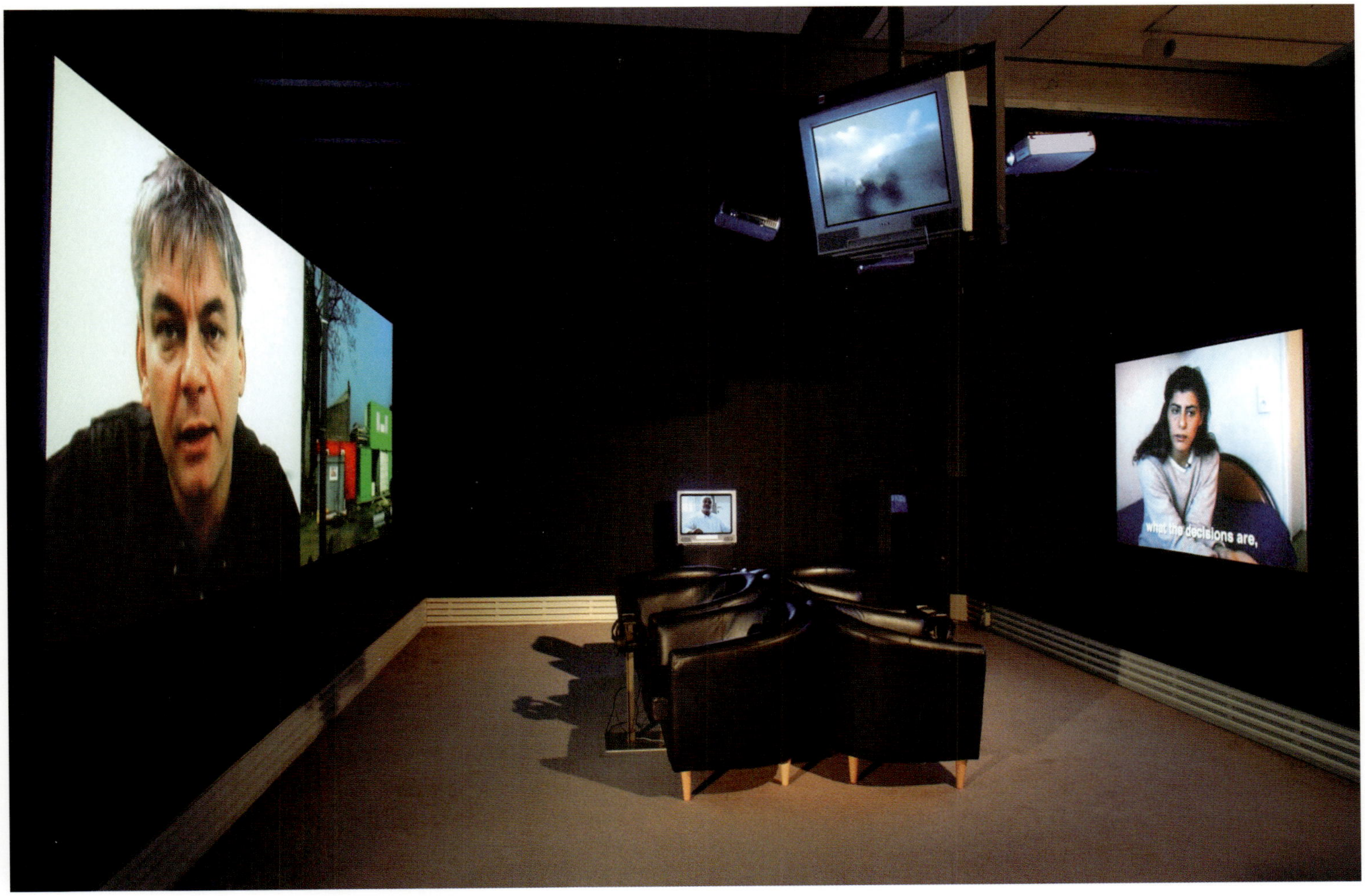

everything and nothing (from the ongoing project, *untitled*), 1999–2001

Video Installation

Thanks to Bernadette Phan, Najat Dajani,
Reem M. Al Nuwieri and Rawi Hage

Collection of the Artist
Photo: H. Foster, © Canadian Museum of Civilization
D2002-16090

taouffik semmad

"For L'Avant-Babel, *I mixed together different alphabets originating in the East, the Far East, Europe, the Mediterranean basin . . . for example, Arabic, Chinese, Latin, Cyrillic and pictographs. By memorizing these alphabets and writing them in a style that resembles calligraphy, I want to arrive at a spontaneous gesture . . . while trying to create a kind of harmony in the writing, as if it were a single language. . . .*

"What I am trying to do is very utopian, for a universal writing is not the same thing as a universal language; each language has its own way of thinking."

(Extract from an interview with the artist)

Taouffik Semmad

Photo: Rawi Hage, 1999

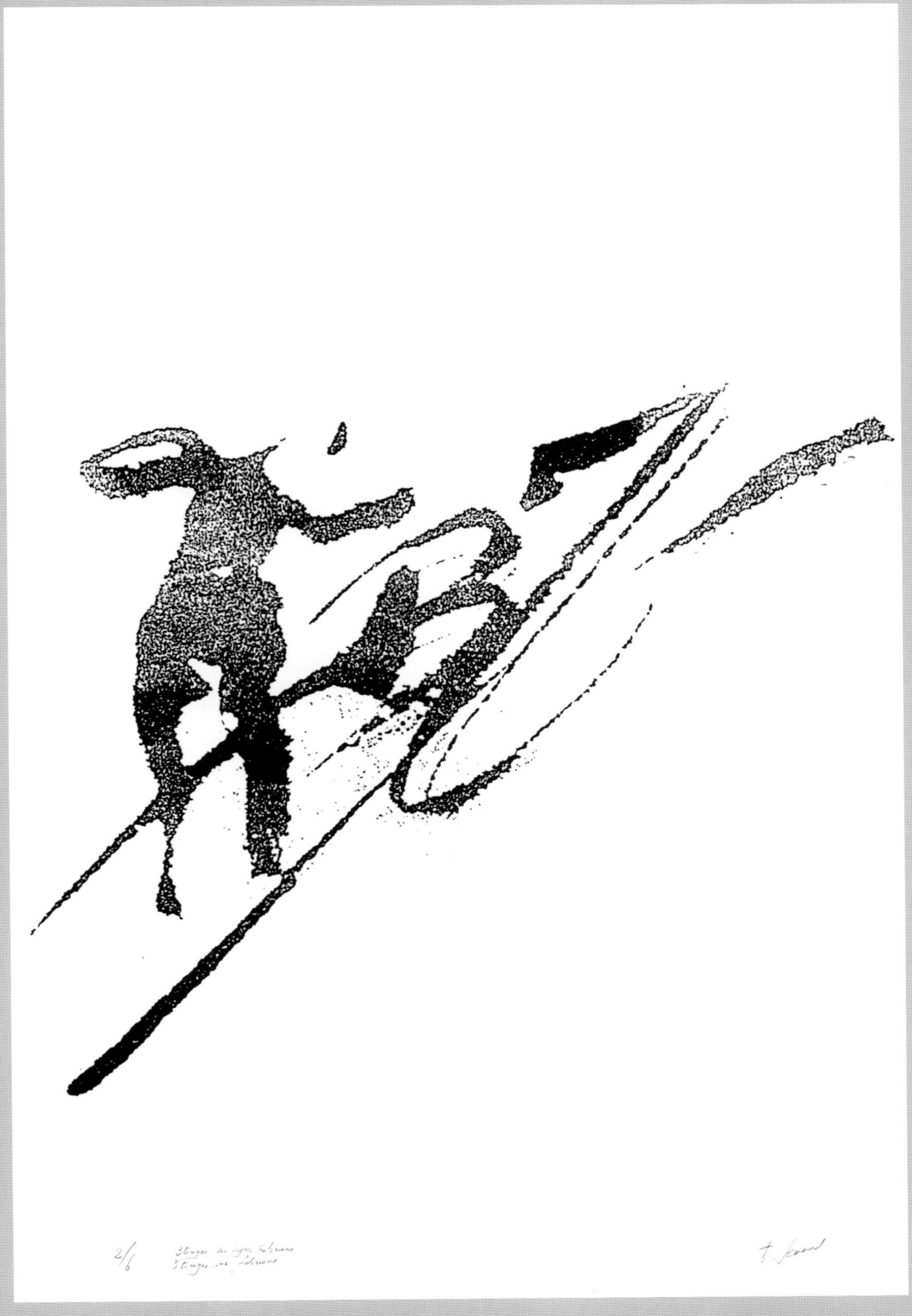

Fresque no 1 (*Fresco no. 1*)
Detail from the serie *L'Avant-Babel (Before Babel)*, 2000

Silkscreen prints on fabriano paper
Limited edition of six numbered copies • 70 x 50 cm

Collection of the Artist
Photo: H. Foster, © Canadian Museum of Civilization
T2002-27

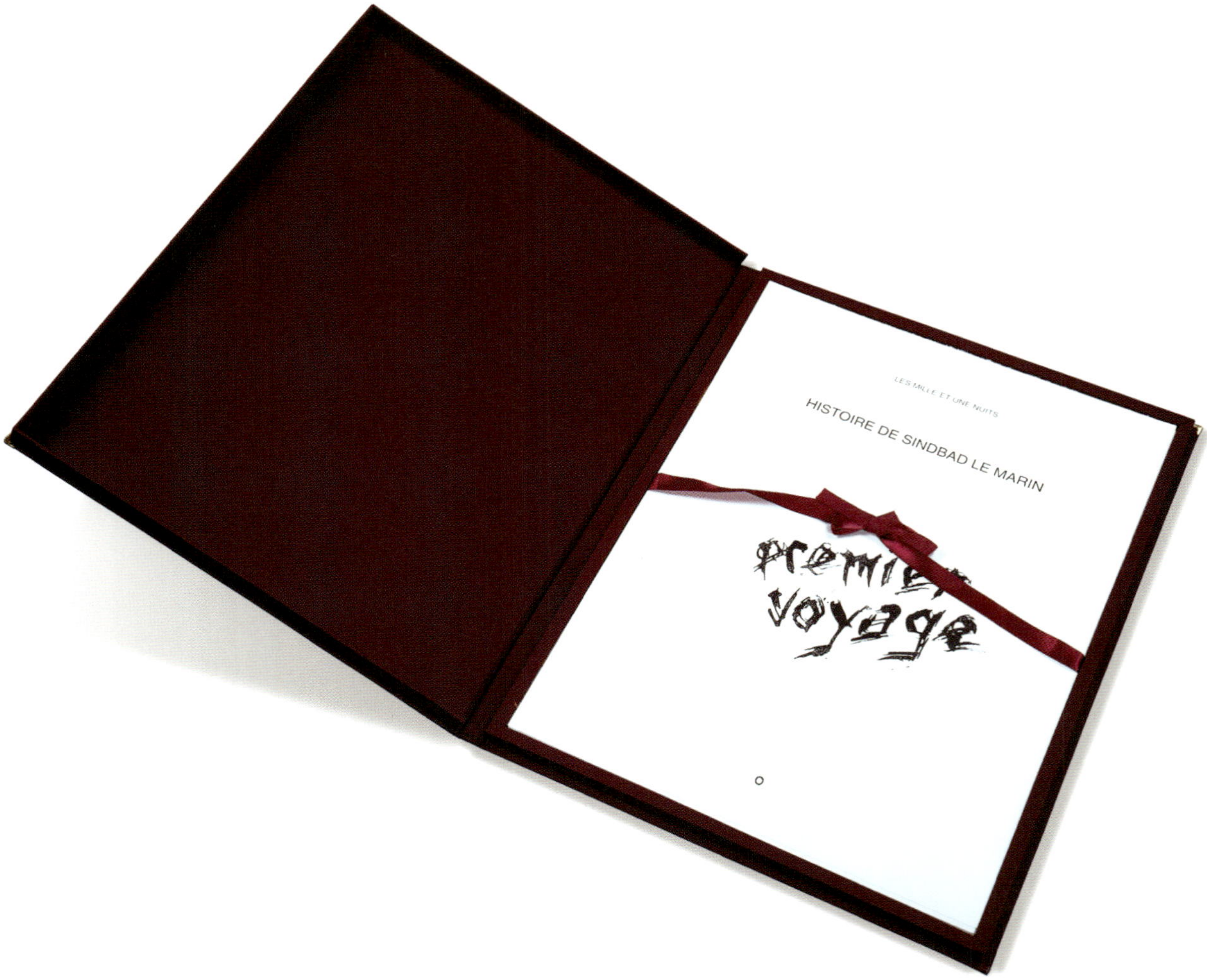

Artist's book
Les Mille et une nuits: Histoire de Sindbad le marin, premier voyage
(The Arabian Nights: Story of Sindbad the Sailor, Maiden Voyage), 1999

Aquatints on holland simili japan paper, silkscreen prints on holland simili japan paper and translucent drawing paper
Copy no. 1 in a case handmade by the artist.

Limited edition of seven numbered copies • 52.5 x 69 cm

Collection of the Artist
Photo: H. Foster, © Canadian Museum of Civilization
T2002-26

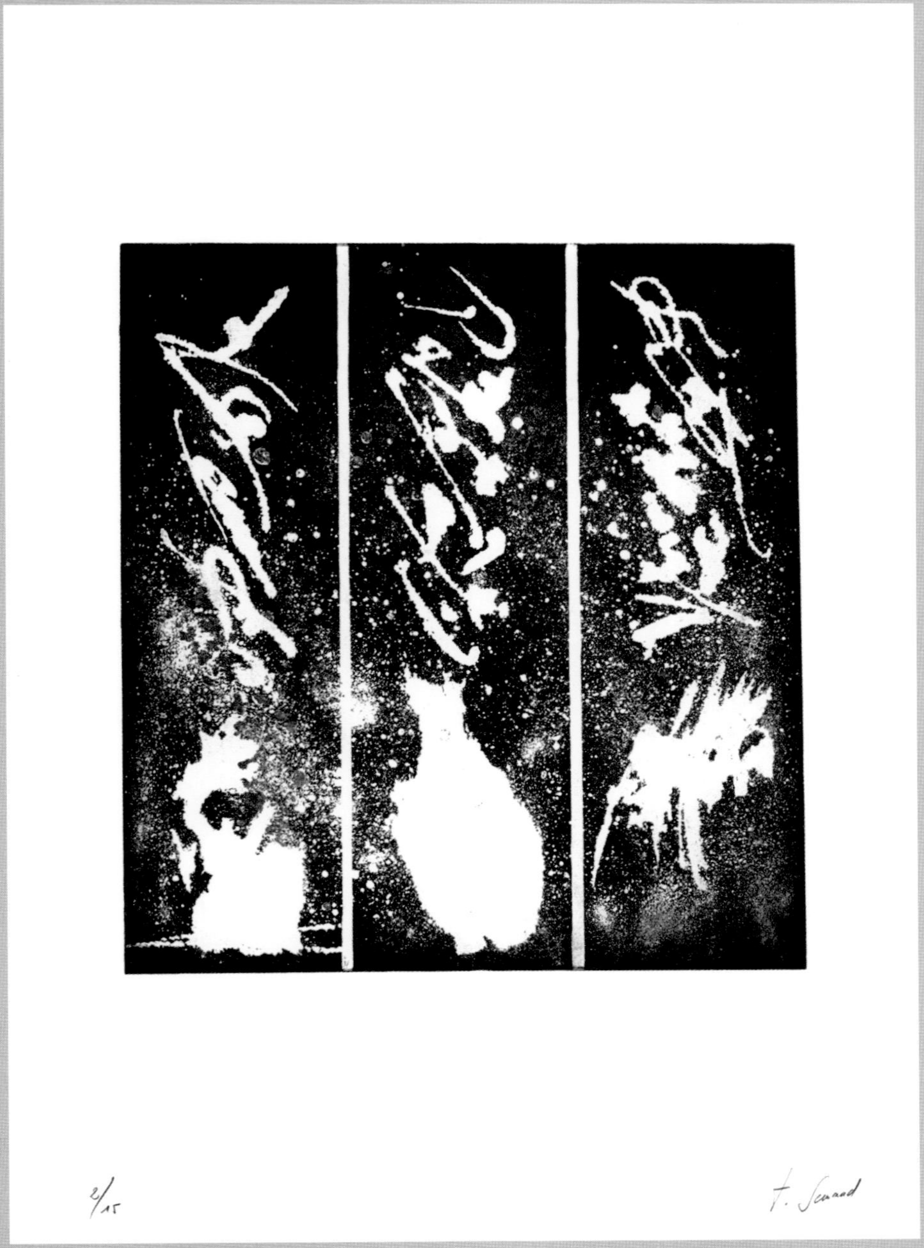

Artist's book
Les Mille et une nuits: Histoire de Sindbad le marin, premier voyage
(The Arabian Nights: Story of Sindbad the Sailor, Maiden Voyage — detail*)*, 1999

Aquatints on holland simili japan paper, silkscreen prints on holland simili japan paper and translucent drawing paper
Copy no. 1 in a case handmade by the artist.

Limited edition of seven numbered copies • 52.5 x 69 cm

Collection of the Artist
Photo: H. Foster, © Canadian Museum of Civilization
T2002-26

shwan

"For certain of my works, I find my ideas by studying Arab proverbs, maxims and sayings, those I know and those I remember . . . I use writing in a popular style, by integrating the inscriptions that I used to see on cars, walls, shop windows and motorbikes. I don't want to write them in diwani *or in* koufi*, nor in any other stylized calligraphy, because that would seem artificial."*

"You can do anything
with Arab letters —
you can make them jump,
you can make them dance,
you can even make them sing!"

(Extracts from interviews with the artist)

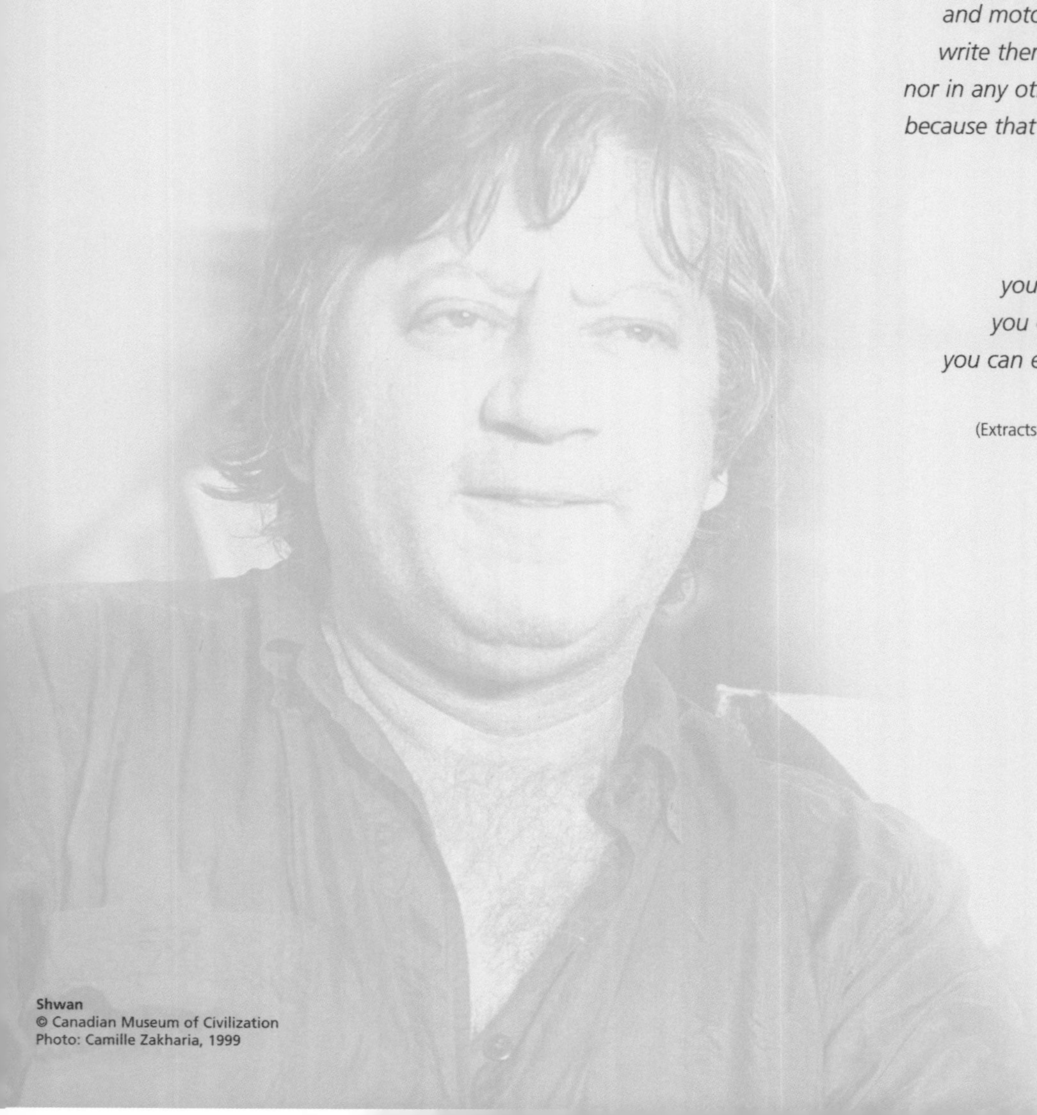

Shwan

Photo: Camille Zakharia, 1999

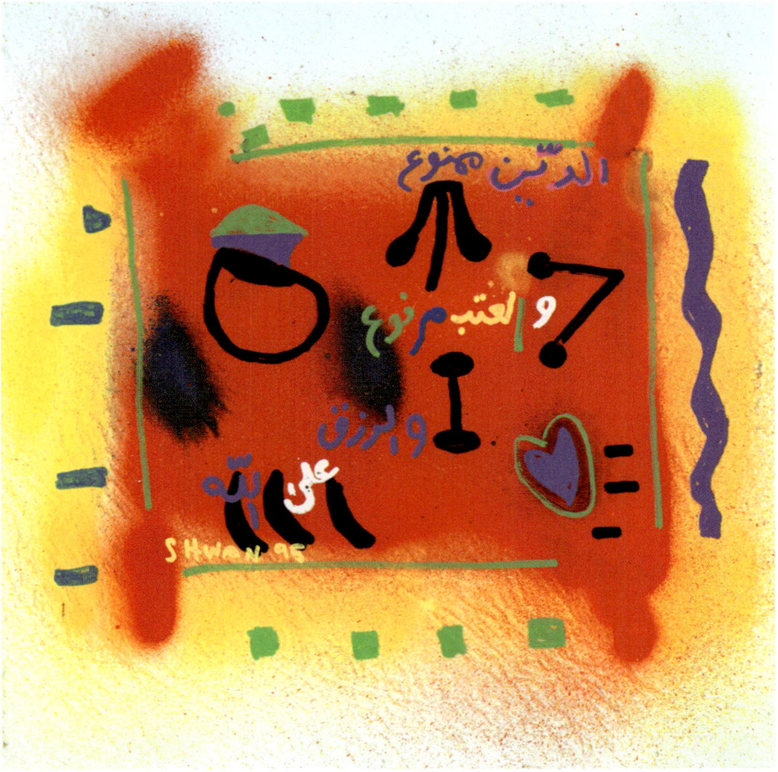

"No credit; no hard feelings; God provides to everyone.", 1995
Expression from Arab popular culture

Mixed media on vinyl tile • 30.5 x 30.5 cm

Collection of the Canadian Museum of Civilization
Photo: H. Foster, © Canadian Museum of Civilization
T2002-33

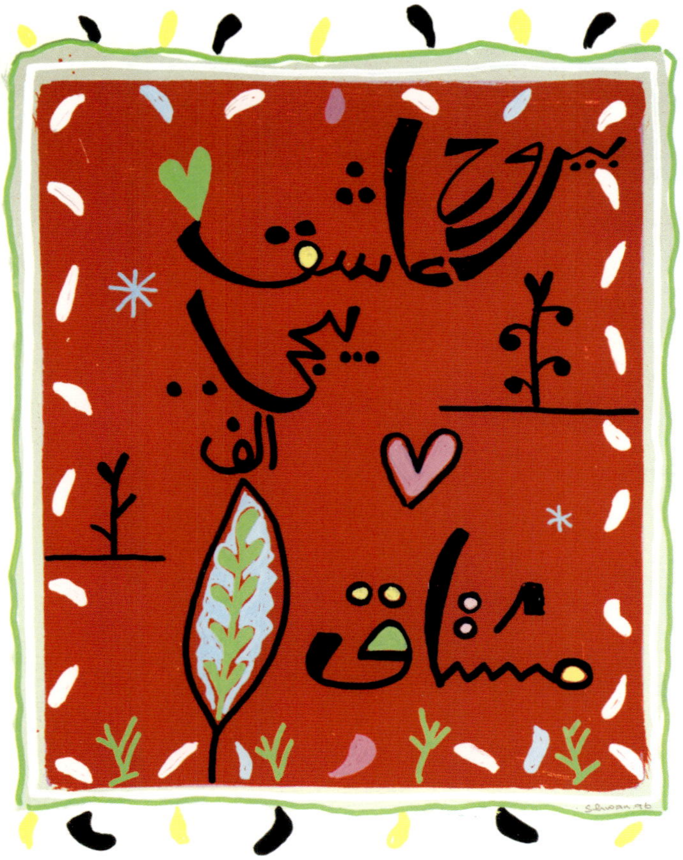

"A lover leaves and a thousand others show up.", 1996
Expression from Arab popular culture

Mixed media on paper • 50 x 40 cm

Collection of the Canadian Museum of Civilization
Photo: H. Foster, © Canadian Museum of Civilization
T2002-34

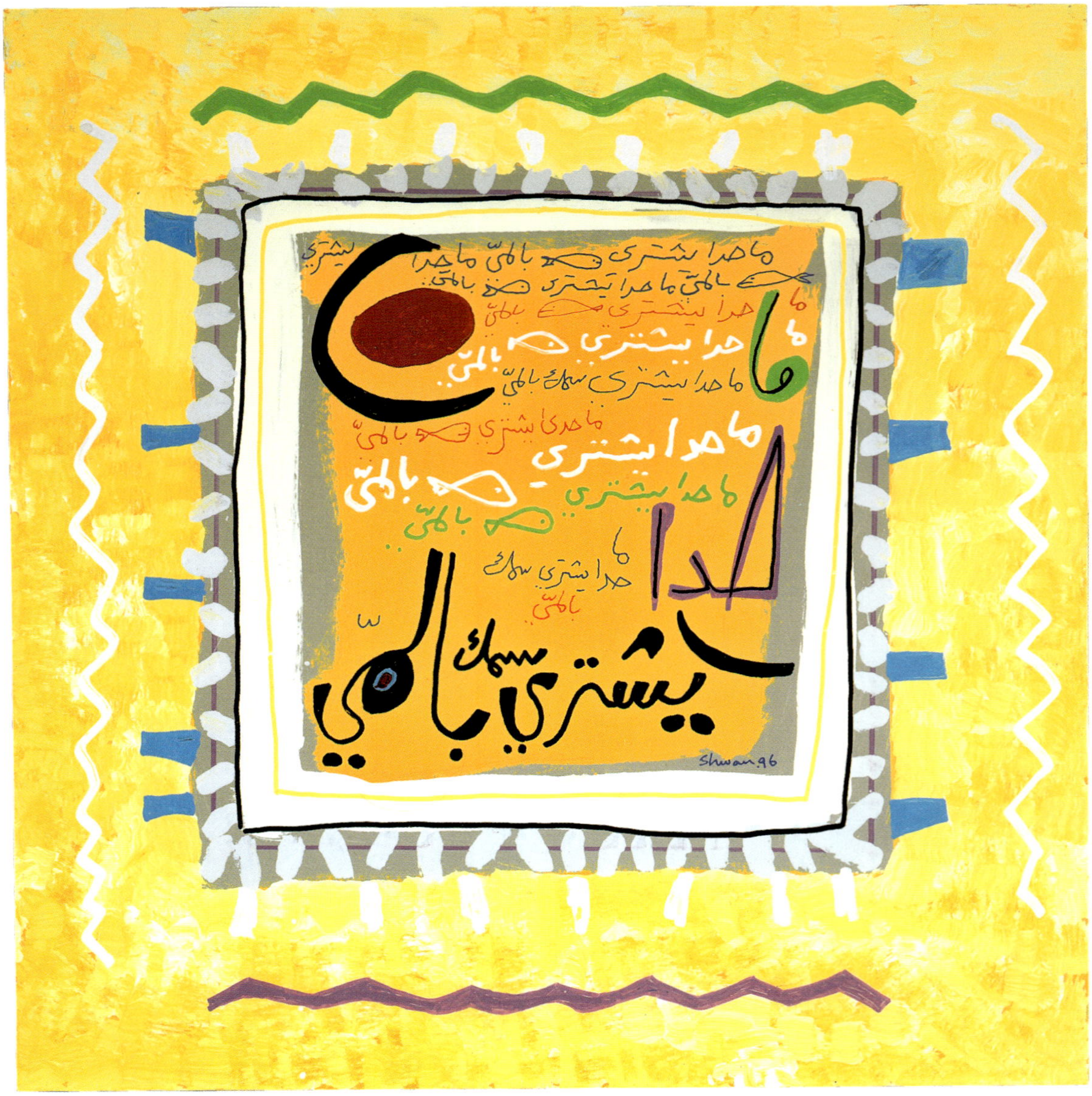

"Nobody would buy a fish in water.", 1996
Expression from Arab popular culture

Mixed media on paper • 50 x 40 cm

Collection of the Canadian Museum of Civilization
Photo: H. Foster, © Canadian Museum of Civilization
T2002-35

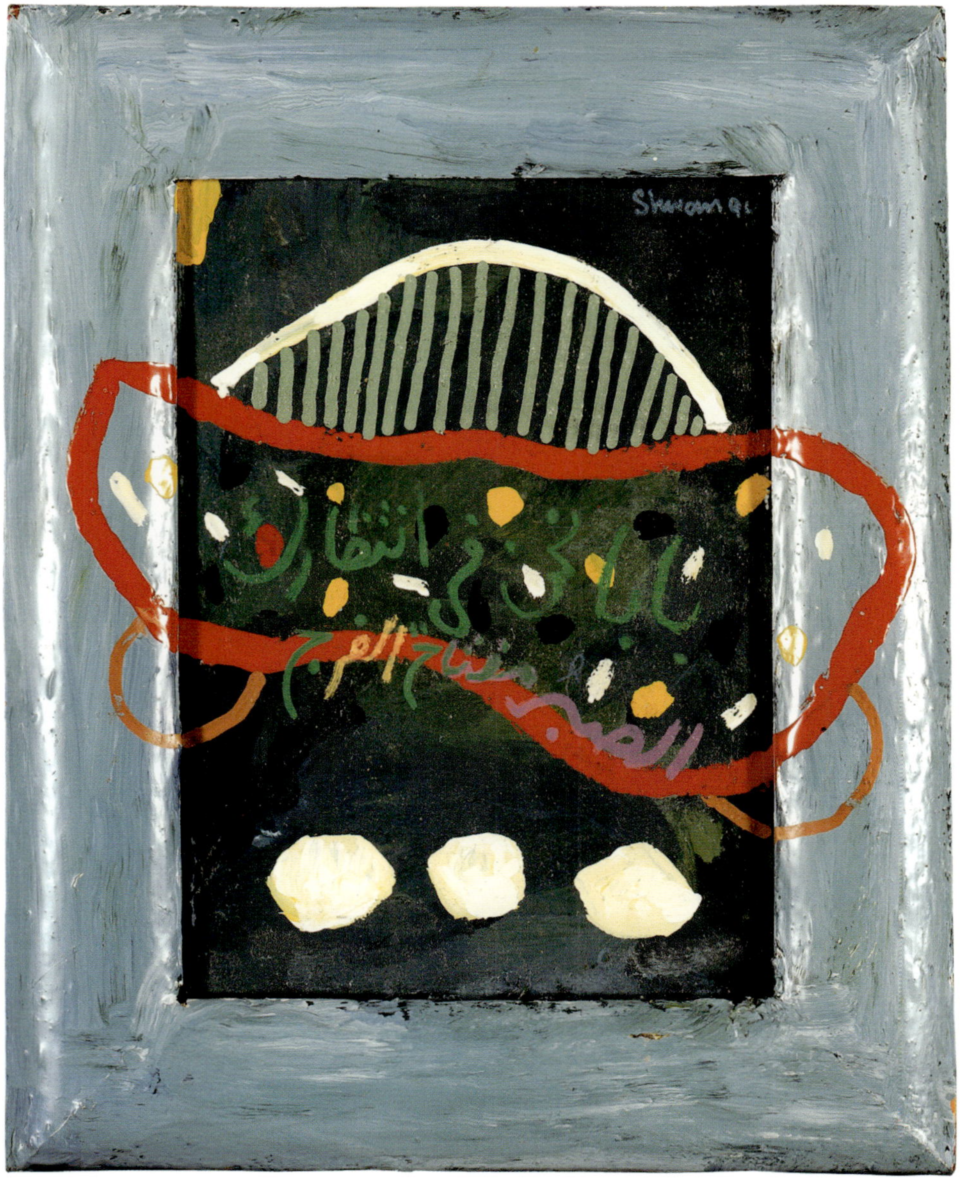

"Daddy, we are waiting for you.", 1994
Expression from Arab popular culture

Mixed media on paperboard and wood frame • 20.5 x 26 cm

Collection of the Canadian Museum of Civilization
Photo: H. Foster, © Canadian Museum of Civilization
T2002-36

sanaa m. wassef

"For the calligraphy, I choose verses from the Koran. Sometimes the idea influences the form of the work; sometimes it's the form that suggests the verse. In each case, reflection is necessary. One is in harmony with oneself, with one's senses and one's spirit. It is that which creates bahja, *pleasure."*

(Extract from an interview with the artist)

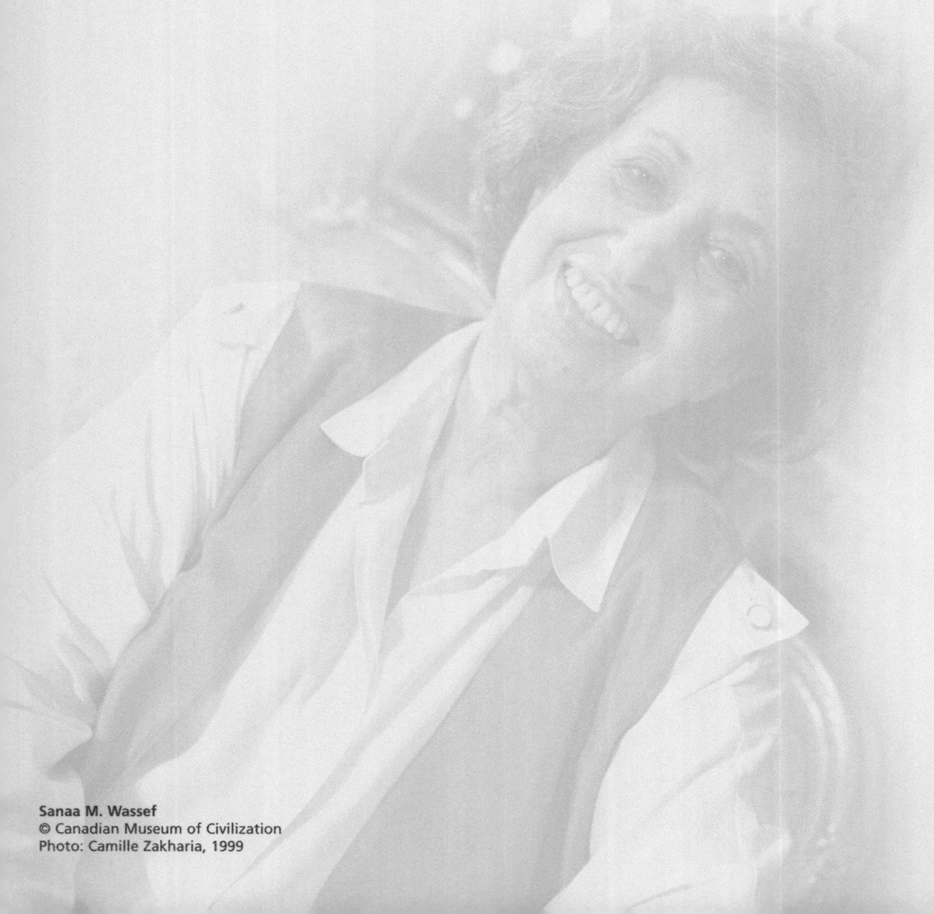

Sanaa M. Wassef

Photo: Camille Zakharia, 1999

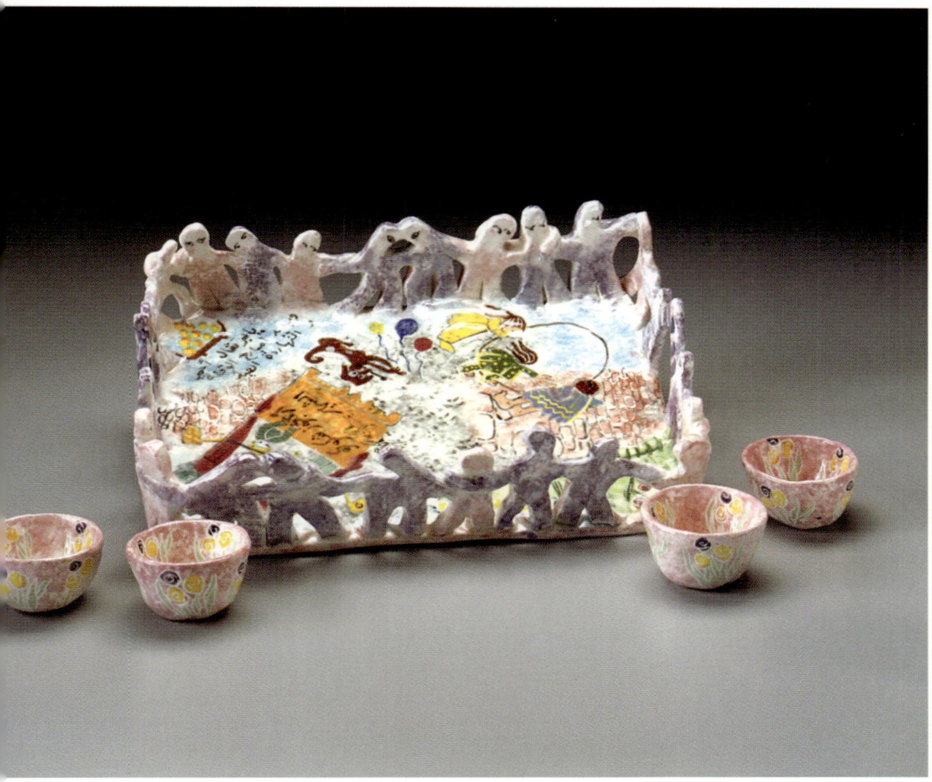

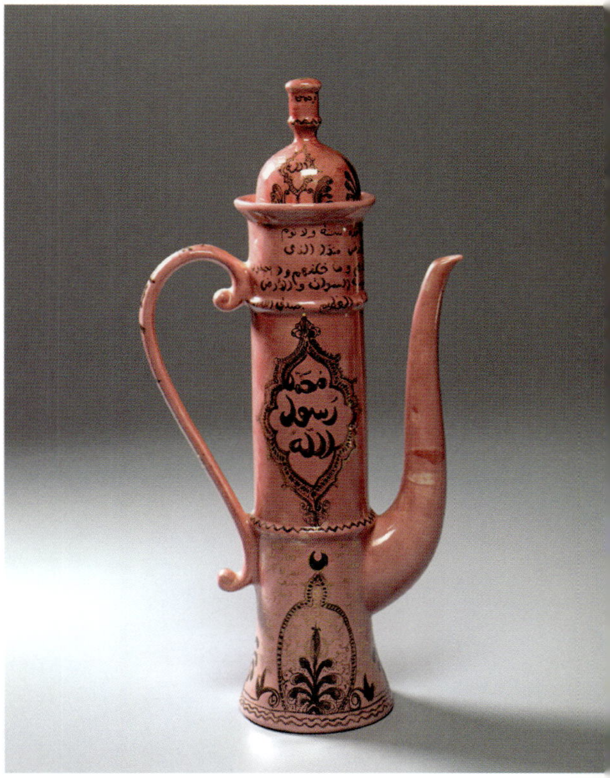

Memories of El Eid (Memories of the Feast), 1995

Earthenware
22.3 x 32 cm (tray)
7 x 6 x 7 cm (each cup)

Collection of the Artist
Photo: H. Foster, © Canadian Museum of Civilization
T2002-37

Pink coffeepot with verses from the Koran, 1980

Earthenware • 8 x 16 x 4 cm

Collection of Zalina Ali
Photo: H. Foster, © Canadian Museum of Civilization
T2002-38

camille zakharia

"The project is about a passenger being driven by circumstances, an unplanned trip, being here and remembering where I once belonged, being torn between cultures, a fading memory of an experience once lived, a celebration of a space ahead of me."

"Maybe the fragmentation of my identity accounts for why I always ended up working with collage."

(Extracts from the artist's statement and an interview)

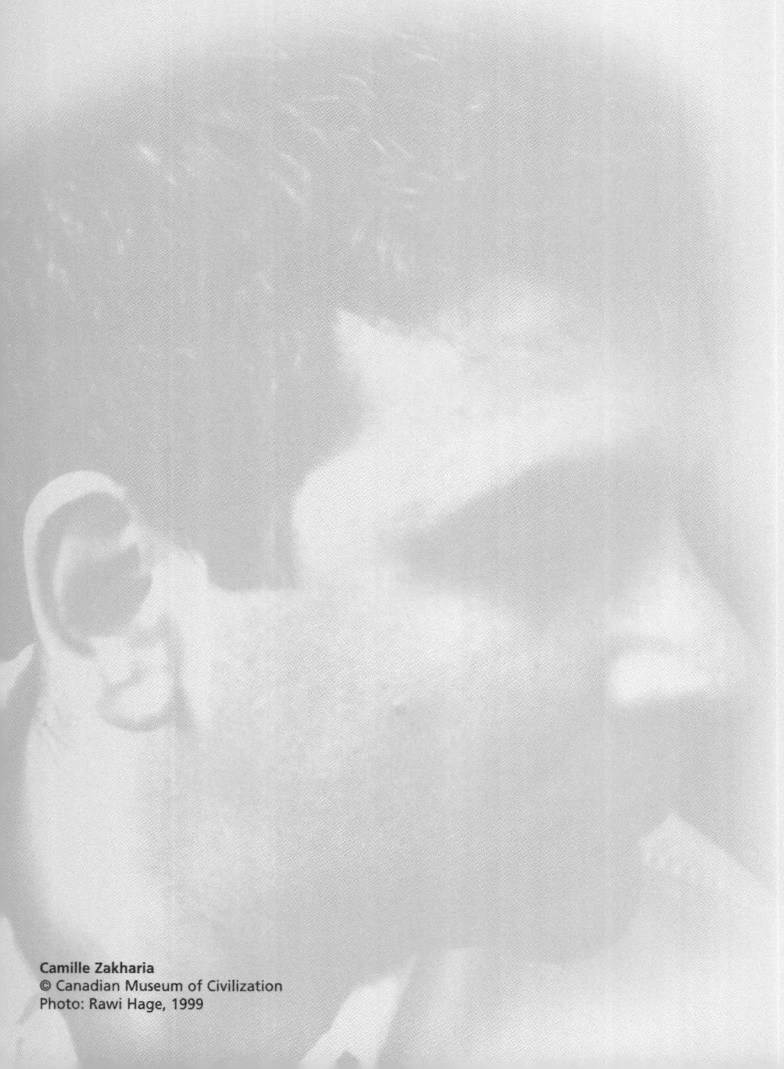

Camille Zakharia

Photo: Rawi Hage, 1999

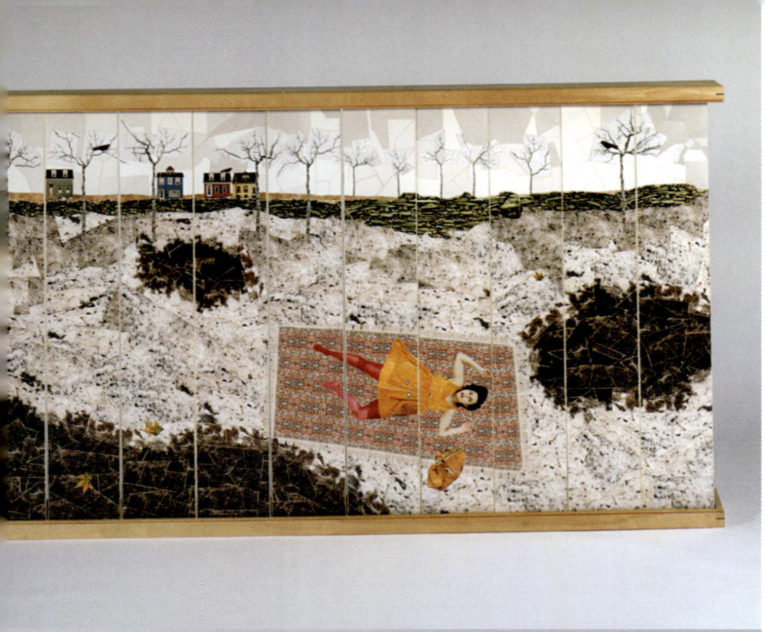

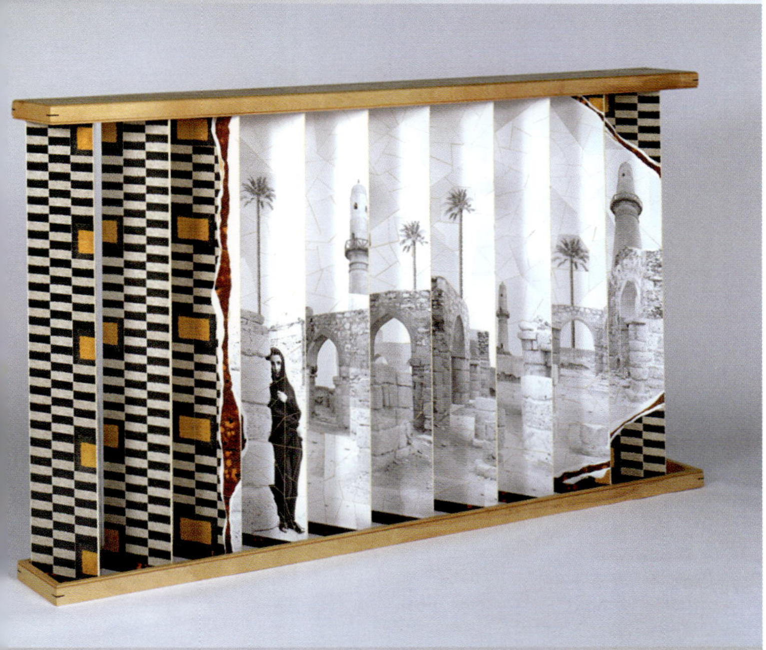

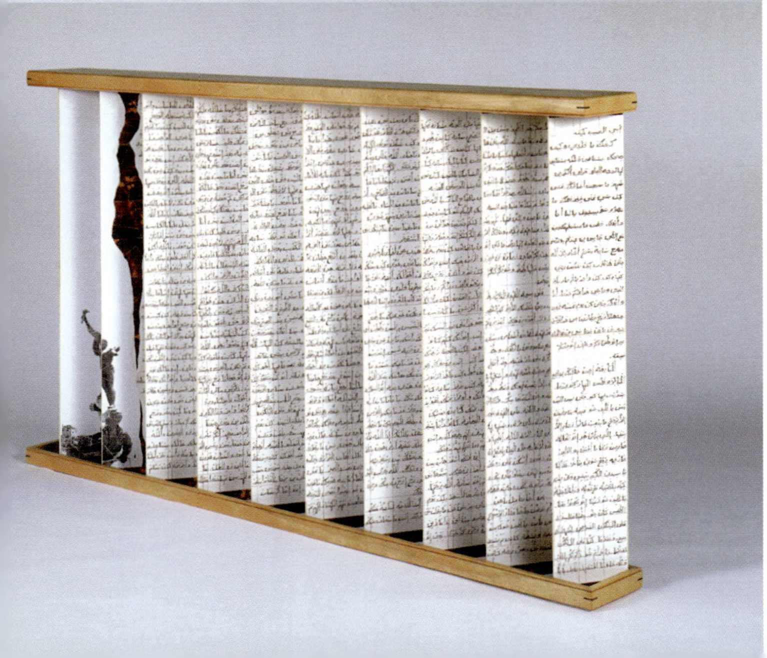

Lebanon-Canada, via Bahrain (Liban-Canada via Bahreïn), 1998

Photocollages and gouache on paper,
affixed onto triangular wooden columns • 203 x 122 x 25.4 cm

With the support of the Nova Scotia Arts Council
and of the Canada Council for the Arts

Collection of the Artist
Photos: H. Foster, © Canadian Museum of Civilization
T2002-17, T2002-18, T2002-19

See Appendix I for text which appears on this work.

Nicolas Zeitouni

". . . whenever I had time, I found myself visualizing all the scenes of my native country that I had been able to observe during my childhood. And as if they were stories, I set about illustrating my memories."

(Excerpt from a text by the artist)

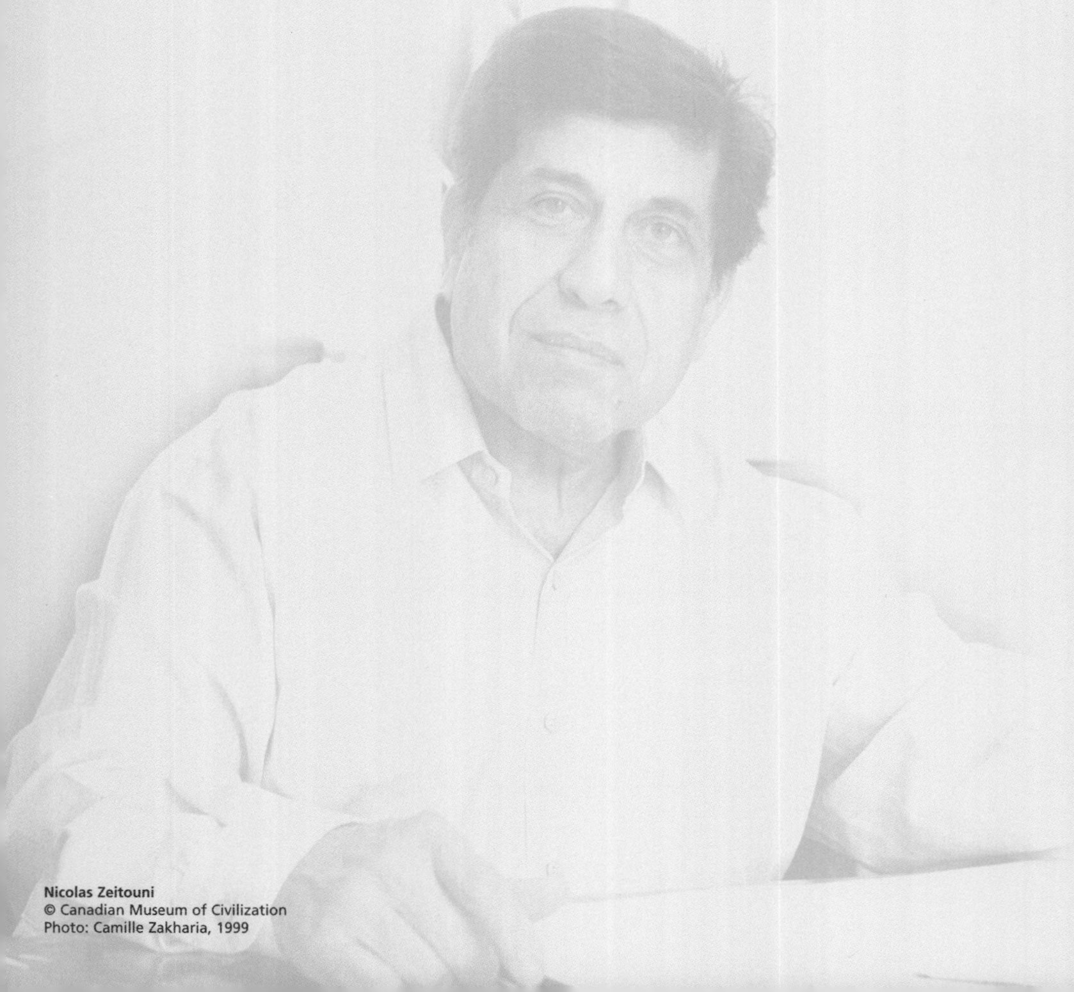

Nicolas Zeitouni

Photo: Camille Zakharia, 1999

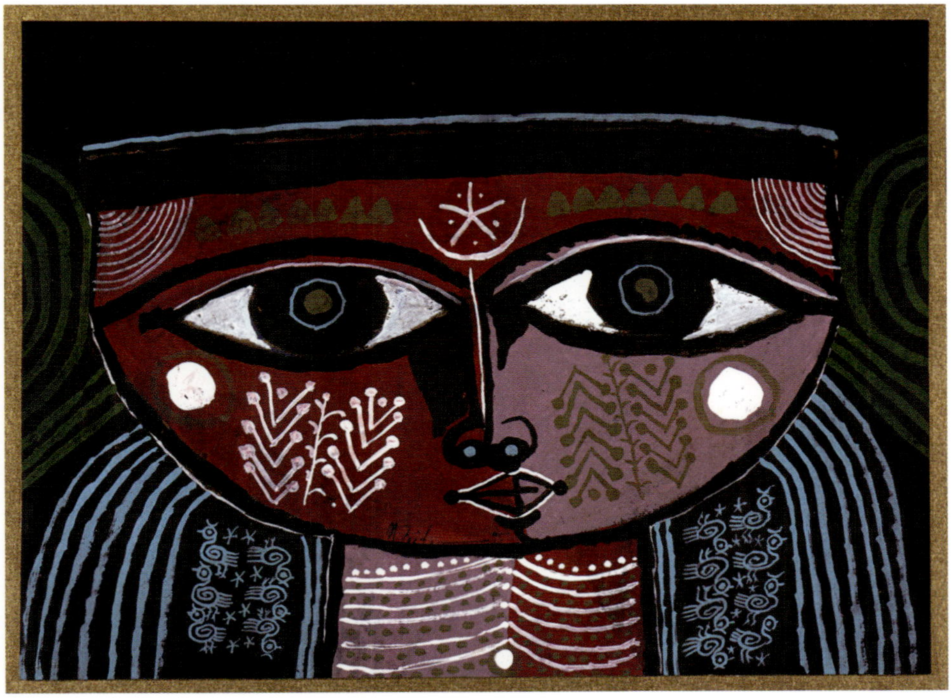

Le Regard (The Look), 1995

Gouache on paper • 45 x 55.5 cm

Collection of the Artist
Photo: H. Foster, © Canadian Museum of Civilization
T2002-1

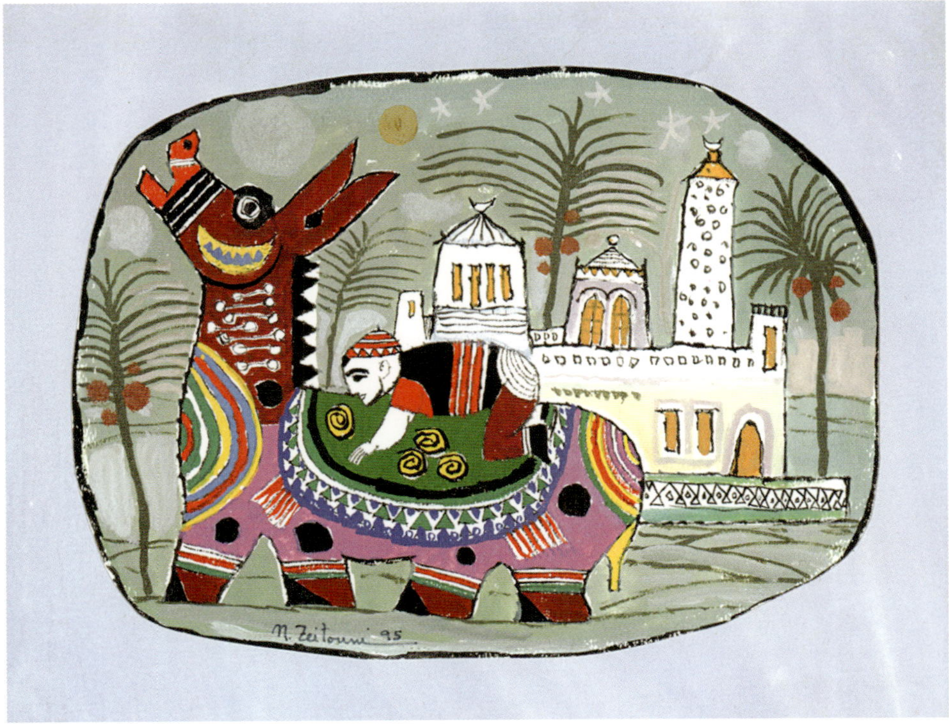

L'Apprentissage (The Apprenticeship), 1995

Gouache and watercolour on paper • 52.2 x 42 cm

Collection of the Artist
Photo: H. Foster, © Canadian Museum of Civilization
T2002-2

sami zubi

"Jerusalem: A Gate of Hope *expresses my love for Jerusalem and my hope for peace. Historically, the gates of the old city — strong, solid, heavy — were built to protect the inhabitants against a common external threat. Modern politics has constructed a symbolic gate, superimposed over the old; invisible and impenetrable, it serves to contain the people within a conflict that appears insurmountable."*

(Excerpt from the artist's statement)

Sami Zubi

Photo: Camille Zakharia, 1999

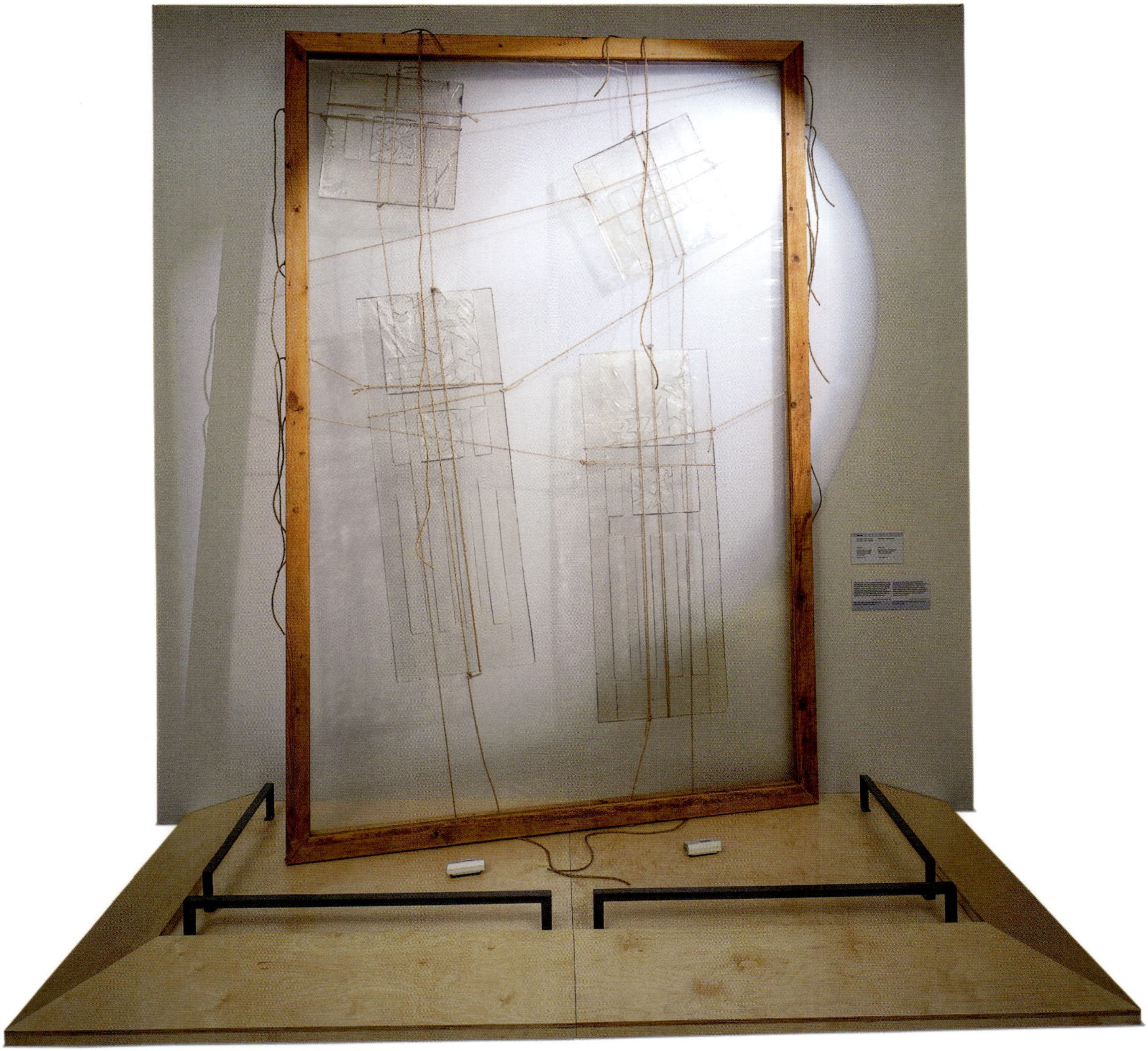

Jerusalem: A Gate of Hope, 2000–2001

Wall Installation: molded acrylic resin mounted
on a wooden structure, plastic sheet • 213 x 61 x 305 cm

Collection of the Artist
Photo: H. Foster, © Canadian Museum of Civilization
T2002-40

ARTISTS

Artists

BIOGRAPHICAL NOTES

ADEL ALNASER

Adel Alnaser was born in 1954 in Babylon, Iraq. As the child of a large family, he learned his father's coppersmith trade early on, and decided to become a painter. To pay for his courses at the Fine Arts Institute of Baghdad, he did copperwork every evening after school. Once his courses were completed, he left Iraq and its political climate to pursue studies in visual arts and to broaden his horizons. He went to Italy, studied at the Fine Arts Academy of Rome, founded an association for Iraqi artists in exile along with other students, and travelled across Europe.

In 1984, the Iraqi government did not renew his passport, and Italy refused him citizenship. Adel Alnaser then appealed to the United Nations, which encouraged him to turn to Canada. Arriving in Toronto in 1989, he began a journal in the form of drawings. Later, since he couldn't find work that was sufficiently well-paid and that would allow him to draw (ink and pencil) and to paint (oils and watercolours), he chose to live in Montreal, where he managed to earn his living by drawing.

After an epic period characterized by "scenes dripping with blood," Alnaser's work became more self-critical: "One doesn't deal with war through [images of] war . . . I found a method to express my suffering and the suffering of the people I come from, as well as their political and social problems, in a more aesthetic way." He went on to explore the links between Mesopotamian civilization and Muslim heritage, and began to better familiarize himself with North American art.

Adel Alnaser's works have been exhibited in Canada, Italy, France and the Middle East. The Canadian Museum of Civilization has acquired one of his works.

HANNAH ALPHA

Born in Cairo in 1944 to parents of Lebanese origin, Hannah Alpha has lived in Egypt, Lebanon, Algeria and Saudi Arabia: all stages of a long journey that eventually led her to Canada. She has lived in Montreal since 1981.

She began her training as a painter at the Heliopolis School of Art in Egypt, and took courses at Beirut's American University, as well as at McGill University upon her arrival in Montreal. She has also led drawing and painting workshops in Lebanon and in Montreal (Saidye Bronfman Centre). It was in Saudi Arabia that she began to distance herself from realistic representations, in order to involve herself in abstract art and the expression of pure emotion.

Preoccupied, above all, with the problematics of surface and depth, she also integrates writings in different languages — and even Pharaonic hieroglyphs — into her art. Painting has been for her a means to exorcise pain, as her series on Lebanon and on the Gulf War clearly depict: "When I arrived here, I painted a series called *The Sinking Ship*, and it was really Lebanon that was going under . . . harsh colours and water." Since that time, her approach to art has become more personal and more serene: "As one matures, one returns to oneself."

Hannah Alpha has several solo exhibitions to her credit in Saudi Arabia and in Canada, and has participated in numerous group exhibitions. Her works are also included in various public and private collections.

MIRELLA APRAHAMIAN

Born in Beirut in 1939 to Armenian parents who had survived the genocide, Mirella Aprahamian left Lebanon to study art in Switzerland. She then lived in Greece, Morocco and, for 13 years, in the United Kingdom. Established in Canada since 1984, she now lives in Montreal.

She began her training as a professional artist in Beirut (ALBA), further pursuing her studies through courses and workshops in the many countries she lived in, including at the Cass School of Art in London and the Pratt Graphics Center of New York. Above all, she has concentrated on the techniques of engraving. "I am an engraver even when I paint," she says.

This "Mediterranean person", as she calls herself, has found a new "white light" in Canada: that of winter. "When I arrived here, I was using very pure, very violent colors . . . and little by little, all that snow . . . and the desire to adapt, the fear of being myself . . . . Later, I found my own pace. And everything changed, the inspiration, my style . . ." A theme that recurs in her fictitious landscapes, her engravings and her painted furniture is the small red-roofed house of her native country. "I have lived in so many countries that I have not yet found my home; I search for it still.

"Many artists dream of their past, but can only express it when they are living in another country. I find myself in the same situation. These images can all be created because I live here, away from my country. Otherwise, it would not be possible."

Mirella Aprahamian has numerous exhibitions to her credit in Canada and abroad, and her works are found in many museums and institutions, including the Lodz Museum in Poland, the San Lozzaro Museum in Venice and the National Library of Canada, as well as the Bibliothèque nationale du Québec.

YASSER BADREDDINE

Yasser Badreddine was born in 1942 in Al-Nabatyia, a city in South Lebanon. Introduced to traditional poetry by his father, at a very young age he developed a lively interest in both poetry and calligraphy. He was only 14 years old when the merchants in his neighbourhood began coming to him to order their shop signs. He learned the trade by studying other signs in the city, and through contact with sellers of artist's colours and brushes. In 1960, he enrolled in college and began to create and produce political banners. He first began writing poems when he was in his early twenties. Much later, after his arrival in Montreal in 1990, his verses would be greatly inspired by the Canadian landscape.

After studying law, Yasser Badreddine published poems and obtained his first stable employment as a calligrapher. From this time onwards, he perfected his knowledge of the Riq'a, Naskhi, Farisi, Thuluth and Diwani styles, and rubbed shoulders with masters of calligraphy, including Mr. Sammame, Cheikh Nasr and Mr. Al-Baba. The latter, with whom he became friends, even entrusted him with the retouching of one of his important works.

The year 1972 marked a turning point in Yasser Badreddine's artistic journey, when he met Dr. Dahesh, a writer and aesthete, who asked him to undertake the calligraphy for one of his poetry collections. This encouragement incited the artist to treat his own poems in a calligraphic style, as well as verses from the Koran. His literary work thus became one with drawing: "What characterizes Arab calligraphy is that it is possible to invent many forms from a single word or from a single phrase . . . . It's like a poem — an artist can create many things with the letters." In his work, he uses manuscript illumination, and prefers parchment and leather as supports.

Yasser Badreddine has written and undertaken calligraphy on many volumes of poetry. He received first prize in the graphic design category at the International Arab Book Fair in Beirut, for *Sara* (1997) and *Daftar Al-Ghourba* ("On Exile within the Self", 1999). The Canadian Museum of Civilization has acquired some of his calligraphic work.

LAILA BINBREK

Of Yemeni ancestry, Laila Binbrek was born in Kitchener, Ontario in 1970. She spent her childhood in Saudi Arabia and her adolescence in Egypt, then lived in England, where she attended the Blackheath School of Art and the Portsmouth College of Art. Upon returning to Canada, she earned a bachelor's degree in visual arts from the University of Waterloo, in Ontario, and attended a post-graduate program at the Dundas Valley School of Art. She now lives in Toronto. "When I say that I am going home to see my family, this can be in Kitchener or in the Middle East. One or the other. 'Going home' does not have an established, definitive meaning for me."

The question of identity plays a dominant role in her work, its centrality reflected by the position that the body occupies, both as a point of reference and as a place in which social relationships are articulated: "When people look at my work, they find themselves in unfamiliar territory. Something has been displaced. . . . One can see that there is a parallel here, a link with my own experience of displacement." Always fragmented, dispersed, captured in its traces (body hair, earwax), its functions (elimination, reproduction) and the rituals of grooming and hygiene, the body is evoked through drawings, models and objects (bathtubs, combs) organized within the framework of installations: "That the nude body is judged 'obscene', the sexual organs 'offensive', menstrual blood 'dirty', shows how a society perceives itself."

Another central theme, allied with that of the body, permeates Laila Binbrek's work, and that is the place occupied by women in Western and Eastern societies: "There are different ways to interpret my work. Knowing where I come from opens the door to other meanings, to other ways of looking at my work."

Laila Binbrek's work has been exhibited primarily in Ontario galleries, in solo and group exhibitions.

MARC ELIANY

Marc Eliany was born in the village of Beni Mella, Morocco, in 1948. He has remained deeply attached to his native country — which he left in 1961 for Israel — and regularly returns there. During his years of undergraduate studies in Jerusalem, he also spent some time in Canada. Seduced by the beauty and the peaceful atmosphere of the country, he decided to settle in Ottawa in 1976. He continued his studies there and earned a doctorate in sociology. Hired by the United Nations, he lived for brief periods in California, Austria and France, and was called upon to travel in the Far East and in South America.

Essentially self-taught, this painter has nevertheless attended courses at the Tel Hay College of Art in Israel and the Ottawa School of Art. The influences on his art are many. He admires the spontaneity of Moroccan painters André Elbaz, Maxime BenHaim and Shaibia; the composition of paintings by Klee and Chagall; the use of colours by painters in the Group of Seven; and the lines and shapes of Amerindian painting. Marc Eliany uses Moroccan pigments which he mixes with oil or, more rarely, with acrylic, to create his canvases. He also works with coloured paper pulp and collages of wallpaper — techniques that allow him to produce highly textured surfaces.

"My work, he says, reflects the constant return to the places of my childhood and the search for my roots." He paints Morocco, not figuratively, but rather by recapturing its most visible landmarks in a manner that transforms his memory of it. Additionally, his choice of Moroccan colours and symbols pays tribute to the tradition of tolerance towards strangers which exists in that country.

He has participated in many exhibitions in Canada, the United States and Europe. His works are included in several public and private collections.

RAWI HAGE

Rawi Hage was born in 1964 in Beirut to a family that, in 1978, would go into temporary exile in Cyprus in order to escape the civil war. At the age of 18, he again left Lebanon, this time for New York City, where he lived for nine years. Towards the end of his stay in the United States, he began studying photography at the New York Institute of Photography. In 1991, he emigrated to Montreal, where he earned an Arts Diploma from Dawson College, then a bachelor's degree in visual arts from Concordia University.

It was during this time that one of his professors, Raymonde April, brought him to see photography "as a medium that can become very aggressive, very unjust . . . at the documentary level," because it can be easily manipulated by the media. Hage opposes that pernicious effect on the medium by incorporating his photos — which deal primarily with immigration, war and racism — into fictional contexts in which many voices summon each other. Somewhat like a Vermeer who has metamorphosed, through his art, the images of a camera obscura, he transforms his photographs in order to make them unsuited to hurried consumption or sensationalist use.

In his work *Care of Raymonde*, for example, not only does Rawi Hage transform his photos into postcards that he mails to April, but he also uses them as the basis for an imaginary narrative with exile as its theme: "The images on some of the postcards reflect memories of past existence, while the written texts express the living present or a longed-for past." In this way, he creates "an ambiguous realm, an undefined space between the fictitious and the real, a paradox, a mirror of a persona caught between two existences," or at least between two places, two cultures.

Rawi Hage has participated in solo and collective exhibitions in Canada, Lebanon, France and Colombia. The Canadian Museum of Civilization and the Musée de la civilisation de Québec have acquired some of his works.

ABD HANAFI

Abdelhamid Hanafi was born in 1950 in the Tunisian city of Menzel-Bourguiba, a city built by French colonists. He started to draw at a very young age. As an adolescent, he began painting with gouache, then the artist Béjaoui introduced him to oil painting and mosaic. In 1969, he left Tunisia for France, where he began an apprenticeship with the sculptor Tati. He later lived in the Federal Republic of Germany and in Sweden. In 1977, he decided to emigrate to Canada and took up residence in Montreal. He then completed his artistic training through private studies in the art of engraving at the Centre de conception graphique Graff, and in jewellery-making with the jeweller Léo Beinglas.

From adolescence on, it was the scenes of urban life (daily activities, festivals, social events) that held his attention. He paints them as joyful, vividly coloured and filled with humour: "My aim is to create a painting that makes people happy," he explains. Like the souks of his childhood, his paintings overflow with figures of all ages — actors and observers, native and foreign. In this way he tries to bring together beings and cultures: "I feel as if I am . . . a junction point between different cultures."

Because Hanafi's canvases represent, in condensed form, the daily life of the places that he paints, his role approaches that of a sociologist and chronicler, or a stage director and storyteller. For this reason, rather than a "naïve" painter as the arts establishment has labelled him, he prefers to be called a "popular" painter. "My style is popular, not only because it is accessible, and because people like it very much, but because it is close to the people and represents them."

Abd Hanafi has more than a hundred exhibitions to his credit around the world. For his body of work, he has received, along with other tributes, the Médaille des Arts de la Renaissance Française (1998). His paintings can be found in various private and public collections, including those of the Canadian Museum of Civilization, the Museum of Fine Arts of Sherbrooke and the Museum of Fine Arts of Göteborg, Sweden.

JAMELIE HASSAN

Jamelie Hassan was born in 1948 in London, Ontario. Her maternal grandfather and her father travelled from mountain villages in Lebanon to North America in the early 1900s, fleeing Turkish military conscription and the First World War. After completing her high school studies, Jamelie Hassan travelled to Rome (1967) and Beirut (1968), where she studied art. Upon her return to London in 1969, she continued her studies and, while working in the library at the University of Western Ontario in London, she established her first studio and became very active in the cultural community of her city. In 1978, she travelled to Baghdad, Iraq, and studied Arabic at the University of Mustansyria. Extensive travel continues to enrich her work, which often reflects this artist's respect for popular, traditional and indigenous art forms.

Jamelie Hassan creates a dialogue in her work between past and present cultural references and elements in her own history. In her installations, she combines images and sounds (watercolour, mural painting and photography with video and audio), objects (actual or reproduced often in ceramics), and texts. Montreal-based cultural critic Monika Kin Gagnon has recently written of her work: "A thematic quality . . . of Hassan's oeuvre is her reverence and engagement of everyday, smaller histories, those that deliberately thwart the grander statements of a singular History. From her earliest installations, a quality of tension emerged between the lived aspects of day-to-day histories and how they are eclipsed or effaced by official accounts."

Profoundly aware of the construct of Orientalism and involved in a programme of cultural activism, she found in the analysis of Edward W. Said and Gayatri Chakravorty Spivak, among others, a critical discourse that reflected her concerns around issues of representation and subjectivity. This accounts for the importance she assigns to aspects of language and narration, as well as to diverse forms of cultural "translations". She is among those artists who seek to destabilize the dichotomy of production/distribution through positioning her works *in situ* and in context, whereby she dislodges our simple conception of art as object.

Jamelie Hassan has participated in numerous exhibitions in Canada and internationally. Her works are in many public collections, including the National Gallery of Canada in Ottawa, the Canada Council Art Bank, the Art Gallery of Ontario in Toronto, and the New Museum of Contemporary Art in New York City. She received the 2001 Governor General's Award in Visual Arts.

LILIANE KARNOUK

Liliane Karnouk was born in Cairo in 1944, and is a graduate of the Academy of Fine Arts in Rome, the Université du Québec à Montréal and the University of British Columbia (M.A., 1971). She lived and worked in Europe, Egypt and Eastern Canada while maintaining her home base in Vancouver. In 1980, she returned to Egypt, where she initiated an art programme at the American University in Cairo, and published two books on contemporary Egyptian art.

Liliane Karnouk's art originated in her fascination with plants as symbols and as materials. In her paintings and installation work, she has explored a variety of techniques, ranging from the ancient art of plant-fibre papermaking to macro-propagation of plant cells in vitro. In an exhibition held at the British Museum, she surrounded an ancient Egyptian sarcophagus with a grove of date palms. The trees, cloned from Nilotic originals, were displayed in their test tubes. This work earned her a fellowship in art and science from the National Gallery of Canada in 1996.

More recently, Liliane Karnouk has been approaching art from an Eastern perception, combining the aesthetics of symmetry and floral interlacing with the functionality of applied arts. Her screens and tables derive from her fascination with the integrative potential of Islamic design, into which she weaves European medieval and Amerindian forms to create a fusion with her Canadian experiences: "These works, dated from my return to Canada in 1997, represented my readjustment to life in Vancouver after a very long absence. They mark the transition between the mind-stretching geometric puzzles of Islamic designs, which framed my Egyptian existence, and my sudden exposure to the possibilities offered by computerized drills, among a range of recent and challenging technologies available in Vancouver. The choice of designing furniture was made because I could not find contemporary items which linked my Islamic carpet and my computer table, or passages within my own mind which connected the two worlds of experience. It made sense to adopt the Islamic philosophy of art which united the functional with the aesthetic, and to explore plain geometry and colour, because I needed time to remember and to forget. The panels were hand-painted in what felt like an eternity, but they were cut by a machine in moments. The ritual of transition was complete."

Her work has been shown in numerous exhibitions in Egypt, Germany, Italy, France and the United States.

FAROUK KASPAULES

Farouk Kaspaules is an Iraqi-born Canadian artist, who left Iraq in the mid-1970s for political reasons. Following a brief stay in the United States, he chose Canada as his country of exile. Since his arrival, he has earned degrees from the Visual Arts Department of the University of Ottawa in studio profile (1997) and art theory (1998), and has been active in artist-run centres and community organizations. Although he favours the traditional media of painting and engraving, he also uses silkscreen photography and video in his works.

Farouk Kaspaules's mixed cultural origins — Christian, Chaldean/Sumerian, Islamic/Arab — have not only influenced his works of art, but have also enriched his artistic practices. He uses icons of diverse ancient cultures, and mixes them with symbols and elements borrowed from modern cultures — inspired in this by the American painter and engraver Robert Motherwell.

His interest in personal and cultural displacement is associated with broader geopolitical and social questions. His various representational strategies address issues of war, violence, identity, marginality and gender. During his first European exhibition in London, England, in 1993, he established links with other exiled artists from the Middle East — specifically from Iraq. These encounters led to a turning point in his artistic production, which became more politically explicit.

Farouk Kaspaules has participated in some 20 solo and collective exhibitions in Canada, England, Hungary, Chile and Brazil.

ALI KICHOU

A native of Béjaïa, Algeria, Ali Kichou was born in 1959. He was admitted to the National School of Fine Arts in Algiers in 1978, then to the Academy of Fine Arts in Rome in 1983. He later became a restorer of art in Italy, where he lived for a period of 14 years. The discovery he made, at the beginning of the 1980s, of the little-known art treasures his country harboured — the Tassili frescoes, Berber handicrafts, homes designed by Kabyle women — encouraged him to break away radically from traditional Western painting. He researched new materials, and replaced the canvas as the support for his works: "My work, my artistic approach, is a constant reappraisal of accepted techniques, which are conventional and therefore of a historical nature."

From that point on, Ali Kichou used burlap and glue in order to give his works relief, and revived the "sign", an ancestral mode of expression. He joined with the group Movimento Trattista ("Strokes in Movement"), and created installations that were more aesthetic than thematic, to which he soon added the dimension of sound. There is a parallel between his work and theatre, with its costumes and props and the richness of its artistic setting. He thus tries to rejoin with the universal by drawing from the cultural sources of different peoples. When questioned on his identity, he responds, "Honestly, I don't feel Arab; I feel Algerian. When I dream, I don't dream in Arabic . . . I dream in Berber, I cry in Berber. But I feel concerned because I am part of the Arab world . . . and the Arab world is rejected."

An enthusiastic traveller, he has been to Berlin, Stockholm, Budapest: everywhere that his works have been exhibited. Struck by the population density in Europe, preoccupied by the future of his children, and wishing to improve living conditions for his family, he decided with his wife, the artist Hadjira Preure, to emigrate to Quebec in 1995.

Ali Kichou has participated in nearly 80 solo and collective exhibitions in Europe, Algeria and Canada. Several Italian, Hungarian and Algerian museums have acquired one or more of his works.

BERNICE LUTFIE SORGE

Born in 1943 in Truro, Nova Scotia to parents of Syrian origin, Bernice Lutfie Sorge lived in British Columbia and in several Latin American countries before settling in Quebec. "Being the daughter of an immigrant mother, I have never really known what 'home' means." She has lived in Quebec's Eastern Townships for more than 20 years.

Bernice Lutfie Sorge is a painter and engraver who describes herself as an "explorer". She began her career with landscape painting, only to progressively distance herself from it and involve herself in a more conceptual and experimental process. After earning a bachelor's degree in visual arts from Montreal's Concordia University, she moved to the country to work directly from nature.

"I gather things from the woods . . . I have always had the desire to create something from nothing." This desire was inspired by her mother: a figure who occupied and still occupies a central place in a process in which the question of identity has always been present. "Art has been a marvellous thing for me. It is through art that I have explored my roots, my origins. I have plunged deeper and deeper into the very matter of art, by using materials that come directly from the earth, from the woods."

For Bernice Lutfie Sorge, questions are more important than answers, and it is those questions that she tries to formulate in her installations, her canvases and her engravings: questions that should reach out to everyone. "I love to transform things, and even to transmute them; to make them, in a sense, accessible to everyone. When I do something, I always want to bring it to some sort of universal conclusion . . . although, as far as I am concerned, nothing is ever quite finished."

Founder of the Centre d'art Missisquoi in Dunham and L'Estampille printmaking studio, she is a member of the Conseil québécois de l'estampe and of the Conseil de la peinture du Québec. She has to her credit numerous exhibitions in Canada and in France, and her works are found in many public and private collections.

NIHAL MAZLOUM

Of Turkish-Egyptian ancestry, Nihal Mazloum was born in Paris in 1951 and grew up in Cairo, in an affluent and multilingual family. After receiving a bachelor's degree in anthropology from Cairo's American University, she left Egypt to study ethnology in Paris. She remained there for seven years, then immigrated to Canada in 1978. She lives in Montreal.

Now a jeweller and artisan, she has always been fascinated by metalwork. It was in Paris that she decided to follow that direction, undergoing advanced training in metalwork despite the disapproval of her mother, who was disappointed to see her adopt a craft traditionally reserved for men. "Transforming material . . . that's what pleases me, as much as creating objects does." She opened a workshop in Montreal and began to display her jewellery in 1979. It was in Montreal that she acquired most of the techniques she now uses.

She attributes a sort of sacred value to jewellery, and draws her inspiration from the motifs, symbols and myths of ancient cultures — Pharaonic, but also Greek, African and, more generally, prehistoric. "A piece of jewellery is not only an abstract object that is beautiful. I craft it so as to give strength and power to the person who will wear it," she explains.

Nihal Mazloum participates in various craft shows, as well as in exhibitions in Canada and the United States, and sells her work from her studio and in specialized shops. Several of her jewellery pieces can be found in the collections of the Canadian Museum of Civilization.

JOSEPH MOUKHTAR

Born in Aleppo, Syria in 1930, Joseph Moukhtar is the son of immigrants, his parents having fled Turkey in 1916 following the massacre of the Armenians. He emigrated to Canada with his family in 1981 and has lived in Montreal since that time. "I have lived among many cultures all my life. If I cannot give and if I cannot take, I cannot live," he explains.

Essentially self-taught, Joseph Moukhtar began drawing and painting at a young age — "for the pleasure of it," as he says. As an adolescent, he managed to prepare his own paint colours with pigments and linseed oil. Having attended evening courses for four years at a painting academy in Aleppo, he then took advantage of his encounters with other artists — notably with a specialist in stained glass — to round off his knowledge of art.

The thematic orientation of his paintings changes as he further discovers his host country: "There was a time when I used to stay in my store, in the house. I would put on canvas what I saw in my mind. Now, I go out, I see many things in the city." He says that he wants to free himself from the traditional imperatives of line and motif, to detach himself from the more conventional and nostalgic themes of his early paintings. What appears for him to be a need to blend influences, to cross and unite cultures, leads him, in particular, to re-create the poetry of Canadian urban landscapes — to make their architecture dance and undulate endlessly. "I love the mix of immigrant cultures with Canadian and Quebec cultures. In time, we shall see a new culture emerge. All cultures must be blended together."

Joseph Moukhtar's work has been exhibited in Syria and in Montreal at — among other venues — the Syrian Cultural Centre, and within the framework of the Festival du monde arabe at the Université du Québec à Montréal.

HADJIRA PREURE

Hadjira Preure was born in Algeria in 1954 — the same year that the uprising of the Algerian people led to their war for independence. Following in her father's footsteps, she began studying law, but quickly reoriented herself towards the visual arts. She earned a certificate in the teaching of art in 1981, then a national diploma in 1982 from the École supérieure des beaux-arts d'Alger. The holder of a state grant, she left Algeria with her husband, the artist Ali Kichou, for Italy, where she spent her first year in Perugia and the following 13 years in Rome.

A graduate in painting from the Fine Arts Academy of Rome (1987), she became an assistant to the sculptor and painter Tito. Meanwhile, the situation in Algeria and the birth of children compelled the couple to find a country where their family would not feel like strangers, where they could enjoy the benefits of social rights, and where there would be neither war nor violence. Canada finally accepted them, and she arrived in Montreal with her husband and children in 1995. Migrations, multiple relocations and confined spaces led her to work with smaller surfaces: "But I always hope to give depth to the painting, the impression of something big, even if it is very small. . . . Working in smaller formats allows me to better dominate surfaces."

Interested at first in a realistic approach to painting, she painted animals (in a realistic style) and landscapes (inspired by Monet and Degas), as well as portraits (in the style of Daumier), then discovered primitive art with the cave paintings and frescoes of Tassili. She adopted an expressionism-of-colour style and became a member of the group Movimento Trattista, which promotes the use of the free stroke and the "sign". Through the use of ancient techniques — waxwork, engraving, sculpture and egg tempera — she endeavours to render movement and emotion. For her, "the most beautiful thing is hope, light." And it is to set off that light that she creates the areas of darkness in her paintings.

Hadjira Preure has participated in some 40 exhibitions in Canada, in Europe and in Algeria, and her works are included in the collections of numerous European museums, particularly in Italy.

ALDIN RASHID

Born in Baghdad, Iraq in 1950, Aldin Rashid has followed a long route which has led him from Bucharest to Rome, by way of Berlin, and finally to Canada. He has lived in the Vancouver area since 1991. This multi-talented calligrapher is also a painter, a ceramicist and a restorer of art works, notably icons. In addition to his training in architecture, he has worked as a graphic designer and artistic director of a magazine, and as a design consultant for the Egyptian Gallery of Berlin.

It was in Iraq that he learned the basics of Arab and Persian calligraphy under the influence of his father, himself a calligrapher, as well as under the tutelage of Hassan Massoudy and of the master Hashim al-Khattat, who introduced him to the Kufic style of writing. In 1968, he left Iraq to further his studies, and he has never returned.

"When I left, I carried a seed inside me; maybe it had come from my parents, maybe from the teachings of the great heavenly religions or maybe from someone else. In foreign lands this seed became a volcano fuelled by longing for my homeland and for my people.

"I reached freedom through my calligraphy. My work gives me peace and tranquillity while also passing on the good word of my ancestors to present and future generations."

Since his arrival in Canada, Aldin Rashid has participated in numerous exhibitions in British Columbia. His works are also on display in several public and private collections in Europe and in North America, and can be found in the collections of the Canadian Museum of Civilization.

KARIM RHOLEM

Karim Rholem was born in 1965 in Tangiers, Morocco. He left his country for the first time at the age of 16, to travel through Europe. Three years later, he left again — this time for Canada. He arrived in Montreal in 1985, and first studied languages, then photography at the CEGEP du Vieux Montréal. In 1994, he left for Canada's North (today's Nunavut) with the intention of photographing its landscape. Once there, he became fascinated by the Inuit hunters, and it was the hunters in their traditional clothing that he decided to photograph instead.

From then on, seized with the urgency of depicting minority or threatened communities and individuals nearing the end of their lives, Karim Rholem became a portrait photographer. However, whether he chooses to photograph immigrants living in Montreal (*Si loin . . . si proche*), centenarian Quebecers (*100 ans d'histoires à raconter*), or poor Moroccan porters (*Le poids du destin*), what he shows us is, above all, the human being in all his or her complexity and dignity. For example, the large formats that he favours allow for full-length or close-up photos which portray the person as he or she is. The artist's choice of the black-and-white format reflects his desire not to distract the spectator's eye. In addition, the artist adds textual accounts to his works, which allows the individuals he photographs to speak, and establishes a dialogue between their words and his images: "For me, photography is a door that lets me go towards other people, other places, 'elsewhere', the unfamiliar, all that is unknown to me."

Conscious that he is accomplishing the work of an archivist, Karim Rholem fully acknowledges the influence of the portrait photographers and anthropologists August Sanders and Edward S. Curtis. In doing this kind of work, he comes closer, not only to ordinary people, but also to the history of a people, a community and an epoch.

Karim Rholem has to his credit numerous exhibitions in Quebec. Some of his works can be found in the photographic collection of the National Archives of Canada, and in private collections. One of his works has been acquired by the Canadian Museum of Civilization.

ISHRAK SAHAR

Born in 1949 in Iraq, Ishrak Sahar left Baghdad in 1982. She lived for four years in Kuwait, where she taught visual arts, then for two years in Madrid, Spain, where she devoted herself to painting. The recipient of a certificate in fine arts (1970) and a bachelor's degree in visual arts (1976) from the University of Baghdad, she also received a diploma in textile design from the E. Harlacher Institute of Zurich (1976), which she earned during a two-year study period in Switzerland. She settled in Toronto in 1988.

The evolution of Ishrak Sahar's work is characterized by two approaches. Lacking the necessary means and floor space for painting on an easel, the artist first worked in black and white, using inks. The frames that she makes for her paintings also date from this time. Her current approach, however, has proven more liberating in the face of the difficulties she has encountered as an immigrant. She finds, for example, that using strongly textured colours and a wooden support enhances her ability to evoke her country and childhood. To better retain her fading memories, she paints them in one or more squares that are placed at the core of her paintings.

She also uses geometric patterns — which belong to the Arab pictorial tradition — to frame and reframe the subjects she puts on canvas, giving them a new dimension: "With this texture, with these colours, I have obtained a depth that surpasses what I want to express." Her use of mixed media and her choice of original formats, such as the square motif within a square frame, also contribute to this impression of depth.

Ishrak Sahar has exhibited her work in many galleries and public institutions in Canada, Spain and Iraq. The Canadian Museum of Civilization has acquired some of her works.

JAYCE SALLOUM

The grandson of Lebanese immigrants, Jayce Salloum was born in Kelowna, British Columbia in 1958. After studying arts in the United States, he began his artistic career in 1975: the year that civil war broke out in Lebanon. Already marginal because accompanied by "shock-texts", his first photographic exhibits were rapidly transformed into installations, as he progressively associated his photographs with archival objects and documents, and as he resorted to other media, such as video. Jayce Salloum gives special weight to the constituent elements of representation and, more particularly, to their underlying historical, social and cultural context. This deconstructionist approach allows him, on the one hand, to attempt to "define that place from which I relate with the world" and, on the other hand, to transgress the structures that limit and shape how we look at the world.

A great nomad, he has lived in several of North America's largest cities. But it is Beirut and Lebanon, where he has also lived, that most radically influence his work: "The use of images/representations of Lebanon and Beirut has an extensive history in the West and in Lebanon itself. . . . My own position as an image-maker is situated somewhere between being a family member, visitor, tourist, guide and unwilling orientalist . . . never occupying any one position for too long, fluctuating peripatetically between the act of reproducing and the deconstruction of such an act and its object." Lebanon's historical richness and the power of its metaphorical evocation allow him, moreover, to deal directly with questions that are, for him, central: exile, ethnic representation, and the notion of identity.

Jayce Salloum has participated in numerous solo and collective exhibitions in North America, Europe, Japan and Brazil. Many institutions, including the Museum of Modern Art in New York, the National Gallery of Canada and the Centre Pompidou in Paris, count his works among their collections.

TAOUFFIK SEMMAD

Taouffik Semmad was born in Algiers in 1957. He left Algeria after completing his studies at the École des beaux-arts. After living as a resident student in the former Soviet Union, he also lived in Belgium for a period of 14 years, where he acquired formal training in graphic communications and typography, as well as in engraving. In 1995, he settled in Montreal.

A calligrapher, illustrator and engraving artist, he earns his living by working as a graphic designer and typographer — notably by hand-drawing fonts, which distinguishes him from his colleagues who perform this work with computers. This specialization allows him to bridge the gap between Arabic-Persian tradition (miniatures, classical calligraphy) and graphic design and publishing.

Taouffik Semmad's works of art — illustrations, paintings, engravings — embody his fascination with the "sign" and handwriting in all its forms. In a work entitled *L'Avant-Babel*, he plays with the utopian idea of creating, through calligraphic gesture, a universal form of writing based on the use of multiple alphabets. "A rather modern subject," he explains, "that is inspired at the same time by an ancient tradition . . . a personal interest in the world and in an understanding among peoples."

In another project, an artist's book, he depicts the "Story of Sindbad the Sailor" (maiden voyage) from *The Arabian Nights*. In this piece he is inspired as much by his own experience in life as by the narrative: he graphically translates travels, restless wanderings and the meeting of cultures into an "abstract" calligraphy that combines various Eastern and Far Eastern alphabets and ideograms.

"What fascinates me in calligraphic writing is the gesture. There is an outpouring, a spontaneity, and an element of the unconscious that surfaces, all at once."

A member of the Conseil québécois de l'estampe, Taouffik Semmad has exhibited his art in Algeria, in the former Soviet Union, in Belgium and in Canada.

SHWAN

Half-Kurd, half-Kazakh, Shwan was born in a city in southern Iraq in 1955. At a young age, he already showed a strong desire to learn to paint, but his refusal to join his country's single party closed the doors of art schools to him. Thus, he proceeded to Italy in 1977, and earned a diploma from the Fine Arts Academy of Perugia in 1982. The precariousness of his status, and the fear of being sent back to Iraq, encouraged him to emigrate to Canada, where, he was told, the standard of living was high. He arrived in Edmonton in 1983, but decided to settle in Toronto, where the artistic milieu seemed more dynamic.

During his years of study in Italy, he was attracted to several artists — in particular Bori, Tapiés and Miró — and later to the American Action Painting movement and Willem de Kooning. Wishing to innovate, he systematically copied the works he admired in order to discover their secrets. He was daring in his use of materials and supports — including coffee, wine, nail polish, vinyl tiles and photographic paper — and invented a number of new techniques. He has essentially developed two approaches in his art: the first, more aesthetic, pays particular attention to the composition of the painting; the second, more playful, is inspired by popular Arab culture.

In the latter approach, he brings together, not only motifs and symbols, but also sayings and expressions, such as "The eye of the envious does not prevail," or "Don't follow me, I'm engaged." Such sayings recall scenes of daily life in the Middle East, the prevailing ambience of working-class neighbourhoods, and the inscriptions seen on taxis, buses and motorcycles, which make passersby smile. Not compelled to follow the rules of traditional or modern Arab calligraphy, nor those of classical painting, he makes the letters and colours dance joyfully right up to the painting's frame.

Shwan has to his credit some 50 solo and collective exhibitions — notably in Italy, Canada and the United States. Several of his works can be found in the collections of the Canadian Museum of Civilization.

SANAA M. WASSEF

Sanaa M. Wassef lived in Cairo, Egypt before her arrival in Canada in 1972. Born in 1934, she began drawing at a very young age, encouraged by the artist Ibrahim Gaber, who lived near the family home. To familiarize herself with art, she spent many hours at the Museum of Antiquities in Cairo. She waited until she was granted a bachelor of philosophy degree before studying at the faculty of arts at the University of Cairo, and before beginning to paint in earnest. It was after having settled in Toronto that she discovered ceramics.

Soon influenced by the travelling Tutankhamen exhibition in Toronto, she created ceramic pieces inspired by Pharaonic art. Eventually, however, she grew tired of "duplicating" traditional objects (lamps, vases, jewel boxes) and figurines representing Egyptian gods. She then turned to Muslim art, which she considered to be more intellectually stimulating: "I have found that this art allows you, to a certain extent, to reflect while painting . . . because it is based on calligraphy and ornamentation. For the calligraphy, I choose verses from the Koran; I reflect on their meaning. This gives me a very broad mental outlook." A verse can thus suggest a form, or a form evoke a verse.

She has not, however, completely abandoned painting on canvas. And it is in her paintings that the influence of her adopted country shines through most clearly, particularly in her palette of colours: "Take, for instance, the painting that shows military barracks in the Sinai. When my son looked at it, he said to me, 'Those are not the colours of Egypt . . . of the desert.' I then understood that I had, in fact, painted with the colours of Canada, the colours of its sky and its earth."

Sanaa M. Wassef has participated in some 20 exhibitions in Canada and in Egypt.

CAMILLE ZAKHARIA

Camille Zakharia was born in 1962 in Tripoli, Lebanon. He studied in Beirut, at the height of the civil war, and after various stays in the United States, Greece, Turkey and Bahrain, immigrated to Canada in 1995. His permanent residence is in Halifax, Nova Scotia.

A professional engineer, he has always entertained a passion for photography, taking photographs in all the countries he visited. But it was in Bahrain, in 1992, that a change was triggered and he began to view the world differently, "as if I were seeing things through a prism, in a fractured way." Upon arriving in Canada, he enrolled in the Nova Scotia College of Art and Design in Halifax. He is currently working as an engineer in Bahrain, while continuing to pursue his artistic career.

His favoured medium is the photo-collage: "Maybe the fragmentation of my identity accounts for why I always ended up working with collage," he says. In his photo-installations, he deconstructs the portraits, landscapes and architectures of the countries where he has lived, in order to recombine fragments and splinters of them, borrowing from the motif and dimensional perspective of mosaics and Byzantine icons. His themes have also changed: the nostalgia, the childhood memories depicted in his first collages and gouaches have given way to works based on the experience of immigration and on the life of immigrants — works often autobiographical in nature, even when he is portraying fictional characters.

"The traveller, the outsider, displacement, fragmentation — all these are essential elements repeated in the works I have completed in the last few years. The common thing is identity, the search for a place to fit in.

"[I guess] every place I've been, I have had a room. And maybe if you combine all these rooms in different places, that would be my home."

Camille Zakharia has a large number of solo and group exhibitions to his credit, notably in Bahrain, the United States and Canada, and his works are exhibited in many private collections. One of his works is found in the collections of the Canadian Museum of Civilization.

NICOLAS ZEITOUNI

Of Egyptian origin, Nicolas Zeitouni was born in 1935 in Alexandria. As a child, the ways and customs of his culture seduced him. He was fascinated by "the fishermen dressed in their traditional costumes," by women adorned with bracelets that tinkled, and by popular festivals. Highly attracted by the arts, he enrolled in decorative arts at the School of Fine Arts, received his diploma in 1962, and began to teach visual arts. In 1965, he decided to immigrate to Canada "for a better life." He chose Montreal because "it is a city where one can speak and live in French, and for its richness and its cultural diversity."

The Commission des écoles catholiques de Montréal then hired him, with the proviso that he study for his teacher's certificate. He received the latter from the Université du Québec à Montréal in 1972. During the 18 years he occupied this position, he explored several media: ceramics, enamelling, batik and silkscreen printing. From 1977 to 1981, he studied for a master's degree at Concordia University in the teaching of art, but reoriented himself towards the creation of jewellery in 1983. He then owned and operated his own jewellery store for 10 years.

In 1995, the storyteller in him led him to produce a series of miniatures (gouache, ink and acrylic) originating in his childhood memories: "My paintings represent stories and characters placed outside of time, in an imaginary and fantastic world." To create these paintings, he borrows from symbolic images — such as the hand of Fatma or the eye — in the folk art of Upper Egypt. He does this, however, without sacrificing the theme of his work, and by breaking away from the symmetry traditionally used in decoration. Imbued with sensuality and tenderness, full of life and warm colours, his works also convey the vision of the East and of Egypt that separation has allowed him to gain.

Nicolas Zeitouni's work has appeared in many exhibitions in Quebec.

SAMI ZUBI

Sam Zubi is of Palestinian origin, and was born in Nazareth in 1956. Coming from a poor family, he became conscious of social injustice at a very young age — in particular the oppression of women, and the tensions that were tearing his country apart. At the same time, he progressively distanced himself from a traditionalism that tended to reject Western art. The fashioning of various materials, the creation of images and observation of statues brought him a certain peace of mind: "I could feel that there was something else, an alternative to anger, to dissatisfaction, to real life."

As a young adult, he dreamed of leaving for a foreign country in order to get out of the world he knew and to enlarge his artistic horizons. Sponsored by his sister, he arrived in Toronto in 1978. Once the culture shock had passed, he began to study sculpture at the Ontario College of Art (1980–1984) and became a furniture designer. Thirteen years later, he moved to Canada's capital city with his family, and studied for a bachelor's degree in visual arts from the University of Ottawa (1996). Less strictly technical, this new training allowed him to discover his own style.

For his sculptural works, he favours cement, wood, acrylic resin, plaster and the integration of photographs, while paying particular attention to the linearity, structure and surface of his pieces. He is inspired by the artistic works that he rediscovered during his trips to Jerusalem, such as the old gates with Islamic motifs, but also by certain symbols and ornamental elements of Arab culture. Art represents for him, not only a means of expressing social and cultural preoccupations, but also a powerful instrument for social and political change.

Sami Zubi has participated in many exhibitions in Israel, the Palestinian Territories and Canada.

COLLABORATORS

BIOGRAPHICAL NOTES

collaborators

ALEXIS NOUSS

Alexis Nouss is a professor in the linguistics and translation department of the Université de Montréal. His primary areas of research and study are the aesthetics of modernity, the literature of witnessing, and the issues surrounding cultural intermixing, exile and the Diaspora. His publications include *La modernité* (PUF, "Que sais-je?" collection, 1995) and *Métissages. De Arcimboldo à Zombi* (with F. Laplantine, Pauvert, 2001). He also works as a translator and has written the librettos for two operas.

DOMINIQUE BOURQUE

Dominique Bourque has crossed numerous frontiers — notably by living abroad (Germany, Spain, Japan) and by focusing her attention on marginal cultures (immigrants, artists, people without papers). She holds a doctorate in French literature from the University of Ottawa and has published articles in a number of periodicals, including *Voix et images* and *Tessera*. She has also produced and hosted radio programmes on literature and art, and led media workshops.

ABLA FARHOUD

Born in Lebanon, Abla Farhoud emigrated to Quebec in the 1950s. Following her early experience as an actress — she did television work for Radio-Canada — she decided to study theatre in Paris, where she lived from 1969 to 1973. She subsequently became a playwright. In 1992, she was awarded the Prix Théâtre et Liberté by the Societé des Auteurs et Compositeurs Dramatiques, and the following year received the Prix Arletty from the Université de la langue française. In 1995, her play *Jeux de Patience* received top honours at the Soirée des Masques. The central focus of both her plays and her novels — *Le bonheur à la queue glissante* (Prix France-Québec in 1999) and *Splendide solitude* (2001) — is the theme of exile.

RAWI HAGE

Born in Beirut, Lebanon, visual artist and writer Rawi Hage currently lives and works in Montreal. He holds a B.A. in fine arts from Concordia University. Hage's photos, which deal principally with immigration, war and racism, are set in fictional situations and are transformed by multiple narrative threads which preclude a hasty reading. His writings have appeared in a number of publications, and he has exhibited his work in Canada, Lebanon, France and Colombia.

AÏDA KAOUK

Aïda Kaouk is a curator and researcher at the Canadian Museum of Civilization and is currently head of the institution's research on Canadian women from Northeast Africa. She was in charge of the Museum's Southwest Asia Programme from 1992 to 2002, and was curator of **The Lands within Me**. After earning a Ph.D in cultural sociology from the École des hautes études en sciences sociales in Paris, she undertook postdoctoral studies at the University of California, Berkeley. Over the years, she has conducted research at a number of universities in the Middle East, France, the United States and Canada, and is the recipient of a number of prestigious research grants, including Fulbright and Ford Foundation grants. In addition to artistic and cultural practices, Aïda Kaouk's research and activities centre primarily on questions related to immigration, cultural identity, cultural intermixing, social relations and minority groups.

LAURA MARKS

Laura Marks is a theoretician and curator of films, video and experimental media. Her work takes a sensual and materialist approach towards art and the world, with particular emphasis on issues related to cultural exchange. Her current research includes the history of Arab and African mathematics, as well as alternative models for the culture of informatics. She is the author of *The Skin of the Film: Intercultural Cinema, Embodiment and the Senses* (Dukes University Press, 2000) and *Touch: Sensuous Theory and Multisensory Media* (Minnesota University Press, 2002), and has developed several audiovisual programmes for international festivals and artist centres. Laura Marks is the Dena Wosk professor of arts and culture at Simon Fraser University in British Columbia.

SERGE OUAKNINE

Born in Morocco, a child of the Jewish Diaspora, Serge Ouaknine spent two years in Poland before settling in Quebec in 1977. Active as a painter, writer and stage director, he is also a professor at the theatre school of the Université du Québec à Montréal. In addition to writing poetry and short stories, Ouaknine is the author of numerous essays on contemporary art and on Eastern and Western thought. In 2000, he published *Café Prague et autres récits de voyage*.

LAMBERTO TASSINARI

Lamberto Tassinari, who graduated in philosophy from the University of Florence, has lived in Canada since 1981. Active in Italy as a teacher, he also worked in communications, notably at FIAT, and in publishing at the publishers Mondadori and Etas Kompass. In 1983, he helped found the magazine *ViceVersa*, remaining its editor until it folded in 1996. A professor at the Université de Montréal, he published a novel in 1985, and a collection of his essays, *Utopies par le hublot* (Carte blanche), appeared in 1999.

CAMILLE ZAKHARIA

Camille Zakharia was born in Lebanon and educated in Beirut during the civil war. Trained as an engineer, he lived in the United States, Greece, Turkey and Bahrain before immigrating to Canada in 1995, where he studied photography at the Nova Scotia College of Art and Design in Halifax. In his photo-installations, he deconstructs portraits, landscapes and architectural images captured in the countries where he has lived, recombining the fragments and shards using the motifs and non-perspectival space characteristic of mosaics and Byzantine icons. His work has been shown in numerous exhibitions, notably in Bahrain, where he currently works.

APPENDICES

AP
PEN
DICES

LEBANON -CANADA

TEXT FROM CAMILLE ZAKHARIA'S
LEBANON-CANADA, VIA BAHRAIN

My dear son Camille,

How are you, my child? How is your health? We miss you; by God, we miss your beautiful face! It has been over a month since I received your latest news. I hope that everything is fine. You cannot imagine how worried we are, your father and I, when people coming from your place bring us no letter and how relieved we feel when we receive news from you. Cursed be the war which scattered my whole family. Each one of you lives at the other end of the world from us, and none of you is near. Your father and I spend every day in the evening secluded between these four walls, and there is nobody to talk to. We do not expect anything anymore from this life other than to know that you are safe and that your health is good.

Yesterday, your aunt came early in the morning and spent the whole day with us. I insisted that she stay for the night, but she is so stubborn, she did not agree to stay. That woman likes to sleep only at her own place. We feel safer now because the situation here is better, and one can return home a bit later. My dear son, today we had for lunch stuffed vine leaves and "*kibbeh* in a pan" with tabbouleh and fried potatoes. Oh God, how we wished that you were with us! The weather was nice, and we set the table on the east balcony. I dressed your grandmother warmly, and we all sat out on the balcony and ate. Poor Grandma, how she thought so well of all of you! I swear to God that we tried our best to call at least one of you in the afternoon, but, as usual, we failed. May God curse those phones and their owners! Never have we been able to satisfy our wish to talk to you! They have promised us to install new telephone lines next summer. We hope that this time they are sincere and that they are not lying like to us as they did last year and the year before.

After lunch, we made Turkish coffee, and, as usual, your aunt insisted on reading the cup to predict the future. She told me that one of you would come for a visit soon. I hope she is right and that I will see you all.

Speaking about coffee, in your last letter you asked me how to prepare it. It is very easy. Let us suppose that you are preparing coffee for three people. You pour four cups of water in the pot; then you put the pot on a low fire. Put four full teaspoons of coffee in the water. If you like your coffee medium-sweet, add one-and-a-half to two teaspoons of sugar. Stir the water from time to time. Let the coffee rise once, then a second time, and the third time remove it from the fire. Let it sit two or three minutes to allow the coffee grounds to settle to the bottom of the pot. Then pour the coffee the way you like it and enjoy it. They say that if you have froth in your cup, you will receive some money.

Our news is the same. Our poor neighbour Wafa' died last week. She was very organized and dynamic. She was still working in the fields while she was sick. Her garden was like paradise. I long for her voice in the morning, when she used to feed her chickens. Her voice would remind me of the muezzin when we used to live in El-Mina. We used to open the window in summer, and the voice of the muezzin was like clear music that woke me up early in the morning. Oh God, those days were so lovely! You were all gathered around me. I have a photograph of all of you when you were small. I have it before me in the living room. Every day, I burn incense by it so that the Lord may protect you and your brothers from all evil and harm. In the picture, your aunt's husband, may he rest in peace, is standing behind you with his arm around your shoulder like an affectionate father. He used to love you more than the others. He did not take anyone fishing but you. All your brothers used to misbehave with him. Everybody in the picture is smiling except you. You were serious even when you were a child. You always took things seriously. You would get mad when your brothers and cousins played without you. Your aunt used to call you the "tail of the gang". They would always leave you behind in order to lose you, but you would catch up with them and not let them enjoy themselves without you.

Your cousin Asaad had a daughter, a very beautiful daughter. They called her Samia, like his sister, may she rest in peace! Asaad is unique; every other day he drops in before heading for the village and asks me if I need anything. God bless him! He knows that your father is not able to carry anything heavy. He always installs the gas container, and he taught me how to operate the generator when we first got it. May God preserve his health and his family! These days, the electricity has become better; it is supplied four hours in the morning and four hours in the evening. At least, we can stay up a little longer; we had been going to bed early for years by candlelight.

That is our news. Son of my heart, tell me about you! Tell me about your health and how things are for you. Look after yourself, my son. Tell me, are you happy in Bahrain? I hope this move will be beneficial for you. Do not stay long in the sun. Always cover your head. A sunburn is very harmful. Drink as much fluid as possible. From what you told me, your salary is good, thank God. It is a blessing that the company provides you with accommodations. My son, I do not need to advise you to save as much money as possible. What you earn today, you might not earn in the future. God willing, you will buy soon a piece of land here, in the village, and you will build a house where you will settle down with your family. May God hasten the day when I rejoice with you and your brothers!

I hope that some other Lebanese work in your company. I do not need to worry about you. You make friends quickly. I swear to God that all the people who went to the Gulf have built palaces here. Our neighbour Jamil has bought an apartment in Raouche. I do not know for what price! He also bought for his son in Canada a building to rent out. Every year, he says that it is the last year he will go to Saudi Arabia, yet he goes again. He comes here, stays a month or two at the most, then gets bored and asks his wife to pack his stuff. He is used to living abroad. He is not able to sit between four walls without work or activity. In the village, if you do not have friends, you get bored to death. Since the war, only children and old people are left here. Some people have left for the Gulf; some have left for America. Even Canada has opened its doors and is attracting educated people like your brother Bassam and his wife.

A week ago we received a letter from your brother Bassam. He sent it with our neighbour, Nabil, who lives in El-Mina. Nabil came back to visit his parents. Thanks be to God, your brother and his wife are doing well! They are renting a two-bedroom apartment in the downtown area, so they do not need a car. They say that it is very cold in Montreal; winter is colder than one can imagine. They say that sometimes the temperature drops to 20 degrees below zero. My God, I wonder how people can live out there! How do they manage when there is a power failure? Your brother is working in a company which is about one-and-a-half hours away from his place. He travels by bus to work. There is a bus stop by his apartment, and the bus arrives exactly on time. He does not accept his wife going out to work. He wishes that she would stay at home until the boy is born. He is afraid that she might slip on the ice, and I do not blame him. He sent a message that he would like us to go to Montreal for a visit and to be near him at the time of the child's delivery. Your father got mad when I read the letter to him. And, as usual, he started cursing about the world and the angels. It is hard for us, especially for your father, to go to a country whose language we do not speak. I can manage, for I spend my time cooking and cleaning and taking a bit of a walk in the morning. But your father sits idle, confined to the room the whole day. I swear that he made my life miserable during our last visit to your brother in New York. Your father is used to seeing olive gardens when he opens the door in the morning, and to drinking his coffee on the balcony before leaving home. Every day in the afternoon he wants to play cards with his friends in the village, with his hubble-bubble beside him. At your brother's place, he used to feel as if he were in a sardine can, choking. It is hard for people our age to adapt to a new country. You are still young, and each one of you, may God protect you, would land on your feet wherever you are.

My son, I am sending you this letter with your cousin Walid. He is going to Saudi Arabia in a week, and he told me that I could send anything with him. But I do not like to impose on him. I am going to send this letter with him as well as a few photographs of his wedding. Your father would have liked to send you some nut mixture from Jillab's, but I did not let him. Walid's wedding was like a dream, may God grant them happiness! The newlyweds suit each other very well. I hope that you also marry some day. The reception was at Al-Manara. They had drums and flutes, and everybody danced the *dabka*. They spent a lot on food. Now Walid is going back to Saudi Arabia, and will arrange the visa for his wife so that she can join him. In Saudi Arabia, all the Lebanese live together in residential neighbourhoods, and they socialize together. I pity her mother. She was weeping all during the wedding. It was hard for her to think that Jumana was going to leave her soon. She reminded me of how I felt when your brother left for America and then you all left, one after the other! In the end there were no tears left in my eyes for me to cry. We feel sad because you are not near us, but at the same time look at the youth here. They are bored and idle. Look at the engineers. They accept any work at the lowest wages, and the big companies are taking advantage of them.

My dear son Camille, I have to say goodbye. I would continue writing endlessly, but I have to prepare food for your father. You know how impatient he is. He wants everything to be ready the moment he gets home. I hoped that he would become more patient as he aged, but on the contrary he is becoming grumpier and grumpier. My son, may God protect you, do not stop writing to us. We live for your news. Send us some photographs; I have made an album for each one of you. Your poor grandmother always asks about you. Send her a small gift. You cannot imagine how much she would appreciate it. She still remembers the time that you spent a summer at her place in Beirut when she was sick. You used to carry water for her nine floors up in her apartment building during power failures. She still remembers how patient you were, and how affectionate with her. Before I forget, Camille, I would like to ask you for another favour. Your cousin has passed the baccalaureate, and your brothers sent him 25 dollars each. Why would you be an exception? It does not matter, Camille; the few dinars you send would not affect you. But it should not be more than 20, and may God give them back to you. Your uncle deserves it. He called us a few times in America to inquire about us.[1] The last time, Bassam had . . . at that time we had asked . . . at your brother's . . . which means that . . . the reward, and it . . . first degree . . . for his children and . . . you . . . in the hand of God . . . gives . . . the second . . . finally . . . I hug you . . . to my chest . . . and kiss you . . . thousand . . . with your father . . . I ask God . . . the highest . . . to give you health . . . success and . . . in all your work . . . and to keep away from you . . . all evil and harm. I pray . . . for you.

From your mother who misses you always,

Alice

[1] Translator's note: What follows are sentence fragments arranged on the panel, with photographs filling the rest of the space.

I THINK OF MY MOTHER

I THINK OF MY MOTHER
WRITTEN AND RECORDED
BY GLORIA SORGE, AND AN INTEGRAL
PART OF BERNICE LUTFIE SORGE'S,
A PLACE FOR ROSE

INTRODUCTION

Dear Bernice, for this unique project I offer some stories that I hope will add another dimension to your beautiful mural, enclosed in the magnificent red wood frame constructed by Julien. I've entitled my part, "I Think Of My Mother".

It consists of a series of vignettes which I hope will capture the essence and presence of our mother from the maze of my memories of childhood experiences; experiences that have defined my world and played a role in framing the woman I am. They are the sensory memories reminiscent of the joys and fears that every child experiences, each in her own unique way. Ours are also unique to us because our mother was Syrian, unable to read or write, and widowed with four young children. Out of necessity she had to work, and out of necessity we had to live in a village where there were, to my knowledge, no other Syrians. Her work took her away from us during the day and sometimes into the late evening. Her absence enhanced her presence and created a loving bond between you, our brothers, and me.

MY MOTHER'S TRUNK

My mother had a trunk. I don't know when she acquired it and I don't know whatever became of it, but it seemed to travel with her throughout her life. Perhaps it was the treasure trunk of this child bride, holding mementoes of home and family — things to take with her as she travelled to a new land with a new husband. The image of the trunk frames my memories of my mother. As I search these memories, fragments of my mother's life pass before me as scenes before the traveller on a moving train. I smell the familiar dust that rises whenever the contents are disturbed. It's warm and cold and draws me in as it holds me back in suspense. It cloaks me in mystery and wonderment.

At times, my sister and I were allowed to open the trunk to survey its contents. We would take out the mauve robe that came from Syria. The silk-like material had a subdued sheen. The edges along the front opening and around the neck, as well as the wide edges of the sleeves, were machine-embroidered with flowers and scrolls. It was beautiful to look at and, when bunched in our hands, it felt cool and light as a cloud. We would try it on and walk around dragging its too-long length behind us. Little princesses in a far-off land.

Now, transported, we remove the cloth bag, untie the knot and peek inside. A white ball of sequined material. Should we take it out? Yes, but carefully, for it may disintegrate. The weight of the sequins and the fragility of their foundation prevents us from holding it up. Just hold it in your hand, roll it from one to the other. Watch the light shift. Each luminous sequin gleamed with the promise of rainbow-like beauty; and when our need to touch it and feel it had lost its potential to mesmerize, the remains of our Mother's wedding dress were put back into the bag.

There was another dress. This one in the flapper style, made of a pink satin under-shift covered with black see-through lace that was decorated with sequins arranged in an all-over Art Nouveau pattern. This was a gift from our father. He had bought it for our mother when they were in Paris while en route to Canada. She wore this dress to dances. It is not difficult to imagine our fun-loving mother in this dress, dancing to the music of the late twenties and early thirties. This dress was still complete and, although still elegant, it did not hold the same enchantment as the wedding dress.

What to examine next? Oh yes, the baby shoes. Little black patent leather Mary Janes with straps held in place by a round black bead. There is a cutout pattern on the toes and they are stuffed with tissue paper to hold the shape, but the tissue paper pokes through the toe of one shoe. My left foot is still my measuring stick when I need new shoes. Now my baby shoes are in my dresser drawer, the tissue paper still poking through. My mother said they were my first pair of shoes. Also in the trunk, there was a picture of me standing on the sidewalk looking like a little orphan, and I am wearing those shoes. They tell me that I was once so small that my mother could pick me up and hold me in her arms. They tell me that when I wore them and took my first steps on that sidewalk and began to walk towards my mother that I also began to walk away.

From time to time, there were other treasures added to the trunk. When we were still quite young, and after our father died, my mother worked in a hat factory where she sat all day picking imperfections from the felt with tweezers, before the hats went on to be pressed into shape. One day she brought home two miniature hatboxes, each containing three tiny fedoras. One box contained red ones and the other, yellow ones. Why did they make them so small? Are they dolls' hats? Now one of the red hats sits on the dash of my car to help me identify the car whenever I am lost in a large parking lot.

The one thing in the trunk I didn't like was a fox stole. Even though its fur was so shiny and so silky, inviting the touch, its eyes always looked straight at me while its paws dangled lifelessly whenever it was picked up. I remember that sometimes when the trunk was opened, my mother would fling the fox stole around her neck and strike a pose of refined elegance. These were occasions when she enjoyed the memories stored in the trunk. Later the fox stole disappeared to the pawnshop to be ransomed for rent money. I think that she always regretted that — not so much because she was so poor that she couldn't pay the rent, but because the fox stole represented some special memory for her.

Only mommy can open the faded envelope; we can only look. So, very carefully, she takes out the brown, silky lock of hair, curled gently like the wing of an angel. She had a baby who died at the age of nine months from a high fever. His name was Vicki. The brown envelope made her sad so we didn't look at it too often.

For me, the most fascinating thing in the trunk was a box of carnelian-coloured beads of different sizes. My mother told me that they were amber beads. At one time, they had been a necklace which my father had bought for her in Alexandria, Egypt, when they were on their honeymoon. When the beads broke, she placed them in the box and put them in the trunk until she could have them restrung. One time I tried to restring them for her using some twine. This task proved too difficult with the thick twine, so the job was left unfinished. When I was older and on my own, I would occasionally ask about the beads, just to make sure they were still in the trunk. I often suggested to my mom that she should give them to me so that I could have them restrung for her. She always refused, saying she was going to have cuff links made for the boys, my brothers. I wondered, "How many pairs of cuff links do they need and would they wear reddish-orange cuff links?" A few years after I was married I asked for the beads once again, suggesting that I would have them restrung because long necklaces were back in style. This time my mother gave them to me. With assurances that I would do something with the beads and not lose them, I eagerly removed the box from the trunk. All of the beads were still as I had left them, including the white twine. At home, I put them in my dresser drawer where they remained for many years. Sometimes, my mother would inquire about the beads and I would assure her that I still had them. Every now and then, I would take them out of the box just to look at them and to feel their smooth coolness in my hands. I could never decide exactly what I should do with them.

In the summer of the year that our mother died, my sister turned fifty. Her family planned a large party for her. I wanted to give her something special. One day as I opened my dresser drawer, I realized what the perfect gift would be. I had a jeweller make two necklaces with matching pairs of earrings. On the necklaces, our mother's beads alternate with small fluted gold ones. Each earring has a gold bead above a small oblong one from the original necklace. When my sister opened her gift, she was struck by the beauty of the necklace. "You remember the beads, don't you?" I asked. My sister, being two years younger than I, had no recollection of the beads, so I told her the story. Since then, my sister and I always wear our necklaces and earrings at our family gatherings. The wearing of the beads on these occasions seems to heighten the spirit of our mother, present and watching as we fumble through the preparation and enjoy the eating of the Syrian food she so loved to prepare for us.

THE HOBO

The days of my early childhood were the post-war days in Canada and, as in the years of the Depression, people were on the move looking for work. Because the railway passed through our village, it was not unusual to see a hobo from time to time. I remember the day when one came to our door looking for something to eat. We could hardly feed ourselves but my mother never turned anyone away. In fact, she always said, "God is good", meaning God would always provide for us, so how could she turn away a stranger? The hobo looked grimy, but he had a broad smile with a ruddy complexion. He sat at the table with us and we had breakfast together. I don't think I ate; I just looked. I distinctly remember my mother saying to the hobo, "You can eat with us, but afterwards I will have to sterilize the dishes you use." Somehow my mother could say things like that and it would not sound insulting. I can see my mother, with crystal clarity, putting the utensils in a pan of water, then into the oven. For my part, I marvelled at the idea of putting forks, knives and spoons into the oven to bake, and I watched in wonder as she slid the pan in and closed the oven door. In her later years, when she was dependent, for the most part, on her "old age pension", she sponsored a child under the Foster Parents Plan, sending ten dollars every month. It seems as though my mother was always sharing something she had, whether it be food, or advice, or something more tangible.

My first significant memory of giving of my own volition was when the Salvation Army came to our village. They gathered in front of Ron's Garage with their huge, shiny brass instruments and began to play and sing. I recalled my mother often having mentioned their goodness. I was swept away by this early evening concert. So when the collection began, I dashed home and emptied the bottle holding my life's savings. I ran back as fast as I could taking my spot in the line just as it was my turn to give, and I proudly placed my sixty-seven cents in the middle of the hat. When I am moved to give unconditionally for the sheer joy of giving, I know that I am my mother's daughter.

THE TREE

A few years ago, I drew a tree because I was thinking of my mother. I used nice paper and chalk pastels. The tree has brilliant yellow roots that clutch the soil, anchoring it as it stands strong and straight. The branches of the tree are bare of leaves. Instead, they are decorated with various ornaments — birds, bells, an angel. One must look closely at the drawing to see the ornaments. Their ethereal, whimsical quality is reminiscent of my mother's love of knick-knacks, especially of birds and animals. But trees and plants are good totems for my mother, as she was always tending a garden, either inside or out. I remember when my mother borrowed a little corner of the Postmaster's garden plot. He always grew gladioli, rows and rows of them, and I think it was his flowers that graced the front of the church on summer Sundays. But my mom grew vegetables: carrots, beets, beans, radishes, lettuce. In that first garden, she planted, along with the usual seeds, some vegetable marrows — the promise of stuffed *koosa*. When the little marrows began to form, my older brother put one of the young marrows inside a milk bottle to see if it would grow into the shape of the bottle. In the evening after supper, my mother would weed her garden. We would either help or get in the way, and we kept an eye on that marrow. I remember clearly the night we noticed the little marrow pressing its tender green surface against the inside of the bottle, like a child's tongue licking hard against the inside of a window while being watched from without. My mother laughed at the puckishness of my brother and I was truly amazed.

The interconnectedness of all of nature, the nurturing of the food we grow to eat, the joy and the gratefulness we feel when we share the fruits of our labour with others is part of the legacy my mother left to me.

When my daughters were young, we didn't grow vegetable marrow, we grew zucchini — the promise of zucchini bread — enough for the whole neighbourhood.

THE STORYTELLER

When my sister and I are together we often recall the stories our mother used to tell us of her life in Jdaidet-Artouz, her village in Syria.

We had a ritual. At night, when my sister and I were in the bed we shared, and before we drew the imaginary line down the middle to mark off our respective territories, our mother would lie down with us and tell us stories of when she was a young girl, and then we would say our prayers together — the Lord's Prayer, always ending with "And God bless all the little children all over the world."

Our mother only went to school for one day. She said that there was a word she could not pronounce properly and the teacher humiliated her so, that she begged her father not to make her return. In fact, I think she bribed him because she offered to look after the sheep and goats for him if he would grant her this wish, which he did. She would lovingly describe the sheep that she said were unlike the sheep we have in Canada. Her sheep were black with heart-shaped tails that stood upright and fanned out. And she would gesture with her hands to create a picture of these tails for us. On very hot days, she and her flock of sheep and goats would find shade in the olive groves. One day, the thought of a good olive became very tempting, so she climbed a tree and shook it until most of the olives fell to the ground. She always laughed mischievously when she remembered her father's wrath at the lost olives, which were not quite ready for picking; but he could never be angry with her for long. For us, she framed a picture of a curious, free-spirited child, often left to her own devices and often in minor trouble — like the many times she would take some bread and skim the coveted cream off the top of the milk, creating a sumptuous lunch for herself and leaving her mother with no cream.

She talked lovingly of her father, who would regularly read bible stories to her from his big books, and of her mother who was kind and gentle and who was frequently asked to sing at weddings.

When I was very young, I used to sing for my mom: "Beautiful Beautiful Brown Eyes" and "Jimmy Crack Corn and I Don't Care; My Master's Gone Away." She always told me that I had a nice voice, so I sang for her, as my sister and I sat on the couch, while she mopped the kitchen floor.

In her village, my mother said that, when she was young, the priests helped decide legal matters. One time, a grave crime had been committed, and a village man was charged. My grandfather, who was well respected in the community, believed the man to be innocent, so he said to the priest, "If you support this guilty verdict, I will leave the Church." The priest supported the verdict of guilt so my grandfather left that church, and half the people in the village left in support of him. My grandfather and his supporters decided to build a new church opposite his home. Because my mother was not in school, one of her duties was to take water and food to the men who were working on the new church. When it came time to lay the cornerstone, the workmen said that, if our mother could lift the stone, they would put her name on it. To my knowledge, the church across from my grandfather's house has a cornerstone that bears our mother's name: Wardeh Lutfie.

Shortly before she left Syria, she and our father visited a holy place where she said water came out of the stone on the side of a mountain. It did that because God had opened the mountain to help a little girl escape some danger. As she, our father and the nun who was their guide, walked through the underground shrine, our mother — who was in awe of this story and this place — gently swept her hand across the surface of a door as they passed by. The door swung open. The nun then told our father that his bride must be a "holy person" because that door was always kept locked.

Our mother never took advantage of her good standing in the ranks of the "Holy", but she did, in a time of great need, call upon St. George, the patron saint of her village. As she recalled, after she was widowed, her landlord threatened to obtain a court order to have her evicted for failing to pay the rent. Although she was being falsely accused, she felt vulnerable and feared losing us, her precious children, to the Children's Aid Society. So she prayed to St. George to help her. She promised St. George that if he would help, she would never ask anything of him again. The judge believed our mother, and we were not evicted.

Many years later, having forgotten her promise to St. George, our mother prayed to him again. This time she desperately needed rest and relief from the pain in her perpetually swollen feet and legs. The pain subsided, and a restful sleep soon embraced her. During the night, she was awakened by the bed shaking so much that it bounced off the floor, and the picture of St. George that always hung on her bedroom wall was swinging back and forth. This time St. George spoke, reminding her of her promise of long ago. She begged him not be angry with her, then all was quiet and serene. She said she felt badly that she had forgotten her promise, and she hoped that God and St. George would forgive her, but she seemed to also feel comforted and special.

One of my last visions of my mother before she died is of her sitting up in bed, her legs stretched out before her, and her praying hands before her bowed head. I stood in the doorway of her bedroom, watching and listening to her repeat the Lord's Prayer, as she had done so many times with my sister and me. This scene of deep faith and childlike trust brought tears to my eyes. There were many things wrong in her life then, as there had always been, but she never lost her unyielding faith that "God is good" — words I had always heard her say whenever life seemed unfair. But somehow things seemed to have a way of working out. I think God had a lot of help from our mother.

So my mother, when I think of you, the first thing I see is your wide, beautiful smile, white even teeth, and wrinkles of joy about your beautiful, beautiful brown eyes. I picture you as though I were looking at a framed photograph — it never alters from that frozen moment in time. This vision may, at times, recede, but it never fades. And when all things come together, I capture something that is mine. Mine to keep. Mine to share. Mother, daughter, daughter, mother mine.